Finding Our Way

Finding Our Way: A Newlywed Couple's Peace Corps Odyssey in 1960s Korea

Printed in the United States of America
by Peace Corps Writers of Oakland, California.

For more information, contact peacecorpsworldwide@gmail.com

Peace Corps Writers and the Peace Corps Writers colophon
are trademarks of PeaceCorpsWorldwide.org.

ISBN-13: 978-1-950444-43-4
Library of Congress Control Number: 2022916199

First Peace Corps Writers Edition, September 2022

NORTH KOREA
SEA OF JAPAN
Sokcho
Kangnung
Ulungdo
Han
Bukhan
SEOUL
Han
SOUTH
Pukpyung
Ulchin
YELLOW SEA
Yechon
Geum
Taechon
KOREA
Pohang
Taegu
Kyungju
Nakdong
Seomjin
Kwangju
Pusan
Yosu
Western Channel
Strait
Korea
Eastern Channel
Cheju
JAPAN
0 25 50 km
0 25 50 mi

INTRODUCTION

Recalled some 55 years after the fact, this is the story of how Linda and I, a young couple barely in our twenties, embarked on a great adventure. Away for just over two years, we volunteered to live and work halfway around the world, in a land we knew little about, and with a family we had never met. During that time, we encountered people and situations with which we had no familiarity. Those experiences at times challenged our beliefs and helped us learn lessons that altered forever the course of our lives. This is the story of how our adventure unfolded over half a century ago.

The idea of the United States establishing a volunteer corps of young people to serve the needs of developing countries had been discussed on a national level as early as the 1950s. Senator Hubert Humphrey first introduced legislation to establish such an agency in 1957. At that time, the idea did not generate sufficient traction in Congress, but the seed was planted.

Several years later, during the summer of 1960, the influential progressive labor and civil rights activist Walter Reuther visited presidential candidate John Kennedy to advocate establishing a volunteer program to send young Americans around the world to peacefully assist people in other countries. The idea fit with Kennedy's goal of broadening opportunities for youth to serve the nation, and he incorporated it into his presidential campaign. In his memorable 1961 inaugural address, President Kennedy hinted at the future when he said, "And so, my fellow Americans: ask not what your country can do for you – ask what you can do for your country."

Once in office, the President acted. By March, an executive order had established the Peace Corps. By August, the first volunteers went overseas. By September, spurred by Senator Humphrey, a bill establishing the Peace Corps as a permanent agency of the government was signed into law. Five years later Linda and I applied to become volunteers in that program.

Peace Corps' initial three goals have remained consistent over the years: help meet local technical and manpower assistance needs in developing countries; promote a better understanding of America among the citizens of those countries; and foster an enhanced awareness of overseas cultures on the part of Americans. A fourth result emerged for us during our service: the Peace Corps experience taught us a great deal about ourselves and helped shape our future. The two years we spent living and working in a culture other than our own influenced choices we later made about vocation, lifestyle, and values. Our experience suggests that other Peace Corps Volunteers would say something similar.

The cohort of volunteers with whom we served was one of the first Peace Corps groups to serve in the Republic of Korea. During the late 1960s, the Peace Corps and the government of Korea experimented with how best to address the country's economic needs. Initial goals included improving English instruction and upgrading public health practice, both seen as essential to the country's development and its ability to engage in international trade.

When we arrived, Korea was a country relatively unknown to most Americans, including us. Despite training for three months, we had only a minimal awareness of Korea's history. We knew little of its cultural contributions over the centuries, from art to language to near universal literacy. We learned nothing of Japan's forceful annexation of the Korean peninsula (1910–45), its division into two different political systems following WWII, or the brutal three-year civil war with the communist north that ended with an armistice in 1953.

With the end of armed conflict and the imposition of a truce, economic development became one of the southern Republic's top priorities. During our tenure there, we found South Korea's people to be energetic, creative, and bold. Their aspirations eventually transformed an impoverished economy into what became known as the "Miracle on the Han River."

The South Korean government invited the Peace Corps to play a part in the early days of its economic expansion. Between 1966 and 1981, over two thousand Peace Corps Volunteers (PCVs) served in South Korea. Those Volunteers all have their own stories. The one I recount here is unique to us. It is not meant to be reflective or even similar to the experiences of other PCVs. For us, the experience was profound. What we learned about ourselves, and what we learned from the Koreans with whom we lived and worked, awakened new beliefs and altered the direction of our lives. Since the 1960s, South Korea has remade itself. That transformation began during the time we were there, and as the country began to change, so did we.

In the pages that follow I recount events that marked our journey of discovery as we sought to find our way in a different land. The memories are vivid, but we couldn't have recounted them without the letters we sent home, photographs we took, and the shared recollections of Korean and American associates—friends we have known for over fifty years. During the twenty-one months we lived in Korea, Linda and I sent one or two letters to our parents almost every week, letters they saved for us. Those letters have allowed us to dust off our adventure, bring it back to life, and shed some light on its importance to the rest of our lives.

While the writing throughout these pages is in my voice, the memories are ours. Linda contributed mightily, helping me flesh out the events and impressions recounted in each chapter and making editorial suggestions that enhanced the telling. Ours is largely a story of love for the Korean family who welcomed us into their midst, love for the friends we made while in the country, and admiration for the Korean people whose spirit, work ethic, and fortitude were, and continue to be, an inspiration to us.

Steve Gallon
Corvallis, Oregon
May 2022

Chapter 1

THE LAUNCH

Linda and I had been married just eight days on July 16, 1967. It was a warm Sunday afternoon, one day after we returned from a whirlwind honeymoon spent in picturesque spots on the California coast. Nervous, exhausted and excited, we huddled with our families at Los Angeles International Airport, preparing to say good-bye and board a red-eye flight to Pittsburgh. We were to begin a new chapter in our lives the next day, a ten-week program to prepare us for a two-year overseas volunteer assignment in the United States Peace Corps.

Prior to our wedding we had each lived in the same Los Angeles suburb, attended the same church, and gone to the same university. With Linda being a year older than I, we ran in different social circles. Our paths didn't cross meaningfully until spring break 1965 when we both volunteered for a project to renovate a San Francisco correctional halfway house. During that week a mutual attraction sparked but didn't fully ignite until we both arrived back on the UC Santa Barbara campus in the fall. By winter term, when I was a junior and Linda a senior, we were steady companions.

During our courtship, the two of us shared picnic lunches several times a week on the campus bluff overlooking the Pacific and hung out together on weekends. For us, the mid-sixties were carefree. We knew the music of the Beach Boys by heart, danced to Johnny Mathis, and loved the folk protest tunes of Peter, Paul and Mary. We lived sheltered lives on an idyllic beachside campus.

Early in 1966, the reality of life beyond college loomed closer. Linda was on schedule to graduate at the end of spring term. Social, popular with her peers, and full of confidence, she was thinking about her future. I was a year behind and not quite as certain of myself. My focus remained more immediate: classes, work-study job, and pitching on the Gaucho baseball team.

As Linda considered life beyond UCSB, we broached the possibility of getting married following my graduation a year later. We shared visions of what we might want to do if we started a life together. My thoughts had not gone beyond graduate school, while Linda had more far-reaching fantasies. She shared a story of a hometown neighbor who had joined the fledgling Peace Corps in 1963 and traveled to Morocco to live and work. Inspired by stories of his adventures, she started to nurture a desire for adventure herself. She wanted to see other parts of the world and make person-to-person connections in those places. Joining the Peace Corps had become her dream.

As we talked, Linda asked if I would consider making a two-year commitment to live and work somewhere overseas before going to graduate school. Living and working in another country was something I had never imagined. The idea of taking a break from school sounded good, but all I knew of the Peace Corps was that it was a program President Kennedy envisioned as a way of giving service to our country. I began investigating by reviewing the countries where PCVs served and the kind of work they did.

Considering our ages, I had questions. It seemed we had little to offer beyond youthful enthusiasm. As it turned out, that was exactly what Peace Corps was looking for at the time. Later that spring, when Peace Corps recruiters visited campus, we were encouraged to apply. By that point, the idea of working overseas stoked my fire. We started to hatch a plan.

Following her graduation, Linda moved to her parents' home in Santa Paula and found a social work position at the county hospital about an hour south of the UCSB campus. That summer, I worked a construction job in Los Angeles. We saw each other on weekends, worked on wedding plans for the following July, and filled out Peace Corps applications.

The application process took some time. In addition to completing multiple forms, we were asked to take a language aptitude test, send in transcripts, secure letters of reference, have FBI background checks, and apply for passports. We wanted the decision-makers in Washington, DC to know that, while we were applying as singles with different last names, we would be married shortly after my graduation the following June. Therefore, we included "Please consider us for the same assignment," in all our correspondence. We imagined a two-year grand adventure speaking a different language in some faraway place. An assignment in a Spanish-speaking country somewhere south of the border was what we thought most likely. Latin America seemed logical since we had both taken several years of Spanish.

When I returned to campus in the fall of 1966, Linda continued planning for our July wedding. We kept our fingers crossed, hoping for a Peace Corps assignment. With all that was on my plate and realizing we would need to investigate other possibilities if our Peace Corps dream did not materialize, I decided to forgo my senior season on the baseball team.

Neither of us will ever forget the day that spring when envelopes bearing the Peace Corps logo arrived in our mailboxes. Linda's letter came to her parents' home in Santa Paula, mine to my UCSB apartment. I tore open my letter, curious to see what it said. There, at the very bottom, was the key sentence inviting me to train for a teaching assignment in the Republic of Korea. Linda's invitation was the same.

So far, so good!

At least we had been invited to the same program. But, hold on...Korea?? We had mixed emotions; being selected thrilled us, but being considered for an Asian country, a region of the world largely mysterious to us, was a complete surprise.

The surprise actually enhanced our enthusiasm. Later, over the phone we said, "Sure! Let's go for it!" We wanted a new experience, and Korea would be that. We each sent back our confirmation and added 'packing for a post-honeymoon summer-long Peace Corps training program' to our to-do list!

Our plan unfolded just as we had imagined. Three weeks after my graduation, we had a beautiful wedding at our hometown church. That evening, we set out on a weeklong honeymoon up the California coast. Our feet barely touched the ground that week as we began to experiment with life together. Then, just eight days after our wedding, we gathered up our pre-packed luggage, left family and friends at the airport, and boarded a big jet bound for Peace Corps training in the Allegheny Mountains outside Altoona, Pennsylvania. We were to embark on three months of high-intensity language study, cultural education, and technical training that would prepare us for work we had never done, in a country we had never visited, and about which we knew very little. Our assignment was to become English conversation teachers in Korean secondary schools.

The red-eye flight that Sunday was long and ended with a harrowing landing. We circled Pittsburgh in the pitch dark for the longest time. Outside, the fog was so thick we couldn't see the plane's wingtips. Finally, the plane began to descend. I sensed the loss of altitude, but the descent seemed to take forever. Then, suddenly, the nose of the plane shot up at a steep angle. The force of the acceleration snapped our heads back, plastering us to our seatbacks. When we leveled off, we heard the pilot say wryly over the intercom, "We'll have to give that another try." After circling a bit longer, and with wingtips still not visible, the plane started down again. To great applause, we landed safely. As we stared out the window a dense fog shrouded the terminal.

Once on terra firma, our anxiety gradually abated. We weren't through flying, though; we still had a commuter flight to Altoona ahead of us. Most of the passengers waiting to board that flight were about our age. We made tentative inquiries and discovered that most of them were bound for the same place—Peace Corps training at a place called Blue Knob.

We were wary as we boarded the Allegheny Airlines plane. It was much smaller than the United 707 we had flown from L.A. The takeoff was uneventful, but soon Linda tapped my shoulder and pointed out the window. A blue flame was shooting out the rear of the starboard engine. We didn't know what to make of that, so I checked with the flight attendant. She dismissed it, seeming unconcerned, or if she was, she didn't show it. Unconvinced of our safety, we remained vigilant. When we landed in Altoona at mid-morning without incident, we were glad to be finished with flying for a while.

Next up was a bus ride to Blue Knob, a hilltop in southwestern Pennsylvania, home to a former military radar installation. Transformed to a modest ski resort during the winter months, it served as a Peace Corps training site in summer. We would be spending the next three months on Blue Knob. When we arrived in the early afternoon, we had been in transit for nearly twenty-four hours. Red-eyed and sleepless, we were, nonetheless, giddy with anticipation. Despite our fatigue, the bus ride from the airport was a real gabfest as everyone made introductions. Ours was one of several buses, filled with a total of 117 Peace Corps recruits, most of us young, recent college graduates.

Before the buses disgorged their eager passengers, a female staff member hopped up the steps, welcomed us, and asked, "How many of you are married couples?" When a number of us raised our hands she left to check the other buses. Minutes later, she returned looking a bit perplexed. Sixteen couples had identified themselves. The roster only showed eight.

All our extra precautions during the application process had not made it through to the training staff on the ground. Half the newlyweds were still recorded as singles. "Hmm," the staff member said, "It appears you married folks will have to double up, two couples to a room."

Oh, dear! Tears welled up in Linda's eyes and slid down both cheeks. I heard her whisper, "I want to go home." Instantly, I felt nauseated and panicked. Whatever security I had assumed as we embarked on our big adventure was quickly shaken. Quitting before we even started was something I couldn't imagine.

In response to gasps and groans throughout the bus, the staff person who had announced the possibility of doubling up said she would explore other options and get back to us. The crisis of the moment was put aside for a short while. Then, after a brief tour of the facilities, the storm clouds abated. Several thoughtful single men volunteered to double up into quad rooms, and the staff managed to convert several dormitory storerooms into habitable spaces, thus finding the additional eight rooms necessary to allow each couple its own domicile. We were immensely appreciative! The new arrangements assured us of privacy and I was able to let go of my imagined nightmare of having a wife, no job, no housing, and no idea of what our next steps might be. I had begun to fear we had leaped into the unknown without a parachute. With Linda's equilibrium restored, my fears quickly faded and I was able to focus on getting settled into our new digs.

Our room on the second floor of a two-story building was quite stark: a bare room lit by a single overhead bulb, linoleum floor, two built-in dressers, a small closet, and a floor-to-ceiling pile of metal government issue bed frames along one wall. Ours, we suspected, had been one of the storerooms. The gang toilet and shower rooms were down the hall. The whole place had the appearance of just what it was—an aging military barracks. It was to be our first home as husband and wife. While it was no palace, given the fears from which I was still recovering, I was one hundred percent in favor of making it work. And Linda seemed okay with it, too.

An unforgiving sleeping arrangement was the most physically uncomfortable feature of our modest new home. On bare linoleum, we placed two goose-down sleeping bags we had received as wedding presents from my parents. That was it—no pad, air mattress, or comforter. We had to make do. The only thing between hips and hard linoleum was the bottom half of a nylon bag filled lightly with tiny feathers. The old squeaky bed frames stacked against the wall were taboo. As was the custom in Korea, we were required to sleep on the floor. We knew that, in the short term, we were in for some uncomfortable nights. When the staff made supply runs to nearby Altoona, the first thing we ordered was a foam pad or air mattress, something that would make sleeping on the floor a bit more tolerable.

The facilities at Blue Knob consisted of a half-dozen boxy, two-story clapboard buildings, one of the larger ones converted to resemble a ski lodge, though only faintly. Scattered throughout what appeared to be barracks were classrooms, a cafeteria, offices, and lodging rooms that overlooked a thick deciduous forest on the flanks of what was really a hill rather than a mountain, at least from our West Coast perspective. Lush, green fields dotted the landscape in the distance. Our new home was in rural, agrarian, and humid Pennsylvania.

Our Blue Knob Room

Chapter 2

TRAINING

Long days soon became the norm. For five full days each week and a half-day on Saturday, training began at seven o'clock in the morning, often not ending until after nine at night. Each day, we had five hours of Korean language studies, plus classes in teaching methods, cultural issues, and occasionally stories from Americans with experience living in Korea.

Language classes formed the core of the program. Since few Koreans knew English, we would need to understand the rudiments of spoken Korean to get along on a daily basis. Drills in conversational Korean were supplemented with learning to read the unique symbols that comprised the ten vowels and fourteen consonants of the Korean alphabet. We were delighted at the near total lack of exceptions to Korean pronunciation and spelling rules as compared to the ubiquity of oddities in the English language.

Within the first month of training, we could sound out and pronounce Korean words; what we could *not* do for the most part was understand the meaning of what we read and heard. We needed to build our vocabulary, learn the complex grammar rules that governed speech, and then tune our ears to the very different sound of spoken Korean. We soon discovered that sounding out a word or sentence was one thing, while understanding that same vocabulary in the context of spoken speech was quite another.

The membership within language classes was reshuffled each week according to performance. Trainees most adept were grouped together. Discerning the pecking order of language groups was not difficult. Linda was usually part of one of the upper groups while I was somewhere in the middle of the pack. Korean language has a reputation of being a real challenge for native English speakers. The structure and sounds are strikingly different from our everyday speech. Our Korean instructors, newly arrived from Seoul, were patient as we practiced scripted conversations.

We were learning a different alphabet, new vocabulary, sentence structures, grammar, and proper articulation, all simultaneously. We learned a formal style of speech—one used most between people of equal social status. What we didn't learn was a more honorific style used when speaking to elders and people of higher social rank, and a less formal style used with children. Everything about spoken Korean was quite different from English.

The Korean Alphabet

Vowels	ㅏ	ㅑ	ㅓ	ㅕ	ㅗ	ㅛ	ㅜ	ㅠ	ㅡ	ㅣ
	a	ya	ŏ	yŏ	o	yo	u	yu	ŭ	i
Consonants	ㄱ	ㄴ	ㄷ	ㄹ	ㅁ	ㅂ	ㅅ			
	k, g	n	t, d	r, l	m	p, b	s, sh			
	ㅇ	ㅈ	ㅊ	ㅋ	ㅌ	ㅍ	ㅎ			
		ch, j	ch'	k'	t'	p'	h			

Linda had a talent for language; she adapted to new ways of expressing ideas, and her accent was often pitch perfect. I, on the other hand, had a less flexible tongue. Despite my best effort, my accent was more reflective of Southern California. Those of us who had the hardest time couldn't quite get the sounds right. One of our fellow trainees had a particularly difficult time with a phrase that, when Anglicized, sounded like, "*moolown eet chio,*" meaning something close to "*of course*" in English. His attempts unfailingly sounded exactly like "*baloney joe.*" He became legend for his fractured Korean utterances, endearing him to us. Alas, he didn't make it to the end of training. Being more of an average language learner, I didn't fear not making it through training, but I grew concerned about my ability to communicate when we arrived in Korea. I knew I was going to have to push myself to keep improving.

Saturday's training schedule was abbreviated, ending at lunch-time. By then we were all ready for a break. The daily schedule was so packed that we didn't have much free time during the week. We often had laundry to do on the weekends, reading to catch up on, and friendships to nurture. Most of us enjoyed getting outside. It was summertime and the weather warm. We took hikes and played games like basketball, ping pong and Frisbee golf.

Halfway through the summer, we began to receive vaccinations to boost our immune systems in preparation for encountering a whole new bacterial and viral environment in Korea. Typically, those shots were administered on Saturday afternoons, leaving us achy and uncomfortable, so much so that we did not look forward to the weekends quite as much as we had earlier in the summer. Our least favorite was a short series of gamma globulin shots, which left me with the sensation of having had a hot golf ball injected into my backside.

When a gamma globulin shot was on the schedule, a humorous thing occurred. The amount of vaccine we received was based on our weight, so all week prior to the scheduled injection, some trainees tried to limit what they ate, hoping to drop enough weight to lessen the amount of vaccine they would receive. Still, we all suffered no matter how much was injected into our bodies. On Saturday nights following those inoculations, Linda and I would often lie on our thin mattress pad, trying to find a comfortable position for sleep. Fortunately, those after-effects were short lived; by mid-day on Sunday, we were usually pain free.

Our meals during training were never very popular. The cooks in our cafeteria were contractors, and to prepare us for what we would find in Korea, Peace Corps had requested they make something akin to a Korean diet. Everyday Korean cuisine traditionally consisted of homemade soup, moist and sticky rice, and spicy kimchi complemented with a variety of mostly vegetable side dishes. The basic menu was the same for each meal of the day. To introduce us to such a diet, the cooks served us Lipton chicken noodle soup and Uncle Ben's instant rice, both out of a box. Side dishes didn't make it to the menu, except maybe some toast at breakfast.

The decision-makers couldn't have gotten it more wrong; our meals were not even a close approximation of Korean fare. We all collectively voiced our complaints, trainees and Korean language instructors alike. The instructors often didn't eat what the cooks prepared; some resorted to preparing meals in their dorm rooms. After much discussion, the cooks reverted to a cuisine with which they were more familiar, one that was only slightly more palatable.

As we soon discovered, our disappointment with the food was a predictor of other curious things to come during training. One was a lack of available information about Korea. The topic of Korean history seemed to be off limits, especially that regarding the first half of the 20th century when Korea was occupied and literally annexed by Japan, beginning in 1910. Koreans were forced into supporting Japan's war effort in the 1940s. After the war their country was partitioned into two regimes, one in the north and the other in the south. Before long, early in the 1950s, civil war ravaged the entire country. However, none of that was presented to us during our class discussions. Korea's political climate and economic situation that followed the 1953 truce were never raised. The other trainees and I sensed something was missing, but we never pressed the apparently taboo topics. Our language and technical studies kept us busy.

We did receive a warning to avoid discussion of Korean or American politics with any of our language instructors, who had all arrived recently from Seoul. That seemed reasonable. We assumed Peace Corps wanted us to remain neutral as cultural ambassadors for the United States. We did not fully realize at the time how much we had yet to learn about life on the ground in Korea in the late 1960s.

As the summer progressed, weekends were not without a little mischief among our fellow trainees. The consistent undercurrent of dissatisfaction with our meals became widespread. Often the cooking was bland and the servings scant. Linda and I didn't voice a complaint, but we knew others who felt more strongly. More than once, several of our fellow trainees raided the kitchen pantry after hours, sometimes finding leftovers to which they helped themselves. There was speculation among our ranks that the kitchen staff was shorting our servings and saving food for their own use. If so, that could explain why, despite having left evidence of their clandestine visits—things like chicken bones in the trash—no negative consequences ever befell the late night raiders, at least none that were discussed. The head cook may have simply chosen to absorb the losses without reporting them to administration. In any case, the topic was never raised at any of our meetings.

During eleven weeks on Blue Knob our training group became quite tight-knit. Lifelong friendships were kindled as we struggled together to learn the Korean language, methods for teaching English

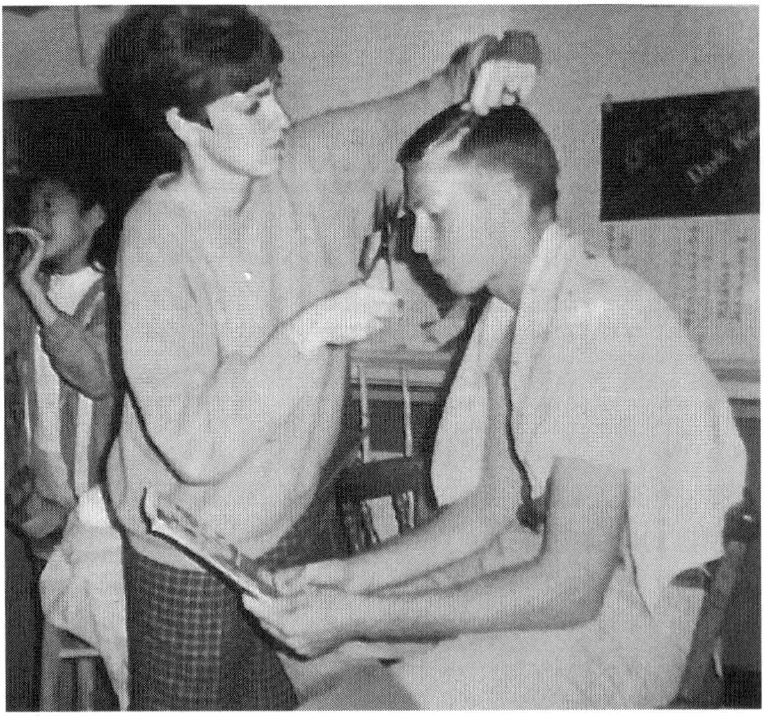

Linda Giving Me a Trim

as a second language, and ways to relieve the stress of a packed calendar in our free time.

Being isolated on a remote mountaintop without public transportation helped to assure the development of interdependence among all of us. We organized shopping lists that staff fulfilled on their weekly trips into town and made appointments for Sunday haircuts in the lodge with a couple of volunteers acting as barbers, one of whom was Linda. Trainees stocked and staffed a snack bar to enhance, and sometimes supplant, the meals that were never applauded.

Perhaps the group's greatest extracurricular accomplishment, however, was securing approval and the necessary liquor permits to establish a weekend nightclub. We converted a windowless unoccupied cinder block bunker located just down the hill from our barracks into a club we called the "*Kahtchee Kapsheeda*" (Korean for "Let's Go Together"). The *Kahtchee* was a place to mingle, enjoy a beer or a glass of cheap wine, and dance to current tunes that wafted from a scavenged jukebox. Those weekend evenings provided a respite from the daily grind and intensity of training activities.

Initially, we didn't realize that being invited to training did not assure us of selection for service in Korea. Throughout training, our fitness was continuously assessed, but the ultimate criteria for being selected were never made clear. In fact, the selection process seemed shrouded in mystery. We assumed decisions were based on how we performed in language classes, our response to the cultural and instructional technology discussions, and the impressions staff members had of our character and behavior over the course of the summer.

Linda and I had different reactions to our realization that we weren't shoo-ins to become PCVs. Linda, adept in picking up the Korean language and making friends, never experienced concern over being assessed for suitability. She assumed we would make it through and gave it little thought. I, not nearly as confident or as good with the language, did have some anxiety, owing in part to my own historical sense of insecurity. During my years growing up, I consistently saw myself on the social margin, without close friends. Keenly aware that bright, accomplished graduates of prestigious colleges and universities all across the country filled our training group, I wasn't sure how I measured up. My anxiety, though not a significant preoccupation, stayed with me throughout the summer.

Some trainees were concerned about the influence of the staff psychologist, a secretive man who was viewed with suspicion by many. We all had to meet with him at least twice over the course of the summer. We suspected he had some influence on our future; how much was a matter of speculation. Meeting with him was, for some, a dreaded experience, fueled in part by his aloof, distancing manner. To make matters worse, he asked us to make judgments about other trainees. He once asked all of us to provide three names for each of these four statements:

1. Will do an excellent job in Korea.
2. Is likely to fail in Korea.
3. I would be willing to be assigned to the same city as this person.
4. I do not want to be in the same city as this person.

Exercises such as that, plus the requirement that we take the controversial MMPI (Minnesota Multiphasic Personality Inventory), often used to help diagnose psychiatric disorders, made us feel as if we were constantly under a microscope.

Anxieties within the group were piqued when there was attrition in our ranks. Some trainees exited the program for personal reasons while others were involuntarily "deselected." We never knew why people left or exactly how decisions to remove certain trainees were made. We most often had little opportunity to debrief with those who left. They would just be gone one day. When trainees left the program, everyone assumed the psychologist had a hand in the decision. Whether that assumption had merit or not, his was a thankless job, one to which I personally did not think he was well suited.

How we learned of our selection was another exercise that proved unsettling. Late in the training program, on decision day, staff informed us that individual envelopes would appear under our doors early in the evening. Unbeknownst to us, two different letters with instructions to report to one of two different buildings were delivered. Upon opening our envelope we headed off to our assigned room where a crowd of staff and a few trainees greeted us with celebratory whoops as we entered. They immediately congratulated us for being selected as Peace Corps Volunteers.

After the stream of arrivals became a trickle and then completely ended, we realized we were missing several of our fellow trainees. A combination of confusion and sadness tempered our initial joy as word spread quickly around the room that some didn't make it. We were thankful to be selected, but worried about what would happen to those who would not be joining us.

As I noted, the psychologist's role in the decision to "deselect" some members of the group was a matter of speculation. He was not well-liked, not only by trainees but also by some of his fellow staff members. Toward the end of summer, he became the target of pranks. One occurred the week before the selection announcements when his red motor scooter went missing. After a short search, it was found close by in the woods. We didn't know who was responsible but the incident seemed to spark the imagination of others.

The day after the selection announcements were made, the scooter disappeared again. We heard that someone(s) had hoisted it onto the roof of the women's dorm sometime during the night. I don't recall how it was recovered, but I do know that time has not altered the feelings within our group toward the psychologist. I personally felt some empathy for him, having been a psychology major myself. His was a difficult task — that of judging which trainees were stable and capable of adjusting to the challenges we were expected to face, and which were not. His manner did not help his cause. Aloof and non-supportive, his behavior played a role in the dislike and suspicion many felt toward him.

With our status as PCVs confirmed, I sensed a big weight lifted from my shoulders. Training, however, was not over. We still had a couple of weeks before we were to depart Blue Knob. As language classes continued, the reality of going to Korea began to hit home. Peace Corps provided each of us a large sturdy trunk, and a list of suggested items to purchase and pack—things likely not available in Korea. We made a long list of personal hygiene products, winter and summer clothes, grooming aids, gifts for our host family and other things we thought we might need over the course of the next two years. After a couple of shopping trips to Altoona, our trunks were filled.

About a week before we departed Blue Knob we capped the summer at the Kahtchee, our weekend club, with a wild nightlong celebration. The party was a chance to blow off the steam built up in advance of selection day. Organizers collected a larger than normal kitty for the purchase of beer, wine and party snacks. We all gathered, volunteers and staff, that Saturday before the sun went down. Everyone was in a festive mood. The music blared, and speculation circulated about what secret ingredients might have been added to the sangria-like concoction in the punch bowl. Unfortunately for Linda and me, our evening was cut short when one of us went a bit overboard at that mysterious punch bowl. It was still dusk when I helped a very wobbly Linda, who rarely consumed alcohol, back to the dorm. We spent the rest of the evening there as she apologetically watched the ceiling spin and made frequent trips to commune with an alternative bowl in the bathroom down the hall.

Sadly, there was another casualty that evening. A member of our group broke her arm while trying to perform a gymnastic move she would never have attempted had she not visited that same punch bowl quite so often.

We all departed in the middle of the following week, including our friend whose arm was encased in plaster. Ours was to be the third group of PCVs to go to Korea, thus our group designation was K-III. Of the 117 prospective trainees who had arrived on those busses back in mid-July, Peace Corps ultimately selected 88 of us to be Volunteers.

The first group, K-I, had begun their service a year earlier, in the summer of 1966. K-II had followed a few months later. Both groups that preceded us taught English in secondary schools, just as we would be doing. Peace Corps eventually broadened its mission in Korea in subsequent years. From 1966 to 1981, just over two thousand volunteers in fifty-one different groups worked in education, health, agriculture, and tourism, all at the invitation of Korea's government.

Since the K-I group had not yet finished a full year in Korea during our summer on Blue Knob, news of their experience did not filter back to us; we really didn't know what to expect as we prepared to cross the Pacific. Our introduction to the language, the people, and the work we would be doing was still new and superficial. While we doubted our readiness, September turned to October, our trunks were shipped and our travel schedule announced.

During the first week of October, Linda and I flew back home to California for a week to reunite with family and friends and say our final good-byes. We would not be seeing any of those folks again for nearly two years.

We were to regroup with our fellow K-III PCVs in Seattle on October 11. The next stage of our grand adventure was set. We knew the trajectory of our lives was about to change. Just how, we could not imagine.

Chapter 3

THRUST FROM THE NEST

The day before we were scheduled to rendezvous with our group, Linda and I flew to Seattle. Following an unforgettable "last supper" of the best-ever chicken cordon bleu at an airport hotel, we frantically dashed off last minute thank-you notes for the mostly stored wedding gifts we had received three months earlier. The next morning, after dropping our evening's work in a postbox, we greeted our fellow travelers in the departure lounge at SeaTac International Airport. I had butterflies in my stomach as we told stories about our home visits and speculated about the adventure that lay before us.

Parting with family was double-edged; it was wrenching to know we would be gone for nearly two years but exciting to be headed off to find our way in the world. Under the surface, we harbored a healthy dose of anxiety. Korea was still a mystery. We had no accurate picture of where we were going and what to expect when we got there. In retrospect, we were engaged in a trust exercise of the highest order. We were about to launch on a voyage of discovery. Peace Corps, we presumed, would provide a safety net as we experimented with life in a new land, struggled to communicate in a still unfamiliar language, learned the ways of a different culture, and did work we had never done before. We chicks were about to leap from the comfort of a familiar nest into the unknown.

As I mentioned earlier, throughout our discussions at Blue Knob we received precious little information about contemporary Korea. We knew there were tensions with Japan, owing to the way the Japanese disregarded and mistreated the Korean population during the thirty-five years they ruled the country following the 1910 annexation. Then, after WWII, dissatisfaction was rampant with the division of the peninsula into different governments, North and South. Ultimately a brutal civil war took place, one that ended with a truce, but not a true peace. The North became a totalitarian socialist state with ties to both Russia and China, while the South birthed an authoritarian democracy, with military and financial support from the United States. The Korean people were left divided; many yearned for reunification. It was into that cultural tension that we were poised to enter.

Our flight to Seoul had two legs. The first stop was an overnight in Tokyo. We had nearly forgotten our anxiety about flying following our July experience. We were in a plane with a large group of friends, preoccupied with what lay ahead; thoughts of airplane trouble were a distant memory. After a long and uneventful flight, the plane touched down in the dark at Japan's Haneda Airport.

After making our way through Customs, we were dropped at a hotel in a business district not far from the airport. We ventured out immediately to stretch our legs and see what we could see. The fact that we had landed in a different country was evident. The smell of the cool evening air was different—not unpleasant, but to our noses unusual. The neon signs shone brightly in a language we found a total mystery. Written Japanese was a curious array of lines and squiggles, very different from Korean. On one block, construction on a high-rise continued into the night. The scene was lit like daylight as locals walked briskly down crowded sidewalks. We wandered for a while, marveling at the newness of it all, checking out the window displays of garments, electronics, and travel posters.

Hesitant to roam more broadly that night, we grabbed a bite to eat back in the hotel and retreated to our room. We didn't speak the language and wanted to avoid getting lost. We were a bit intimidated by the lack of anything familiar. Exploring our room's radio, I was surprised to find an English language broadcast of game seven of the 1967 World Series. It was a treat to listen as the Cardinals beat the Red Sox on a Bob Gibson 3-hitter.

Sleep was fitful that night, no doubt owing to a strange bed and our impending arrival in Korea the next day. The following morning we still felt tentative as we rose early to venture out with a few of our friends. Keen on purchasing a quality Japanese camera, we hoped our inability to speak the language would not thwart us. The hotel concierge pointed out a nearby shop on our map and off we went. A helpful shopkeeper who spoke excellent English guided us to a camera that looked right to us — familiar name brand, affordable, and not too complicated. Ideal! With that successful purchase under our belt, we hustled back to the hotel to check out and catch the bus to the airport. We had not eaten, but food was the furthest thing from our minds. Questions filled us: How would the mystery of Korea unfold? Would Seoul look remotely like the little we had seen of Tokyo? What complete unknowns awaited us?

The early afternoon flight was short. Seoul was just over an hour away. As we approached Kimpo Airport, everyone in our group rubbernecked at the windows to get a glimpse of what was waiting for us below. What I saw surprised me. The landscape was monochrome; agricultural fields and buildings all seemed to be various shades of the same color—brown. Seoul, what we could see of it, lay sprawled across a flat plain at the base of a mountain range to the north. The surrounding hills were brown as well and mostly devoid of trees.

While we all strained to get our first glimpse of Korea, Linda was the lone exception. As the plane descended, she developed an excruciating, stabbing headache. The pain brought her nearly to tears. Shaken, I had one of those '*Uh-oh!*' moments not knowing what might be wrong. Thank goodness my anxiety was short lived. Once we landed and the cabin pressure normalized, Linda began to recover, and by the time the plane finally came to a stop, her pain had subsided. What a relief!

It was a warm Friday afternoon, October 13. As I stepped into the sunlight at the top of the plane's stairway, I looked out over a big crowd on the Kimpo tarmac. It was a time long before airport security limited access to arrivals. Greeting us at the base of the stairs were members of the Peace Corps staff, local PCVs, Korean Ministry of Education personnel, a high school band, and nearly a hundred high school girls wearing black and white school uniforms, each holding a corsage. As the band played, a corsage was pinned to my jacket. We each were welcomed personally by our hosts, both Korean and American. We were off to a warm and festive beginning.

Kimpo Welcome

The bus ride into Seoul was eye opening, with much to take in: the people, their dress, the landscape, the ways of getting around, the buildings. Kimpo was several miles from the city, located in what seemed to be an area of transition between agricultural land and the beginnings of an industrial zone.

Korea, at the time, was a poor country, still emerging from their horrific civil war fourteen years earlier. Seoul was not the modern metropolis it is today. The dusty dirt road teemed with pedestrians, men on sturdy bicycles piled high with goods, others pulling two-wheeled carts loaded with construction materials, women walking with large, heavy-looking tubs on their heads filled with produce, and children of all ages running about. No sidewalks existed; all those folks made their way along the roadside as buses, taxis, heavy trucks and Jeeps sped past in the middle of the broad expanse. The road, despite its width, lacked any marked lanes.

Traditional dress was common. The women carrying the heavy loads on their heads wore long gathered skirts with short bolero-type jackets, many toting babies secured to their backs with what appeared to be quilt-type blankets. Men wore baggy trousers, t-shirts and straw hats. Most men, women and children all wore low-cut slip-on rubber shoes. Elementary age children wore shorts and colorful t-shirts or blouses, while secondary school students walked in small groups wearing black and white uniforms—skirts and blouses for the girls, dark pants and high collared black jackets for the boys.

What stood out most to me was that *everyone* seemed to be very busy, and *everything* looked very old. The carts, buses, trucks, and even the crude wooden A-frame backpacks, looked worn out. The people, too, appeared stressed as they bustled about at a quick pace. Many men had a grizzled appearance as they toiled in dirty work clothes. The women looked intent and purposeful. Much of the population I saw that day impressed me as impoverished, and nobody was overweight. What decades later became known internationally as the economic "Miracle on the Han River" was, at that time, in its infancy. Based on what we saw that afternoon, modernization looked to be a long way off.

The city of Seoul sat on the north bank of the Han, with planted fields visible on the south side of the river. Seventy percent of Korea's population in 1967 was engaged in agriculture. Seoul's population at the time was something over three million. Over the next four decades, the city would grow to nearly ten million, and the metropolitan core would spread to the other side of the Han. During that time, the percentage of the citizenry involved in farming would shrink from seventy percent to just seven percent as agriculture became mechanized and the country industrialized to become one of the world's leading economies.

The buildings we saw as our bus rolled along the dusty road were single-story. Houses sat just off the roadway next to fields recently harvested. Uniformly the color of unfired clay, they were dull and brown with thatched roofs. Many shack-like shops appeared to barely stand upright with big signs atop their facades written in Korean, words we could pronounce but not understand, our vocabulary still woefully small. Some shopkeepers spread their wares outside on the ground bordering the street.

As we got closer to the city, the dirt road became pavement and buildings grew in height. Houses looked more refined, almost all with tile roofs and high surrounding walls. Tall apartment houses and office buildings came into view, many in a state of partial construction. In the city proper, traffic increased and crowded sidewalks became more common. Architecture was a mix of multi-story office buildings and traditional single-story structures with roofs of tile, often turned up slightly at the corners. All the structures appeared to be painted in varying shades of gray and brown. To me everything looked drab.

Nowhere did we see signs of the war that had devastated the country more than a decade earlier. The prosperity that Korea would eventually achieve was, however, nowhere in sight. Seoul would one day challenge Tokyo's modern urban skyline, but in 1967 it did not come close.

Our bus crept slowly down streets barely wider than alleys, crowded with pedestrians, bicyclists, and hand-pulled carts. We pulled over to the curb on a narrow lane. A Peace Corps staff member who had been riding up front rose and welcomed us to Seoul. He announced that we'd be staying in the *yogwan* (inn) just adjacent to where the bus had stopped. On the far side of a nearby intersection he pointed out an office building, the home of Peace Corps Korea's headquarters. Each of us on the bus was handed a packet as he announced we were free for the weekend; nothing was scheduled. Our next responsibility was to report to the Peace Corps office at 9 a.m. on Monday to begin several days of orientation.

We were asked to open our packets. Inside, we found sightseeing tips, health precautions, a city map, and five thousand *won* (equivalent to about $18.50 US). We had no clue how far that money would go. The price of goods and services had never been discussed as part of our training. We soon learned that what we had been given was plenty to get us through the weekend. Things were comparatively cheap; a bus ride was ten *won*, a meal typically about one hundred *won*. The exchange rate was 270 *won* to the dollar. That meant Linda and I could both eat dinner, and the total bill would be less than the equivalent of one dollar. Our education about Korea had finally begun.

As we stepped off the bus, the surprise of being suddenly on our own began to sink in. We were in a strange city with very limited language skills and there were no cell phones in those days! It appeared we chicks were being thrust from the security of our nest prematurely. We definitely had doubts about our ability to fly. But we weren't really on our own. Had we been, I think my anxiety would have been higher. Linda and I were young and inexperienced, but our friends were in the same situation, and we all had each other. Together, we were game to explore a place that was so different to us. For me, however, it was a sobering moment. I sensed I was on the threshold of the biggest challenge of my life.

Checking in to our two-story yogwan was like entering another world. Everything was strange: the sights, the sounds, the smells. We had no idea what to expect, but we knew we were about to find out. Our second-floor room, with flowery pink wallpaper and shiny yellow floor, was large and stark. The pile of two folding mattresses, comforters and tiny pillows sat on a low table in the corner. In another corner was a small dresser and mirror to be used while seated on the floor. A window looked out onto the alley below. Lighting was a fluorescent tube on the ceiling. Our dimly lit bathroom was tiled, with sink, shower and a porcelain trough in the floor—a squat toilet. The brown toilet tissue had a crepe paper consistency. We were unaware at the time that toilet paper of any kind was a rare commodity. Newspaper, magazines and school worksheets were more common substitutes. We would eventually debate which was most absorbent.

That first evening, we explored the commercial area around our inn—a warren of alleys lined with tiny, dilapidated shops, protected for security purposes with what looked like mini-garage doors. We paid close attention to the conversations of passers-by, listening to determine if we could recognize any of what we heard. Despite three months of training, we understood almost nothing.

The streets remained crowded as dusk began to settle. Beggars, peddlers, businessmen, and uniformed students all mingled and paid little attention to one another. Sturdy bicycles, used to transport goods, were common; their bells rang frequently, apparently to alert others to their presence. The smells of the city were different, too. Pungent and unfamiliar, they seemed to change around each corner.

Together with several friends, we began to search for a suitable place to eat. We found several tiny, dirty-looking places, some with raw unrefrigerated meat hanging in the window. Not very inviting to us, but popular if judged by the number of patrons being served.

One restaurant that looked better than the rest had two young boys hawking for business on the sidewalk. Unwilling to take "no" for an answer, they ushered us in.

Once seated, we realized we were in trouble right away; we could make no sense of the menu. It was printed mostly in Chinese characters. We knew *bulgogi* (fire meat) was a popular dinner item, so we gambled. Sure enough, the person taking our order didn't blink. The thinly sliced marinated beef arrived on a platter, together with a burner and domed skillet we used to cook the meat ourselves. Rice, kimchi, and a few other side dishes rounded out the meal. Most of us heeded the medical warnings and ate just the meat, rice and whatever we could cook thoroughly ourselves. Despite Linda's protest, I tried a bit of kimchi, but avoided the rest, not knowing what might be safe and what not. The meal was delicious, the portions generous, and the bill for five of us came to under six hundred won, less than three dollars.

Back in our room, we discovered something about older traditional structures, a lesson that repeated itself whenever we traveled. During the night with the light off, we heard rustling from above. Rats, being nocturnal, were noisily scurrying about on the other side of the ceiling while we tried to sleep. At first, we didn't know what we were hearing, but it didn't take long to figure it out. We had an unfounded fear that those little creatures might find their way into the room during the night. In addition, despite a midnight to 4 a.m. curfew when everyone was to be indoors, we could hear sounds in the street below well into the early morning hours. It appeared that at least some of the locals took liberties with the law, at least on the weekend.

Our arrival in Korea impressed upon us that we were in a land totally different from anyplace we had ever seen, heard, smelled, or tasted. For me, I felt we had been deposited in a place where we had minimal navigation skills. We were on our own and our learning curve was about to get very steep.

Chapter 4

FIRST IMPRESSIONS

We awakened at dawn after a restless night. It was Saturday morning, our first in Korea. The sun was not yet up as loud shouts began to emanate from the alley below. Curious, we rose quickly off our comfortable floor bed to peek out the window. We watched as street vendors announced their presence and pushed carts filled with sundry goods we didn't recognize. We took in the sights, strange sounds, and unusual smells. Those very first impressions of Korea – the sights, the people, the sounds, and the smells — were a sensory blast forever seared into our memories.

Our first priority for the day was to find something to eat. We knew the building housing the Peace Corps office, just across the intersection, had a western-style restaurant on the top floor. We met some friends there, ordered breakfast, shared our experience of the night before, and discussed how best to begin our exploration of the city.

We decided to wander awhile and see what we discovered. Off the main boulevards, the streets and alleys were narrow, winding affairs, lined with small open-air shops of all types and hole-in-the-wall restaurants. Still timid, we mostly just peeked into shops as we passed by.

Around lunchtime, we met up with several other members of our group and worked up the courage to venture into one of the larger restaurants. The place we chose had high ceilings, lots of windows, and was far from fancy. It seemed almost industrial, as if it might have been a converted warehouse. Sunlight splashed across the noisy, customer-packed room. A large round table accommodated all of us, and we all ordered the same thing: *bulgogi baek ban* (beef cooked at our table with all the trimmings). Linda and I were curious to compare it with the dinner we had eaten the evening before. However, the main reason for our choice was that it was the only thing we all knew how to order in Korean.

Ajushees (waitpersons) brought platters of raw beef strips with scallions in a soy-based marinade and a bowl full of raw eggs, together with a domed burner upon which we cooked the meat and eggs. Side dishes of kimchi, vegetables and large portions of steaming rice accompanied the meal. It was a feast, much to the liking of everyone at the table. Of all of us, Linda was by far the most careful. She cooked her meat and egg for the longest time and enjoyed it with only the rice—no uncooked vegetables for her. In fact, during the whole weekend, white bread and rice were her staples. She was ever the cautious one and urged me to reconsider if I chose some culinary unknown that to her seemed chancy.

Later, she felt vindicated when the Peace Corps doctors described the risks of eating in commercial establishments. When I did suffer a bit of digestive discomfort, she delighted in needling me, pointing out that she had yet to suffer any ill effects from what I teasingly described as "her anemic white diet."

Outside, on the broad downtown thoroughfares, traffic resembled a free-for-all. Bicycles, hand-pulled carts, and pedestrians all vied for space in the city with buses, taxis, trucks, and a few black Jeeps used by government officials. As chaotic as it seemed, we never witnessed an accident. Buses were the most common conveyances; those most crowded appeared to be the oldest, and as it turned out, the cheapest. They were no-frills and heavy-duty, the only seats being benches around the perimeter of the interior. As a result, most passengers stood. There were two doors, one at the front and one at the rear, each staffed by a girl in a powder blue smock. In addition to collecting fares (ten won, the equivalent of about three cents), the bus girl's responsibility was to keep passengers, often crammed inside like sardines in a can, from falling into the street. When the buses were most crowded, the doors remained open. The bus girl at the rear door stood in the stairwell, gripping the handholds on either side. When it was safe for the driver to step on the gas, she pounded the side of the bus twice, yelled, "*Awriya!, Awriya!*" and away they went. Like many things we discovered in those first few days, we said to each other, "Can you believe this?" It wasn't long, however, before we could be counted among the passengers.

The central downtown intersections were another fascination. When two main thoroughfares converged, the traffic was managed not with signals but huge roundabouts of what seemed like six or eight lanes. Marked by dotted lines, those lanes seemed to serve as mere suggestions for where to drive. Vehicles of all types switched lanes willy-nilly while trying to exit at their intended departure points. If the driver didn't succeed at first, he (never she) would go around the circle again, jockeying for a position to exit the next time around. Witnessing that, we were glad we were not allowed to drive vehicles.

On Sunday, we set out on foot to visit some of the popular antiquities in Seoul. Palaces, gardens, and museums were on our list. As we consulted our map early in our prowl, a group of four young male college students approached us. They seemed to sense we were new arrivals. In halting English, the most assertive of the four said, "We'd like to have intercourse with you." I learned later that line was an apparent quote from a popular book of American English slang.

The students offered to show us some of the sights we wanted to see in exchange for an opportunity to practice their English. From the innocent looks on their faces, we sensed the boys did not fully grasp the meaning of what their leader had just said. They were polite and seemed to genuinely want to show us around. We were all game for the adventure, so we accepted their offer. For the entire afternoon they led us on a most pleasant guided tour of some of Seoul's historical sites, which we found grand in size but rough around the edges, not well maintained. Those boys were delightful; we enjoyed trying to exchange information and giving them conversational tips in their use of English.

Later, as the afternoon waned, we wanted to return their favor by inviting them to a restaurant. Instead, they suggested we rendezvous later at our yogwan. There, they suggested we visit a nearby *tabang* (tearoom). Tearooms were popular places to gather and socialize everywhere in Korea. We spent a couple of hours that evening visiting, learning about each other and Korea. We talked about the boys' studies, university life, and their aspirations for the future. They were curious about our country and our reasons for being in Korea. They had no knowledge of Peace Corps but were unanimous in their agreement that Korea could use more and better English teachers. That experience left us with a positive first impression of interacting with younger Koreans. Students, we had begun to discover, were curious about us, proud of their own country, and very motivated to learn English.

We awoke Monday morning ready to get started with our orientation. We were curious about the Peace Corps/Korea organization, how things worked, and what was scheduled for us next. Filled with stories about our weekend adventures, we all converged at the headquarters. We talked about the places we had visited, the people we met, how we got along trying to communicate in Korean, and the surprises we discovered as we observed life on the streets. We had difficulty quieting down for the meeting that morning.

Kevin O'Donnell, the administrative director of the Peace Corps in Korea, welcomed us. A retired executive from a Pittsburgh steel company, he was enthusiastic, intelligent, compassionate, and thoughtful. He emphasized the importance of what we were about to undertake, assuring us that Korea's future rested on its ability to use and understand English, the medium of international business. Peace Corps, he acknowledged, was a new program to Korea, a partnership between the Korean government and the United States. We were breaking new ground, he said. Americans teaching in Korean schools was unprecedented, and our role was to help meet the country's need for greater English proficiency.

The fiscal officer, Bruce Lawhead, filled us in on money matters. He was a unique character, full of humor, and his personality distinctly different from the button-down, three-piece, wing-tipped style of Director O'Donnell. Bruce dressed flamboyantly in outfits that reflected a different culture each day: African safari, Middle Eastern, European Swiss, Mexican, and so on. We never knew what kind of outfit Bruce would be wearing when we had occasion to visit Peace Corps headquarters. As the orientation progressed, I developed the impression that within Peace Corps/Korea, diversity and latitude in how we approached our work was accepted. I found that empowering.

By far, the presentation with the most significant shock value that morning came from one of the Peace Corps doctors. He was frank about the importance of avoiding diseases that posed a potential threat to our health. We needed to avoid consuming fresh, uncooked vegetables, raw fruit, river fish, water that had not been boiled, and foods from street vendors. Within his remarks was a statement we never forgot. "Just imagine," he said, "A fine fecal veneer covers everything you eat wherever you go in Korea." That got my attention. He talked about Korea's agricultural practice of using raw human waste as fertilizer. It was simply a part of the food chain. While he spoke, I received jabs from Linda again, more forceful that time. The doctor left us with no doubts about the precautions we had to take. His message was crystal clear. At that point I became a believer.

Our orientation during those first days included some memorable cultural events and excursions. A dance show at a popular venue, Korea House, was dazzling. Colorful costumes, traditional music played on unique instruments, and dances that told stories gave us a sense of Korea's rich culture. The performances, all by women, were elegant beyond our expectations, quite a contrast to the impoverished look of people we saw on the street.

Another highlight was a trip to a vast iconic landmark, *Namdaemun* (South Gate), an impressive structure at least a city block in length. Dating back to the 14th century, the gate was a stunning combination of large, carefully engineered stones that framed the huge gate, topped by a spectacular horizontal wooden pagoda meticulously painted in vibrant colors. Once one of three entrances to the ancient walled city, the gate had long since been surrounded by urban sprawl and was well within the city limits; it was a proud symbol of Seoul's historic past.

Fronting Namdaemun was one of the city's largest open-air markets. Everything imaginable was for sale in what seemed like a thousand little booths set within a warren of aisles, all in the shadow of the enormous gate. The atmosphere reminded us of an urban fair, noisy and busy. While there, we decided to test our negotiating skills as we shopped for a couple of small towels and a knife for peeling the tasty local fruit. Prices in Korea, we had been taught, were always negotiable. During our language classes at Blue Knob, we learned phrases to help us negotiate. We tried those phrases out. Success! Our bargaining resulted in a better price than those first quoted for the items we purchased. We undoubtedly paid more than a local, but we were pleased with ourselves, encouraged by the usefulness of our meager language abilities.

In anticipation of our need to improve our conversation skills, the Peace Corps arranged for us to move to a yogwan closer to Yonsei University, where we would have five additional days of intensive language training before heading to our service sites throughout the country.

We had been warned that sometime during our first ten days in Korea, most of us would come down with a short flu-like illness as our bodies adjusted to a different bacterial and viral environment. Typically, the symptoms weren't anything to be concerned about, but some in our group were knocked out of commission for a day or two. Sure enough, I spent a couple of days in gastric distress. I missed a day of language training, which I sorely needed, and an evening dinner hosted by one of the Blue Knob language instructors at his home in Seoul. Being of a solid constitution and admirably more conservative in her culinary choices, Linda did not become ill and didn't miss a beat. I hated to miss visiting the private home of one of our instructors. All the residences we had seen throughout the city were protected with high surrounding walls. I was curious to glimpse how people lived behind those walls. Unfortunately, my curiosity had to wait.

Early in our second week, we received our work assignments. Members of our group were assigned to all sections of the country, some to larger cities and some to remote towns and villages. Linda and I were to be stationed in Taegu, Korea's third-largest city (population six hundred thousand), located about two-thirds of the way down the peninsula from Seoul. Linda was to teach in a public girl's school, and I was assigned to a private boy's school. We would both be teaching seventh-graders in their first formal year of English study. Taegu, we were told, was an industrial city surrounded by mountains, with a reputation for having the country's warmest summers and coldest winters. That description gave us pause, but we were eager to get there.

Questions filled us as we traveled south by train from Seoul. We wondered: "*How will we like Taegu?*" "*What will our school assignments be like?*" "*How will we be received?*" And of paramount concern, "*Where and with whom will we be living?*"

The four-hour train ride introduced us to the countryside. The fields and rice paddies were not like the geometric shapes we were accustomed to seeing in California. Appearing artfully crafted, most were small, terraced and contoured to the shape of the gently sloping hills. As I watched the scenery pass, I wondered how the farmers worked those fields, what they planted, and what their homes were like.

Clustered together in small villages, the houses were like those we glimpsed on our first day's trip from Kimpo Airport to downtown Seoul — earthen structures with thatched roofs and small windows. As the train rolled along, some of my questions about how the people lived began to be answered. It was harvest time. Ox-drawn plows and handheld scythes were abundant. The work appeared backbreaking. We seemed to have entered a time warp when farms were not yet mechanized, and farmers — men and women alike — were accustomed to strenuous physical labor. But, of course, it was not a trip back to the past; it was present day Korea.

An emotional reminder that we were, indeed, in a distant land came not long after we departed Seoul. Our train traveled swiftly in open country when suddenly it came to an abrupt, jarring, almost screeching halt just outside a small hamlet. Wondering what had happened to cause us to stop, we looked around for somebody to answer our questions, but found no one. After perhaps twenty minutes, the train began to ease slowly down the track. A clue to the reason behind our brief stop presented itself when we rolled by the covered body of what appeared to be a small elderly woman. Speculation soon spread among passengers that she had been struck by the train and killed. I immediately felt sick and confused. How could such an accident happen? As the train picked up speed, the accident dampened our spirits, and I began to wonder what other unexpected, troubling experiences we might encounter while living in such a distinctively unique land. After a while, I again became engrossed with the scenery outside the train window, but the fragility of life and the reality of our vulnerability stuck with me.

Life in Korea, I realized more clearly, would be different. We would encounter people and events we had not experienced before, some of which would be difficult to understand. Values and beliefs would be new to us. We had seen disturbing things in Seoul, things that troubled us. Beggars on the streets, dirty and dressed in rags, some with lost limbs or congenital birth defects, seemed desperate. We were told that the population largely rejected such people. Consequently, they had no access to services.

Another more trivial realization was that travel within Korea would be different. Public transportation would be our primary means of getting around. We saw almost no private cars; instead, residents used bicycles, buses, and taxis. Early challenges for us would include purchasing tickets and negotiating with taxi drivers. Distant trips meant traveling by train or country bus, over dusty, muddy, potholed, or wash-boarded roads. There were few paved roads, no through routes that ran from Seoul in the north down the peninsula to Taegu and on to Pusan on the southern coast. Again, I was mindful of the potential uncertainties and risks.

Antiquities in Seoul.

Traditional Art Performances at Korea House.

Chapter 5

LANDING IN TAEGU

Our train crawled to a stop at Taegu Station in the late afternoon on Tuesday, October 24, our eleventh day in Korea. People of all ages crowded the platform, dressed collectively in a mix of traditional and western attire. Of particular interest were the older gentlemen in baggy off-white trousers, long coats, and black stovepipe horsehair hats. That sight was descriptive of the Korea we were beginning to comprehend, older generations being more traditional and younger ones more modern.

Our Peace Corps regional representative's administrative assistant greeted us at the station. A young Korean gentleman, he spoke excellent English. After pulling about a dozen of us together, he told us that we would be spending a couple of nights at a local yogwan while we attended an orientation conference with all the PCVs in the region, both newly arrived and experienced. Our regional rep, Mel Merkin, who lived in Taegu with his wife and four sons, would host the conference. Mel was to be our resource for administrative support, a person to whom we could ask questions, collaborate with on handling difficult situations, and make special requests.

We were immediately attracted to Mel. An imposing figure, tall, soft spoken and wry-witted, he was patient beyond measure as we peppered him with questions during the next day's meeting. His manner instilled confidence. Moreover, he reassured us of Korea's keen interest in hosting us as teachers and volunteer ambassadors from the USA.

As Mel described our worksites, we began to see how our group of friends would be dispersed across the region. At an informal social gathering that evening, we had a chance to meet PCVs from the groups that had preceded us, those who had been in the country for over a year. We quickly noted that mixing in and getting to know those more experienced Volunteers might not be easy. Like our group, they had bonded with one another and, naturally, seemed more interested in reconnecting with friends they had not seen in a while rather than connecting with us. For those of us assigned to Taegu, that situation changed pretty quickly. The eight of us in the immediate area, a mix of the K-I, K-II, and K-III groups, became fast friends over the next several months.

The following day, Thursday, dawned cool and gray. Those in our K-III group assigned to more distant locations departed for their sites. The new Taegu arrivals, including Linda and I, met representatives from our schools for the first time at a luncheon hosted by the Ministry of Education. From there, we were escorted to our sites to meet faculty and receive a tour of the facilities.

As I met administrators at *Kei Sung Joong Hakyo* (Kei Sung Middle School) my woefully inadequate ability to speak Korean was evident. Beyond a few formal greetings and simple self-introductions, I was helpless. While I struggled, we managed to muddle through when a few faculty members tried out their own limited English. I learned I would be teaching eight classes, each having 60 students in relatively small classrooms with tightly arranged rows of tiny student desks. I would have each class twice per week and my focus was to be on spoken English. The students would have Korean teachers for grammar and reading in separate classes. Despite feeling ill prepared for the task, I was scheduled to begin teaching the following Monday.

Linda's school and mine were quite different. *Chae Il Yo Joong Hakyo* (Number 1 Girls Middle School) was public, an older wooden two-story building set on the edge of a large dirt field. The field was like a parade ground where students assembled each morning before classes began. The grounds were stark, mostly bare dirt. The school did have shrubs and a few trees along the front of the building where several large stones marked the entrance.

In contrast, Kei Sung, my school, was a large four-story concrete building situated on one side of a larger campus that included a high school. A two-story ivy-covered administration building sat between the middle and high schools. Behind those structures was a large flat dirt athletic field. The Kei Sung campus, located behind a five-foot wall and built on a low hill studded with evergreen trees, felt apart from the bustle of the city. It reminded me of a small college campus.

Despite the difference in size, our two schools did share some similarities. The naturally lit classrooms had large windows, sixty small desks in rows, with a teaching platform and blackboard in front. Neither school had a central heating system of any kind; only the collective body heat of students warmed the classrooms. Linda's school did have small pot-bellied stoves, painstakingly installed in each classroom every fall, but school administrators only lit the stoves on one or two days during the winter months. My school never bothered installing stoves in any of the classrooms.

The teachers' rooms at each of our schools were almost identical. Each was large and the only room in the whole school that had heat in winter. Two large coal-burning pot-bellied stoves dominated either end of a long interior space. Those stoves weren't lit until November 15, regardless of the weather. The perimeter of each room was lined with desks, one for each teacher on the faculty. On cold days, teachers would often encircle the stoves to warm themselves upon returning from the bitterly cold classrooms.

The next day, Friday morning, Linda and I reported to our respective schools for our first day of work. An assembly was scheduled during the morning at each school when we were to be introduced to the student body, give a short speech, and then have an opportunity to meet the rest of the faculty and observe a class or two. Even though our language instructors in Seoul had helped us draft our messages, we were both very nervous about trying to make ourselves understood in front of an entire school. When we debriefed later, Linda described her experience in a way that sounded very similar to mine. We both spoke outdoors on an elevated platform. The entire student body stood before us as we spoke in what we knew was elementary, but hopefully understandable Korean.

I suspected Linda's message was far more effective than mine. Her pronunciation, accent, and fluency had always been superior. For me, Korean had not become any easier since my days of struggle at Blue Knob. I was mortified, as I stood in front of about 1500 students.

Student assemblies at both schools occurred outdoors since neither school had an auditorium large enough for the entire student body. At Kei Sung, the weather was cool, and the sky was gray as the school principal introduced me. I trembled as I looked out over a sea of curious young faces, all dressed in their black uniforms and caps. In my halting Korean, I did my best to thank the school for inviting me and apologized for my inability to speak fluently. I described my commitment to helping my students learn English, my three months of training, and my excitement at being in Korea, together with my wife. When I finished, the students responded with polite applause. However, I was pretty sure they left asking each other, "*What did that tall American say? I didn't catch any of it. Such a funny accent! How are we supposed to learn from someone who can't speak Korean?*" I sensed I was off to a shaky start, at best.

Chae Il Girls Middle School

Chae Il Parade Ground

Kei Sung Administration Building

Kei Sung Boys Middle School

Kei Sung Middle School Teachers Room

Chapter 6

GETTING SETTLED

After our introductory school visits, the two of us had one more highly anticipated event scheduled that Thursday afternoon – meeting the family with whom we would be living for the next two years! PCVs in Korea, for a variety of practical reasons, did not live independently. Housing was tightly controlled, and rental property was unheard of. Home heating used pressed coal cylinders that required tending throughout the day. Refrigeration and western-style appliances did not exist, necessitating frequent trips to the market. Homes in Taegu had electricity, but its availability was sporadic, especially in winter. Each home had its own hand-pumped faucet in the courtyard. Internal plumbing was rare. Most homes had an outhouse that was cleaned periodically by "honey bucket" men. As a result of all those conditions, living independently would have been time-consuming, labor-intensive, and require good command of the Korean language.

Given our limitations, living with a family provided the most logical solution. At the same time, however, hosting a foreign boarder was quite unusual in Korea. We never learned how host families were recruited, but most had almost no preparation for boarding an American houseguest. Expectations on both sides — boarders and host family — could be quite different. As a result, Korea's PCVs had a broad variety of living experiences, some mutually satisfactory and some more challenging.

Good fortune smiled upon us when Linda joined me at Kei Sung that afternoon to meet the father of our host family. *Lee Dong Seung* was a chaplain and teacher at Kei Sung, a school affiliated with the

Korean Presbyterian Church. Soft-spoken and of slight build, with close-cut hair and a warm smile, he appeared to be in his early forties. We addressed him as *Moksanim* (Pastor), though between us we referred to him as Mr. Lee. After visiting for a while at the school, we traveled together to his home to meet his family.

During the war between the North and South in the 1950s, Mr. Lee had worked for the United States Army and was able to recall quite a bit of GI English, some of it quite colorful. Although his English was limited, he was fluent enough for us to collaborate on everyday issues as we settled in. The mother of the family, whom we called *Samonim* (Minister's wife), was a kind, warm, shy woman who spoke not a word of English. She welcomed us with a big smile and made every effort to make us comfortable. The most endearing members of the family were their three children: *Pil Gook* (twelve-year-old boy), *Pil Yoon* (ten-year-old girl), and *Pil Wan* (eight-year-old boy). As we all shyly introduced ourselves, our first impression of the whole family was positive. Feeling welcomed by all of them, we made plans to move into their home the following afternoon.

Located on the outskirts of the city, the Lee home sat on a dirt street in a neighborhood where all the houses were close together, each behind a high wall. Many of those walls were topped with broken glass or barbed wire. Secured by a substantial metal gate and separated from the neighboring houses by a narrow pedestrian walkway, their home was a sturdy concrete two-story building with a flat roof. We had the impression that privacy and security were important issues in the lives of Koreans.

The Lee house was unusual in several ways. For one, it had a flat roof and an outdoor patio on a portion of the second story, which served as the roof above the first-floor entry area. The house looked like none other in the neighborhood; all the other homes were of a single-story traditional design with gently pitched tile roofs. Our first impression was that the house seemed quite large, especially for a pastor and part-time teacher.

Inside the metal gate on the ground floor, a small outdoor courtyard featured a hand operated water pump and a platform holding large ceramic storage vessels. Adjacent to the courtyard, along the side of the house were two steps up to a four-foot-wide concrete porch and the home's sliding glass door entrance. Shoes, never worn inside the house, were taken off and left on that porch. The door opened into a polished hardwood entry area, bordered by three rooms and a bathroom. Furnished minimally, no chairs graced the rooms; in traditional Korean homes, people sat on the floor.

Set back from the entry area, the center room contained a tall armoire for storing clothes. That room served as the family dining room and was where the children and household assistant slept. A freestanding chest held the bedding that was removed at bedtime and returned before breakfast. The second room to the right of the entry contained a desk on which sat a big black rotary telephone. That room served as both Mr. Lee's office and a sleeping room for overnight guests. Mr. Lee and Samonim slept in a smaller third room on the other side of the entry area. A small door opened from that room into a sunken kitchen.

A real surprise was the existence of an indoor bathroom. Typical Korean homes did not have indoor plumbing; almost all had a *pyonso* (outhouse). The bathroom in the Lee home had a western-style toilet, tub, and sink. However, the similarity to western facilities ended there. While everything looked familiar, it didn't take long to discover some significant differences. For one, the house had no hot water. Water from the well in the tiny courtyard was pumped up to a holding tank on the roof. Gravity fed water to the sink and toilet. Outflow from the sink drained directly onto the bathroom floor, which sloped to a central drain and emptied into the open street gutter outside. The bathtub was not used for bathing, but rather as storage for buckets and drying racks. Lastly, the seated toilet, another oddity, was not connected to a sewer. It emptied into a shallow concrete tank under the house, cleaned monthly by the "honey bucket" man. His two open buckets of raw sewage, hung from a wooden shoulder yoke, always alerted us to his presence whenever he was nearby. Despite its peculiarities, that bathroom offered far more conveniences than did the homes of most of our fellow PCVs.

We still had one more surprise. The room that would become our second home, following our first at Blue Knob, was upstairs with large windows on two sides and a commanding view over the neighboring rooftops to the hills beyond. Inside we found a wood-framed double bed occupying about half the room. Surprised and a bit disappointed, we had anticipated sleeping on the floor. Foldable and stored away in a corner or a cupboard during the day, Korean bedding would have been far more comfortable than the lightly padded linoleum we slept on at Blue Knob. However, as we understood it, the teachers in our two schools, trying to be as accommodating as possible, had acquired the bed for us newlyweds. It took a while for us to adjust to the idea of sleeping on a lumpy well-used mattress of unknown history.

Our small room, despite the size of the bed, was an attractive living space with a low table and a couple of floor cushions. Outside one window was the second-floor patio, and just down a short hallway bordering the patio were two other rooms, empty and not in use. Those rooms provided storage space for our luggage. Eventually they would become places where Peace Corps friends from different parts of Korea could stay while visiting us in Taegu.

Because we were on the second floor, our room was unheated. The traditional *ondol* system provided the source of heat for the main floor, where the rest of the family lived. A fire in the small kitchen, fueled by a pressed coal cylinder called a *yontan,* connected to a network of flues that ran under the rooms on the first floor. The draft of a chimney on the opposite side of the house pulled heat from the burning coal cylinder, warming the floors.

The system worked well to heat the main floor, but the warmth did not penetrate upstairs. We recalled hearing that the Taegu area was the coldest in the country during winter. It was mid-October and the fall weather already made for a very cool bedroom. Soon after moving in, we requested and received a portable kerosene heater from

Peace Corps to make the room more habitable. With its arrival we hoped we were prepared for the winter cold.

We learned right away that many Korean families had help in running their households. Since homes had no refrigeration and no modern appliances, food shopping took place almost daily, laundry was done by hand, and water was hand-pumped from the well in the small courtyard across from the house's entry. The same pressed coal cylinder that heated the house in the sunken kitchen provided the fire to cook the family's food. Running a household was a labor- intensive effort. To help with all the daily necessities, most families employed a domestic assistant, often a young relative from the countryside, in exchange for room, board, and perhaps a small stipend. When we moved in, the Lees had two helpers, an accomplished young woman in her twenties and a younger teenaged girl who acted as an apprentice. With our arrival, nine souls resided in the Lee home.

Linda and I shared a suspicion that such a large house seemed beyond the means of a school chaplain. Perhaps, we thought, in exchange for their willingness to host a newly married American couple, benefactors of some sort had stepped forward and provided the family with the home. We never knew for certain if that was the case, but the Lee home seemed larger and more Western than any in the neighborhood and contained an entire second floor that was unused prior to our arrival. For unknown reasons we were the beneficiaries of more creature comforts than we expected.

On Saturday afternoon, the day after we moved our luggage into the Lee home, Samonim invited Linda and *Shinja*, the older "kitchen girl," on an excursion to the local neighborhood market, a large open-air affair with multiple stalls and store fronts in a warren of narrow alleys. Always busy, the open-air markets sold everything – fresh meat, fruits, dried foods, herbs, dry goods, traditional medicines, kitchenware, live animals, clothes, and more. With no refrigeration in homes, someone from each household in the neighborhood typically trekked to the market at least every other day. If we could not find what we wanted in the neighborhood, a much larger market was closer to downtown. Busy and active, the markets were great places to test our bargaining skills.

Friends, sometime during our first few months in Taegu, helped us find the local black market, a nearly hidden alleyway in the downtown market. There, we could find goods of foreign origin, not always authentic and often beyond the "use by" date. We didn't frequent the black market often, but there were times when we needed a roll of film or a hit of chocolate.

Linda loved the experience of shopping with Samonim and Shinja. They enthusiastically introduced her to most everything the market offered. Since our room had no closet, we were interested in procuring a cabinet of some sort. We needed a place to hang clothes and store other supplies we'd packed in our trunks, which were yet to arrive. That afternoon, the three of them negotiated for an armoire at one of the market's furniture shops. When it was delivered that very afternoon in a hand-pulled cart, our little room was complete, at least for the time being.

Several days later, our trunks arrived from Blue Knob. That evening we gathered after dinner with the family to share a few gifts that had been packed in the trunks. The atmosphere was festive as the kids learned about the simple games and toys we brought for them, Mr. Lee admired the Kennedy half-dollar key chain and tie tack, and the ladies gushed over the powders and creams Linda had selected. It was an evening filled with spirited attempts to communicate and lots of laughter, despite the language barrier.

During that first week in Taegu, the local newspaper interviewed us and Barrie and Jerry Raik, a couple with whom we had become good friends at Blue Knob. We were all in our early twenties, and recently married. The headline in the paper said something about the four of us deciding to have our honeymoons in Korea, making Korea our first "home sweet home." The journalist wrote of being surprised that we would come and live in their country for such a long time. In those early days, we often heard that Koreans assumed life in their country was too difficult, the conditions too harsh, the amenities too few, and the food too different for Americans. That we liked Korean food, attempted to speak any Korean at all, and were comfortable living on the floor, seemed to surprise and delight many we met.

I had to quickly make some unanticipated mealtime adjustments in the Lee home. Linda and I typically ate our morning and evening meals with Mr. Lee at a floor table in one of the downstairs rooms. As is Korean custom, the women of the house and children always ate later. When sitting cross-legged on the floor, I discovered that my inflexibility made it so I could not get my knees under the table. Linda had no such problem, but I had to sit sideways at first to get close enough to eat. The tightness in my legs began to ease within a few days and it wasn't long before I could sit comfortably with both legs under the table. However, during the first week or two, I was the source of some good-natured ribbing from both Linda and Mr. Lee.

Getting my legs under the table was not my only mealtime challenge. Eating utensils turned out to be another. Chopsticks and a soup spoon were everyday utensils, never a knife or fork. Mastering chopsticks was not something we had practiced during training. Adding to that, I was very left-handed, and Koreans eat only with their right hands. When necessity presented itself, I learned I could adapt quickly. My mother often said I was so left-handed I wouldn't miss my right arm if I lost it. She would have been proud and maybe more than a little surprised to see me, in relatively short order, become semi-skilled at using chopsticks with my right hand.

The pace of our adjustment to life in Taegu had to be quick from the very beginning. The expectation was for us to arrive at our schools by 9 a.m. on our first Monday. Linda's school was a twenty-minute walk from the Lee home. With the help of the Lee children that first weekend, we walked the route. Seeing Americans walking the streets in our section of the city was a novelty, especially for the neighborhood children. We received lots of stares and the kids would often yell, "Hello, 'K!" Other expressions were more descriptive. We would hear in Korean, "Wow, such a tall person!" or "Check out the big nose!" The younger children, we discovered, delighted in our tongue-in-cheek retorts. They giggled when our response in Korean was, "Wow, such a short person!" or "Look, that person has no nose!" Such banter was a playful routine with the local boys and girls until the novelty wore off, and our encounters became a more common everyday occurrence.

My school, Kei Sung, was across town, so I rode the public bus each day, one of those crowded, stand-up, sardines-in-a-can carriers. Sometimes I had to push to climb up into the stairwell, with the bus girl pressed against my backside, preventing me from being expelled by the crush of passengers inside. Then, when all was secure, she pounded the side of the bus twice and yelled, "*Awriyah*" as we moved from stop to stop. I grew to admire those girls. They were tough and strong and did their duty on the coldest days of winter and the hottest days in summer.

The Lee Family

Shinja and Linda

Kihyun in Courtyard

Shinja, Wani, Yooni and Googi on second floor patio

Chapter 7

EARLY CHALLENGES

We spent the first week as faculty members gradually finding our way around our schools. After sitting in on some classes to see how the Korean teachers operated, I met my students for the first-time mid-week. My schedule included teaching three to four classes each day, six days per week. The students were seventh-graders in their first year of English. My goal was not to use any Korean in the classroom. The focus was to be conversational English. My fellow teachers encouraged me to design lessons consistent with the students' text in their grammar and reading classes. We wanted the students to see a connection between speaking and reading. The text, in my opinion, was not excellent; the content and sentence patterns were stilted, not at all conversational. I tried to make the best of the situation and adapt the textbook material in ways the students would find interesting.

One unexpected benefit of teaching at Kei Sung was that faculty members were served a hot meal each school day. I didn't realize how special that mid-day meal was until I compared notes with other PCVs. Nobody I knew had such a luxury. Thanks to those lunches, I was introduced over time to a variety of traditional Korean dishes. I learned the names of foods I liked, which helped in deciphering menus when Linda and I ate out at local restaurants.

The end of October was close at hand when I started teaching. My students were already more than midway through the school year. The Korean academic calendar began in March and concluded the following February. I was to be with my first group of students for just a few months before they moved on to the eighth-grade. I decided to start back at the beginning of the first-year text and see how far I could get in bringing it to life conversationally. To make the classes enjoyable, I crafted visual aids and scripted dialogs, not unlike those we practiced at Blue Knob in our Korean language classes. During those first few months I was experimenting, trying to discover how best to create a productive learning environment.

Linda and I quickly found having detailed lesson plans essential. They made the classroom experience more efficient and helped us maintain a quick pace. The downside of writing out lesson plans and creating visual aids was the significant amount of time it required. With sixty students in each class, however, it was worth creating a classroom in which the students were active and learning to speak.

Despite the large numbers of students in each classroom, behavior problems were not typically an issue. A disruptive or non-conforming student faced grave consequences in Korean schools. The vice principals responsible for meting out discipline had an oft-repeated mantra: "Spare the rod, spoil the child." It did not take long for us to learn the degree to which that principle was applied. Critical incidents unfolded at each of our schools during our first few weeks.

I witnessed more than one incident in which the principal or vice-principal brought a student into the faculty room. The student stood in front of the administrator's desk and was berated loudly for his infraction. Then, as the upbraiding continued, the student endured aggressive slaps, raps on his hands with a ruler, or if the infraction was significant, even punches to his body. Finally, when dismissed, the student, clearly shaken and often tearful, bowed and beat a hasty retreat past faculty members sitting at their desks around the perimeter of the room.

In Linda's girls' school, a misbehaving student typically received discipline in the hallway after being dismissed from the classroom. The student sat on the floor as the vice-principal delivered a stern lecture. He had the student hold out her hands, palms down, while he unleashed a stinging rap across the back of each hand with a wooden pointer, bringing her to tears. We were both alarmed, and a bit shook by those episodes. They did not happen often, but we found them disturbing when they did. Fortunately, most of the time, our respective classrooms were showcases of compliant behavior.

Initially, Linda understood her teaching schedule was to include eight seventh-grade classes taught twice a week, plus a weekly after-school English club. On her very first day, however, she found her schedule had changed to teaching all the seventh and eighth-grade classes, but just once a week each. She knew that such little exposure to spoken English was likely to be of little benefit to the students. After a couple of weeks, the vice-principal asked Linda about how things were going and whether she had encountered any "inconveniences" as she was getting started.

With Miss Sung, her co-teacher and interpreter, Linda mentioned that everything was fine except for teaching each class only once per week. She said the Peace Corps administrator was unhappy the agreement with the school had changed. The contract called for PCVs to teach each class twice per week. As she spoke, the vice-principal became visibly upset. His face reddened and Linda feared she had unintentionally challenged his authority. To make matters worse, she was an American woman and a guest. In response, he took a quick stand. The change, he said, could not be done immediately. Linda would have to continue with the current schedule for some time. During that exchange, Miss Sung was interpreting and found herself very much in the middle of what was becoming an open conflict.

A few days earlier Linda had consulted Mel, our trusted regional rep, about her situation. Mel predicted that the school might drag its feet in making a change. If that occurred, he suggested she tentatively agree and then request a letter from the school to the Peace Corps office, outlining the plan and how long it would be before the original schedule was reinstated. That turned out to be sage advice.

As the meeting progressed, Linda requested the letter. Hearing that request, the vice-principal hesitated, seeming unsure what to do. In Korea, people rarely managed interpersonal conflicts directly.

In discussing this issue openly, the vice-principal likely felt uncomfortable. Linda had questioned his authority in the presence of other faculty members. It appeared a crisis was brewing.

After Linda made her request, with the discussion at an apparent stalemate, Miss Sung abruptly left the meeting. In tears, she returned to her desk, furious with the vice-principal and no doubt embarrassed at being involved in such a public disagreement with their guest teacher. Linda was upset, too. Ever the peacemaker, it was not her nature to get involved in a tug-of-war. She felt caught in the middle. The whole situation was made worse because such problems were often handled indirectly, behind the scenes. Rarely was conflict exposed outright; resolution typically occurred later, often with the assistance of a dispassionate third party. That meeting, though it ended uncomfortably without resolution on anyone's part, had an impact. Things began to change quickly. Contrary to the vice-principal's declaration, Linda's schedule was modified back to the original plan the very next day.

As she began teaching each seventh-grade class twice per week, she feared she might have been guilty of a terrible cultural blunder. The other female teachers, however, were reassuring. They sought Linda out to apologize for the vice-principal's behavior and assured her she had done the right thing by standing her ground. He, she was told, had a reputation for being abrupt and rude. Within the week, her fellow female teachers invited Linda to a movie and a popular local bakery. She felt relieved, supported, and accepted. The vice-principal, however, would never be an enthusiastic supporter of Linda's presence in the school.

During those early days, several of the teachers at our respective schools proved especially helpful as we settled into our assignments. Some went out of their way to engage us in conversation, and we responded with them as best we could, given our frightfully primitive language ability. They asked about our families, wanted to hear about our reaction to living in Korea, and expressed appreciation for our attempts to communicate in their language. Linda's fellow teachers, half of whom were women, told her repeatedly that she seemed even more beautiful when she spoke in Korean. She didn't think so, but I tended to side with the teachers.

The thoughtfulness of our fellow teachers seemed to reach across cultural boundaries. It was unusual for married couples to do things socially together in Korea. Men often had friends with whom they socialized, and women participated in their own social circles. When together in public, men often walked several paces in front of their female partners, paying them no attention. During training discussions at Blue Knob we were briefed on the cultural expectations of men, women and couples. Male volunteers, we were told, were likely to be treated differently than the women, whether single or married. The expectation was that male volunteers would be invited to engage with other men in social activities, while women would face barriers to being accepted and respected, both socially and professionally. School administrators and most faculty members were men. Women held few positions of power. Married couples were led to expect social invitations that did not include the wives. Our personal experience, however, turned out to be different.

Perhaps because of our newlywed status or because of my school's affiliation with the Presbyterian Church, we consistently received social invitations as a couple. Christians tended to party less frequently and typically did not consume alcohol. Couples were more likely to socialize and attend worship services together. If a teacher at my school invited us to dinner or to do something on the weekend, it was almost always as a couple. There were exceptions, of course, when Linda would do things with her fellow women faculty members, and I would participate in activities with male friends at my school. Most of the time, however, we did prefer doing things together and were grateful our community of friends and co-workers seemed to recognize that.

Our first month in Taegu ended on America's Thanksgiving. Multiple invitations to celebrate came our way, and we took full advantage. First, the city's American military base, Camp Henry, opened its doors to all Peace Corps Volunteers in the province. Our friends the Raiks came to town from their remote village, and Linda invited her co-teacher, Miss Sung, to join us. We had great fun at a noontime feast catching up with the Raiks and getting to know Miss Sung. Later in the day, Linda and I joined our missionary friends, the Grubbs, for yet another traditional Thanksgiving turkey dinner.

For me, that first Thanksgiving was less of a celebration and more of an endurance test. Toward the end of our first week in Taegu, I came down with a cold. It hung on and turned into a major sinus infection. Visits to the doctor and a course of antibiotics did not touch it. By the time we returned to the Lees on Thanksgiving night, I was really hurting. My head throbbed, and I couldn't breathe through my nose. That night I barely slept. I was literally knocked off my feet for several days. Linda thought I had lost all color and said I looked ghostlike. Samonim was so concerned she prepared a Korean home remedy of rice gruel. Nothing helped.

I spent the weekend in bed, trying to eat gruel, with almost no sleep. The pain and exhaustion left me in a state of semi-consciousness. I had never been so sick. On Monday morning, Linda reached out to our Peace Corps doctor for help. Dr. Scholten responded right away. He picked us up in his Jeep and we went to the hospital for tests. Based on the results, Dr. Scholten concluded I needed to see a specialist. He knew one, a local physician who had received his medical training in the States.

Seeing a Korean specialist was unusual for PCVs. The local Peace Corps doctor was our source for primary care. Referral to a local practitioner was usually done only in unique circumstances. Dr. Scholten concluded I needed more help than he could provide. So off we went to find the specialist's office in a neighborhood across town.

Fortunately, he was able to see me right away. After reviewing the X-rays and collaborating with Dr. Scholten, the recommended intervention to relieve the pressure in my sinuses sounded drastic. When Linda heard it would include pushing long needles up through my nasal cartilage into the sinus cavity on either side of my nose, she decided to exit and wait outside. The procedure was not without risk, but I was miserable. Thank goodness, it worked; in what seemed like just a few seconds a gush of fluid soaked the towel on my chest. My relief was immediate. By the time we returned to the Lees later that Monday afternoon, I already felt (and looked) much better. By Thursday, I was back in the classroom. I knew my illness had impacted the Lees. Samonim was so caring during my sickest days; she did everything she could to help me feel comfortable. Mr. Lee was concerned and shared my situation with the faculty at Kei Sung. When I returned to work, the teachers welcomed me back warmly; they wanted to know all about the procedure I had undergone. I was appreciative of all the help and caring I received during that difficult time. Fortunately it was the only serious illness I experienced during our time in Korea.

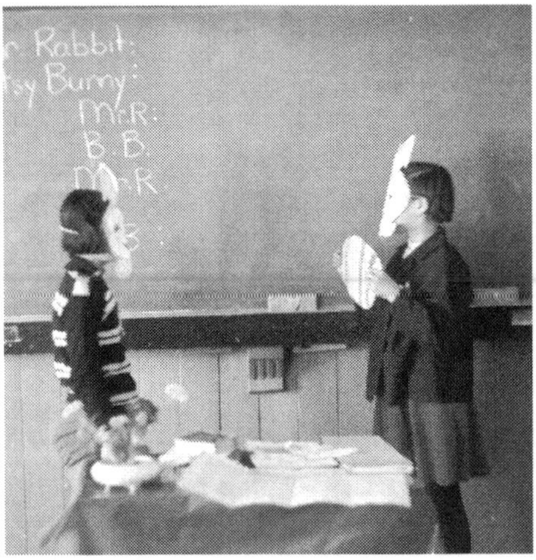

Students dialog wearing masks

Using visual aids

Lunch with colleagues

Linda at work in the classroom

Class begins with a bow

Warming in teacher's room

Linda with Chae Il student

Steve in the classroom

Chapter 8

LESSONS AND LAUGHS

Early December was time for making and storing kimchi, a tradition in every Korean household. Kimchi, which was made in large batches to last the entire winter, was a staple of the Korean diet. Served at every meal, it was a side dish that included, at a minimum, cabbage, hot chili pepper paste, carrots, ginger, and a liberal amount of garlic. Once the ingredients were assembled, the process took an entire day. First, Samonim and Shinja tackled a garden-cart-sized pile of one hundred *baechu* (Napa) cabbages. They were huge; each appeared to be about eighteen inches long and eight inches across — the largest cabbages Linda and I had ever seen.

We both found the process of making a season's worth of kimchi fascinating. Starting early in the morning, the women thoroughly washed each cabbage head and soaked them in a salt brine before setting them aside. Next, they mixed thick red pepper paste in a big rubber tub with the other ingredients. Then, squatting on their haunches on the kitchen floor, the two women painstakingly pulled each leaf carefully away from the base and rubbed in a liberal amount of the paste mixture before folding the cabbage head back together.

Dressed in sweaters and scarves, Samonim and Shinja worked in the unheated kitchen. Handling the wet cabbages and the spicy red pepper paste was brutal on their hands, which looked painfully swollen and red. There was, however, never any complaint or acknowledgment of discomfort. That was a trait of the Korean people that was becoming familiar; they never complained when faced with pain or hardship.

When the cabbage heads were finally fully layered with the red pepper mixture, they were packed tightly into earthenware pots of varying sizes, the largest being about four feet tall and three feet wide at the broadest point. Those pots, called *onggi*, were made with clay that was micro-porous when fired at a low temperature. They didn't leak, but their permeability allowed the kimchi to breathe, ideal for fermentation. Once filled, those pots were stored outdoors on the low platform in the courtyard. Over the months, the kimchi gradually fermented; by spring the taste would evolve from crisp and spicy to tangy. Linda and I liked it year-round but preferred the fresher servings during the first few months of storage.

Kimchi posed an initial dilemma for us. It was such a tradition and, for Koreans, an essential part of their daily diet. No meal was complete without kimchi – breakfast, lunch, or dinner. So, what to do about the doctor's admonishment to not eat uncooked vegetables? All the ingredients in kimchi were raw, but the cultural expectations regarding its consumption were high. We liked both the spiciness and taste of kimchi and knew that not eating it would be a cultural mistake. The Peace Corps doctors had assured us that most fermented foods were safe to consume, their only caution was to avoid river fish, an ingredient sometimes added to the red pepper paste mixture in kimchi. We were fortunate. Samonim, ever mindful of good hygiene, used a kimchi recipe that did not include fish. We enjoyed her flavorful kimchi at every meal and never had a problem. But when we ate out in restaurants or private homes, we were cautious. We never suffered more than occasional GI distress from food we consumed outside the Lee home. Other PCVs were not as fortunate; some did suffer a variety of food-borne illnesses.

With kimchi preparations complete, Mr. Lee's elder brother arrived for a mid-December visit. Arranged marriages were still common in Korea in those days, and he needed help locating a potential husband for his twenty-six-year-old daughter. Being a minister, Mr. Lee was a trusted collaborator in the search for a Christian husband for his niece. December was a popular time for weddings in Korea. With harvest work complete and a winter's worth of kimchi stored away in pots, it was historically a season of plenty, a good time for celebrations.

The opportunity to witness a wedding arose when we received an invitation from a Kei Sung faculty member to attend his December marriage ceremony at a local church. The nuptial was brief. The couple, dressed in elegant *hanbok* (traditional Korean attire), exchanged little more than respectful bows. We saw no indication of joy or happiness on the bride's and groom's faces. We learned later that smiling on one's wedding day had ominous overtones. Tradition held that if the bride or groom smiled on their wedding day, they would not be blessed with any sons, and having male children was of utmost importance in Korean culture. Once aware of that belief, we understood why no eye contact took place between the couple and why the bride's eyes remained solemnly downcast before, during, and after the ceremony. In Korea, those beliefs were strong, and the couple made every attempt to honor the tradition. As we reflected on our own wedding six months earlier, we realized that if there was merit to the belief, we were destined to have a family of daughters.

The national middle school entrance exam was another important annual December event. Taken while students were still in sixth grade, that exam was considered the most critical test students would take during the entirety of their education. The results began to separate the "more able" from the "less able" students, at least in test-taking ability. In Taegu, as in other larger cities, secondary schools were ranked in terms of their quality and prestige. Exam results determined the schools to which a student could apply, and parents wanted their sons to qualify for the best school possible. The more influential colleges admitted only the students who had done well in a highly ranked secondary school. Thus, in many ways, the middle school entrance exam, a test taken by twelve-year-olds, went a long way in determining the student's long-term future education and career opportunities. As a result, students were under significant pressure to do well.

During our first three months in the Lee home, we rarely saw the oldest son, sixth-grader Pil-Goog, whom we called Googi. Six days a week, he attended special tutoring classes both before and after school. Googi always left the house before we ate breakfast and arrived home late in the evening, after dark. When we did catch a rare glimpse of him, he seemed thin and pale. We didn't know if the pressure he felt came from his parents or was self-imposed. Probably both. But after test day had come and gone, we began to see Googi more often. There were no more early morning departures or late-night arrivals. Gradually, as the days went by, he seemed more relaxed and his skin not quite so pale.

It was not long before the exam results were announced. On that day, everyone in the household wore a smile. Googi had done well; he received the second-highest score in the entire province — 796 out of a possible 800. That meant he qualified to attend the highest-rated middle school. Assuming he did well there, he would be automatically admitted to the attached highly regarded high school. Mr. Lee and Samonim were so proud. What we noticed most was that Googi became more relaxed, less serious. His coloring improved, and he began to gain weight. He became playful and began joking with us. He quickly learned the games we were teaching Yooni and Wani. He good-naturedly corrected our Korean and started picking up a bit of English. Just as important, the whole family atmosphere lightened.

Linda and I also became more comfortable in our respective schools as the weeks went by. Our students enthusiastically practiced simple English phrases and seemed to find the visual aids we prepared helpful. After a couple of months, we began to see the light of comprehension click on in the students' minds. Some of Linda's students lived in our neighborhood and regularly accompanied her on their walk home after school. She had a great rapport with her students and fellow teachers alike. The trauma of her early conflict with the vice-principal seemed behind her.

Early December brought the first snow of the season to Taegu, and temperatures dipped quite low. At my all-boys school, the students performed much of the janitorial work. After school, they cleaned blackboards, swept all the classrooms, and mopped the hallways, which were not enclosed but open to the elements on the backside of the building. In washing down and sweeping the concrete hallways, the students sometimes tended to use a liberal amount of water. One morning after a frigid night when the temperature dropped to well below freezing, the hallways had become a sheet of ice. When I arrived at school, I heard boys sliding on the iced corridors. During breaks between classes, many of them would warm themselves by sliding around on the ice. I had to be especially cautious as I navigated the hallways in slippery smooth-soled shoes. The big foreigner (me) invoked enough curiosity without becoming famous for winter corridor acrobatics.

During the winter months, teachers were not allowed to wear heavy coats in the classroom. Our dress was quite formal: skirts and dresses for the women teachers and suit coats and ties for men. Like our fellow teachers, Linda and I learned to layer our clothing for warmth. My usual winter teaching outfit included long top and bottom underwear, shirt and tie, sweater, and wool sport coat. Between classes, the teachers always had a chance to retreat to the warmth of the teachers' room, but students had no such opportunity; they wore layers under their uniforms but they were not allowed to wear gloves in the classroom. All my students had chapped red hands, but again, I never heard a complaint. Their hands looked painful, but those kids were tough. Perhaps that was the point of the policy; children learned from a young age to be stoic and endure hardship.

Linda and I kept our classroom lessons fast paced to keep the kids focused on learning English. We moved quickly between practicing pronunciation, playing word games, learning dialogues, and engaging in short oral quizzes. Our goal was to have no downtime during an hour-long class. To keep things interesting, we used colorful drawings and pictures that we stuck on thin 3'x 4' sheets of plywood covered with white flannel. By gluing flannel pieces to the back of our artwork, drawn or glued on butcher paper, those pictures adhered readily to the flannel-covered board, making them easy to post and remove as we taught. We had a great time making visual aids with the Lee kids that we used in the classroom. They loved helping us draw and color objects or cut pictures from magazines. Those were fun times up in our room with the heater going while we worked together to create things we could use at school.

In the middle of December, a couple of humorous events occurred in the dark of night up in our room. Once, sometime in the wee hours, the bed the teachers had acquired for us came crashing down. Several thin slats that held the mattress in the frame broke, and we hit the floor at an odd tilt, making quite a thud. Our bedroom was located directly above Mr. Lee and Samonim's room on the first floor. Just after the crash, we heard the door open at the bottom of the stairs. Mr. Lee was on his way up to investigate. Dressed in our warm flannels, we all had a good laugh as we propped up the bed in temporary fashion so we could get back to sleep.

I wasn't sure who was responsible, but when we returned from school the next day, the bed was repaired. All was well until a couple of weeks later when Linda was reading in bed. Preparing to get in, I sat on the edge. When I did the entire frame cracked, and a corner of the bed hit the floor at an angle. Again, Mr. Lee visited, and we managed a hasty fix to get us through the night. The next day, Mr. Lee summoned a repairman from Kei Sung to make a more permanent fix. The story of our collapsing bed became one we revisited several times with the family when reflecting, always with a smile, on memorable times in our stay with them.

That first winter, we became aware of a preoccupation that permeated the entire country. The truce that marked the end of hostilities between the North and South was not perceived as a true peace. Infiltrators from North Korea posed a constant threat. Personal, family, and national security were never taken for granted. There was a daily midnight curfew throughout the whole country when everyone was to be off the streets. All around Taegu, the same words were painted in large print on the sides of buildings: *Pan Gong - Pang Chope*. Translated, those words read, "Oppose Communism, Guard Against Spies." Local citizens were exhorted to watch for North Koreans who, with some regularity, infiltrated the South with seditious intent.

Family dwellings in the city were mini compounds, surrounded by tall walls, often topped with jagged broken glass or barbed wire, and secured by a locked gate. Unwanted nighttime intruders, not always Communists, were not uncommon. They were a threat to steal anything of value from homes where vigilance was lax. Pickpockets were also not uncommon. Crowded buses offered an excellent opportunity for pocket-pickers to practice their craft, especially in winter when passengers wore heavy coats. We learned that lesson firsthand.

One cold day, Linda, bundled up with her purse looped over her shoulder on the outside of her coat, boarded a bus that was so crowded that she literally could not move. People pressed against her on all sides. At one point she felt a jostle and suspected that someone might be trying to get to her wallet. With so many passengers pushed against her, she couldn't tell who the culprit might be. Sure enough, when she got off the bus, she discovered her little money clutch had been opened and the contents removed. She hadn't lost much, but such was her pique that she secretly hoped the thief encountered her well-used handkerchief on his way to her loot. She learned that day to keep her purse under her coat.

Within a few weeks, almost the same thing happened to me on my way to school. While aboard a cramped bus, I carried my thin wallet in the internal breast pocket of my coat. The crush of bodies on the bus was so great that I could do nothing when I felt a hand remove my wallet and saw a person wiggle off the bus at the next stop. I knew I was being robbed but I was immobilized, unable to act. I had no idea what to say, and even if I had said something, I didn't know if anyone around me would do anything.

Both thefts left us feeling violated and surprised at the audacity of our assailants. At the same time, we realized that Americans were seen as wealthy and relatively easy targets. So, we considered those experiences educational and did what we could to avoid becoming victims again. For the most part, we were successful.

In those early months, we became aware of more and more

differences between the Korean way of life and American habits. We noticed that in Korea very little trash was discarded. The Lees had a shoebox sized container on the patio where they put out refuse — never food scraps, paper, plastic, or other things that would commonly populate our trash bags at home; practically the only waste items they discarded were the remains of the burned-out coal cylinders used for cooking and heating. Frequent trips to the market always included taking a cloth bag or basket. Markets sold most items without packaging. Newspaper and schoolwork papers were always cut into small squares and used as toilet paper. There was simply not much to throw out.

Trash trucks did not arrive weekly or on any particular schedule. When they did appear once or twice a month, everyone in the neighborhood recognized the sound. Neighbors rushed out to toss their small amount of trash into the truck bed. Most of what was thrown out was spent coal or small broken household items. That realization awakened Linda and I to the excesses that marked life in America. Recycling, environmental protection, and keeping waste to a minimum was valued, expected, and an assumed part of life in Korea. The country was far ahead of America at the time in waste reduction and recycling efforts.

December turned out to provide us with a natural break from what had become hectic days at school. Lesson planning, teaching, and building relationships with our fellow teachers kept us hopping. The days went by quickly, but the month of December afforded us a bit of downtime. Schools closed for several days early in the month for the national middle school entrance exam, which meant free days for Linda. While I was drafted at school to help with test scoring, she had a chance to Christmas shop.

Later in the month was a short winter break when the Lee children were home. They had lost their initial shyness and become regular visitors in our upstairs room. Googi and Shinja always helped enhance our connection with the younger kids, Yooni and Wani. No matter what we tried to share, Googi or Shinja almost always intuitively understood and clued the others in when our Korean wasn't up to the task. Still recovering from the stress of preparing for the middle school exam, Googi's curious, fun-loving personality began to emerge more and more. Shinja, in her early twenties and single, was a bright light in her own right. When able to take a break from her housework, she helped answer questions we had about Taegu, the neighborhood, and how to navigate the market. Both she and Googi quickly became mentors as we adjusted to the day-to-day rhythms of the Lee household.

Baechu cabbage for kimchi

Shinja and Samonim preparing kimchi

Winter fun on second floor patio

Our neighborhood view

Chapter 9

THE HOLIDAYS

With few teaching responsibilities in the second half of December, we looked forward to a number of Christmas celebrations that dotted our calendar. Our Peace Corps doctor, Jim Scholten, and his wife planned several opportunities for PCVs to get together, knowing we would all miss our traditional family holiday celebrations. My school hosted a pre-Christmas party for the entire faculty and their families. The local Mennonite and Presbyterian missions, with whom we had become friendly, invited us to some of their seasonal events. The YMCA held a Christmas Eve service. And to cap it all off, the US Army base invited us to a Christmas Day dinner. There would be little time for homesickness during our first Christmas in Korea.

Just as the holiday festivities began, we had a sobering scare. One of our PCV friends from out of town knocked on the Lee's gate unexpectedly one day, looking quite ill. David, who stayed with us earlier in November, had been immobilized with illness for a couple of days before he felt strong enough to make his way to Taegu and see our doctor. We immediately accompanied him to Dr. Scholten's house and learned he had suffered carbon monoxide poisoning from sleeping on an inadequately sealed ondol floor.

We knew about the risks of traditional ondol floor heating. The danger was in the oilpaper used to cover the floors. If the flooring material was not thoroughly sealed or tiny cracks or tears appeared, carbon monoxide from the flue connected to the burning coal cylinder could escape into the room. Since all Koreans and most PCVs slept on an ondol floor, there was risk, especially if the room was not well ventilated. To compound the problem, many Koreans sealed their windows with plastic in winter to keep out the cold, cutting off any potential ventilation. As a preventive measure, at the beginning of winter the government published in local newspapers the number of deaths that resulted from such poisoning the previous year. Still, preventable deaths occurred.

Luckily, David survived a near disaster. He committed to modifying his sleeping arrangements when he returned to his job site. Unfortunately, Dr. Scholten's charming young houseboy did not fare as well. During our second winter, despite pleas to the contrary, he sealed his room with plastic. He sadly became one of the tragedies of the practice. We all loved him and mourned his passing. The Scholtens, sadly, would always feel remorse for his loss.

Knowing that David's recovery would take a few days. The Lees graciously invited him to stay at the house, which meant he would be with us through Christmas. That act of kindness was so typical of them. As time went by, the Lee home became a welcome place for out-of-town guests who came to visit. We never took their kindness for granted.

After his arrival, David felt well enough to join us, and our friend Kathi, for a baking party at the Scholtens' that evening. We planned to bake cookies to share with other PCVs at the Scholtens' holiday party. Their house was of a traditional Korean design, but it included some western features, including a heated kitchen with a propane stove. After securing baking supplies at the market, we headed there after dinner. David and I were the quality assurance taste testers — tough duty, but we were willing volunteers.

Midway through the evening, the electricity went out – a common occurrence in Taegu. That didn't stop us. The kitchen, powered by propane, candlelight, and good cheer remained a flurry of activity. The lack of power made the evening even more memorable.

After dinner at the Lees' that next evening, with Christmas still a couple of days off, all of us gathered around a potbelly stove, which had been installed on the polished hardwood in the downstairs entry area. We were playing games, chatting, and having fun when Mr. Lee and the kids decided Linda and I should show them how Americans fast dance. What? Us? We liked to dance, but fast dancing was something we had not done since high school. However, after several requests and as many refusals, we finally got up and hopped around to a juiced-up Christmas tune on the radio, trying to look like we knew what we were doing. The entire group was rolling on the floor laughing as we gyrated. Even Samonim, typically not given to light-hearted play, giggled so hard she feigned exhaustion.

Parties at my school and the Scholtens' were scheduled for the same evening, two days before Christmas. First was my school's affair, hosted at a banquet hall downtown to accommodate all teachers and their families from both the middle and high school. From Mr. Lee's earlier description of the event, I assumed husbands and wives would attend together. That was not something we had often seen during our short stay in Taegu. My assumption was correct. About three hundred people arrived in their Sunday best, men wearing coats and ties and most women in traditional Korean *hanbok.* The elegant hanbok included colorful *chima* (full skirts) and *choguri* (bolero type jackets), often made of silk.

The evening was great fun, with games, skits, a satirical interview with me that drew lots of laughs, and a command performance by Linda and me, when we sang "Deck the Halls" in front of the entire assembly. Korean custom often called for guests to sing, especially at celebrations or parties. Notorious for being tone-deaf, I sang at my off-key best that evening while Linda tried to make quick adjustments on the fly. Despite our singing being something akin to fingernails scraping across a blackboard, we received a rousing round of applause for our effort.

The Kei Sung party organizers had a clever way of providing holiday gifts to those present. Each family was given a coupon that represented a fixed amount of pretend cash. Photographs of aluminum kitchen items like pots, pans, kettles, and lunch boxes, all with their values listed, were posted on a big display board. Each couple had a chance to choose as many things as they wished, up to the total value of their allotment of "coupon cash." The atmosphere was festive, and though no items of great value were on the board, all were practical and useful.

When that party broke up, we bid the Lees good evening and taxied over to the Scholten house. We looked forward to seeing our friends, several having come to Taegu from distant sites. We all shared stories about our first couple of months in Korea. It was great fun to catch up and learn what our Blue Knob friends were experiencing and discovering as they settled into life at their work sites. We visited long into the night.

The next day, Christmas Eve, Linda hosted some of the women teachers from her school for an afternoon tea party and small gift exchange. Our friends the Raiks arrived a little later, as did another friend, John Wendland. We would be having four overnight guests that evening, filling the two unheated upstairs rooms adjacent to the patio. The Lees welcomed a literal houseful on Christmas. We tried to lighten their load by going out to dinner that evening, taking in the YMCA caroling service, and then all six of us made a late-night visit to the Presbyterian mission for more carol singing, replete with warm plum pudding. Our Korean family and the Christian missionaries were so welcoming that we felt truly cared for on our first Christmas Eve away from home.

Christmas Day was just as special. Linda had made stockings for each Lee child out of red and white flannel and filled them with small gifts. We stealthily set them around the potbelly stove downstairs on Christmas Eve after everyone had turned in for the night. The next morning, Samonim outdid herself with breakfast for the six of us who had sacked out upstairs. After eating, our friends took off to visit others they knew in Taegu.

When our friends had gone, we brought down our little artificial tree that my folks had sent. Earlier in the week, the entire Lee family had helped decorate it. Everyone sat together around the stove, including the kitchen girls, as we sang "The First Noel" in Korean, shared prayers in Korean and English, and opened gifts. Later, Mr. Lee accompanied us to the English Christmas Day church service at the Army base. The three of us stayed on for a meal hosted at the Officer's Club, and then Linda and I headed once again to the Scholtens' for an evening of more visiting and carol singing.

As our friends departed Taegu following Christmas, we accepted an invitation to join other PCVs for a New Year's celebration in Pusan. Korea's second-largest city on the southern tip of the peninsula, Pusan, was a two-hour train ride from Taegu. Since arriving in October, we had not traveled any significant distance by ourselves; the train trip to Pusan was to be our first solo long-distance journey. We were a bit tentative about going. Our limited Korean language skills made us nervous. Outside of our schools and the Lee home, we rarely encountered Koreans who spoke any English at all. We knew we would have to rely on our Korean to negotiate the train, find a place to stay, and somehow contact our friends once we arrived in Pusan.

An assist came in the form of our friend Lindsey, a K-I volunteer who lived just a few blocks from us. He had planned a winter vacation trip to Japan and would depart from Pusan just after the New Year. He suggested we travel together and stay at a yogwan he knew would be a perfect place for first-time visitors to the city. I'm not sure Lindsey understood the degree of our timidity, but he had an uncanny sixth sense when it came to perceiving the needs of others. In those first few months, he became our friend and mentor as we began to find our way. He showed us the ropes and boosted our confidence as we learned to get around.

We purchased second-class train tickets with Lindsey, which meant reserved seats and a place to stow our luggage. Third-class tickets were also available, but the cars had only benches around the perimeter. When the benches filled, additional passengers stood and often had to negotiate crates of produce and sometimes chickens, on their way to market. Rides in third class could become a true adventure. On the ride to Pusan, as the only foreigners in the second-class car, we were objects of curiosity to the other passengers. They asked questions about what we were doing in Korea, and we did our best to answer, finding it an excellent opportunity to practice our Korean.

Traveling south on the train we saw bare apple orchards, frozen rice paddies, small villages, and brownish mountains barren of trees – a stark, wintry countryside that gave rise to questions. I wondered what those orchards and rice paddies would look like in the spring when the fruit trees blossomed and the paddies filled with young plants.

More cosmopolitan and less industrial than Taegu, Pusan had cruise ships in the harbor and businesses that catered to Western tastes. Located close to the waterfront, the vibrant downtown bustled with activity. The yogwan Lindsey suggested turned out to be only a short walk from the docks. The sounds, sights and smells of the ocean were reminiscent of our college years at UCSB. Lindsey guided us on a seaside walking tour of the docks. The pungent seafood market sold fish of all types, some familiar and some not. New to us, the colorful sea cucumbers were most often consumed raw, and fresh squid-like cuttlefish were typically dried and eaten as a snack. Women, we noticed, provided much of the labor along the harbor, unloading cargo and tending the myriad stalls selling seafood to the public.

As we hiked trails along rocky cliffs east of the city, we saw women free diving for crab, shellfish, and seaweed. Often those women divers were the primary breadwinners for their families. Within diving families, the men performed ancillary household duties like childcare and cooking, a significant reversal of traditional Confucian patriarchal norms for men.

Culinary surprises awaited us as we explored the downtown area. Our PCV friends recommended we visit the Seaman's Club operated by the Royal Asiatic Society. The Seaman's Club served a weekly seafood buffet for less than two dollars. A couple of other restaurants recommended by our friends served fish-n-chips, hamburgers, and ice cream – foods we had only dreamed of eating during the previous three months. No wonder our friends who lived in and near Pusan were so enthusiastic about the city. We liked our situation in Taegu, but Pusan offered a different scene. It was a fun place to visit.

On New Year's Eve, we gathered with about a dozen other PCVs at a downtown yogwan to celebrate and share stories about our first few months in Korea. We discovered Linda was not alone in having to negotiate her teaching schedule. We also learned that others found their living situations to be difficult, sometimes related to their host family's diet, and sometimes owing to the discriminatory ways some families, work sites, and communities treated PCVs. Korea, at that time, had few resident Westerners. We were a novelty and were sometimes viewed with suspicion. Single women had an especially difficult time gaining respect in their schools, either because of their gender or because they were unmarried. Women in general were often not held in high regard as co-workers or professionals. They were thought to be inferior to men. We had not been prepared during our days at Blue Knob for that kind of treatment.

After a third day in Pusan, we were ready to schedule our return. We were beginning to understand that some of our friends were becoming disenchanted with their living situations. For us, Taegu was beginning to feel like home; we looked forward to getting back. When Lindsey left for his Japan vacation, we were ready to go. Purchasing train tickets, getting around town, and tending our bill at the yogwan presented no problems. Our confidence in our ability to communicate and do business in Korean had grown. Buoyed by some of our friends' positive descriptions of historical sights they had visited, our curiosity to see more of the country was growing as well.

Chapter 10

WINTER ROUTINES

Back in Taegu, our schools were still on holiday break. Classes wouldn't start up again until February. Since we had no teaching responsibilities during the interim, Mel suggested we design a project for ourselves. Our primary interest was improving our language abilities, so we contracted with a Korean language tutor. We also learned the local U.S. Information Service (USIS) needed a native speaker to lead an English conversation class for some educators during the short break in the school calendar. Linda and I volunteered to team-teach.

A mix of college and high school teachers made up the USIS group of only five men. We generally found Korean English teachers to be quite limited in their ability to speak the language. At the same time, they hesitated to practice or acknowledge a need to improve. Based on Linda's experience at her school, male teachers fit that description more often than women. Men seemed more preoccupied with a "loss of face" and an accompanying sense of shame. If a man acknowledged a skill deficit, he might be seen as "less than." Most men we met avoided situations where they risked not measuring up to expectations.

Our USIS group was different. The men were not embarrassed by their limited language skills; they were hungry to learn and improve. They had a relaxed demeanor, joked, and even dressed more casually than their more traditional teaching peers, wearing sweaters and wool shirts, never coats and ties. Being a part of that group energized us. We looked forward to our classes with them, three afternoons per week. The men quickly bonded with each other, had a good time, and exhibited noticeable improvement despite meeting with us for just two weeks.

During the break, Googi was preparing to enter his new school. That prompted a celebratory dinner in which we all ate together, a departure from our customary practice of eating with just Mr. Lee. Googi's graduation and admission to Taegu's most sought-after middle school had the family in high spirits.

With more free time in our schedule, an evening tradition developed. On nights we were home, the family invited us to spend time with them. We played games in the warmth of the downstairs entry area, sitting around the potbelly stove on the polished hardwood. We taught the family some games we had brought with us. By January, however, the family was teaching us Korean games. Everyone's favorite, *Yute*, involved throwing six-sided sticks, equivalent to dice, to determine how many spaces a team could advance around a game board. We had some spirited matches of adults vs. kids and males vs. females. In addition to games, we sometimes sang Korean and American songs, compared animal sounds (which was always hilarious), and even taught and learned new skills like sewing and simple cooking.

Our weekly visit to the public bathhouse was another routine we established. Every neighborhood had a public bath and ours was less than two blocks away from the Lee home. A nondescript single-story building in the middle of the block, it boasted a subtle, dimly lit neon sign, identifying it as the *mogyoktang* (public bath).

Most homes did not have private bathing facilities. To bathe at home, water had to be heated in the kitchen over the precious pressed-coal cylinders mainly devoted to meal preparation and home heating. The public bath was both more efficient and a neighborhood gathering spot. As the weather grew colder, we developed the habit of going early, before breakfast. The bathhouse was large, with separate but identical bathing facilities for men and women. There were different gender-specific dressing rooms, with open cubbyholes for storing clothes. The bathing rooms were quite large. Each had three different side-by-side pools, each one capable of holding up to about fifteen bathers. Floor level faucets protruded from the wall every few feet on the wide tiled perimeter that surrounded the pools. Windows, high up near the ceiling, provided natural light.

Bathers provided their own soap, washcloth, and drying towel. The latter was thin, made of cotton, about the size of a thin kitchen tea towel. Bathing etiquette consisted of squatting next to a faucet, filling a small rubber basin with hot water, shampooing hair then scrubbing the body. Often, fellow bathers were asked to wash parts of the back that couldn't be reached. When we compared notes, we discovered complimentary back scrubbing was more common among women than men.

After rinsing thoroughly, bathers then submerged in any of three pools, one cold, one pleasantly warm, and the third quite hot. Not unlike Goldilocks, I found the cold one too cold, the hot one too hot, but the middle one was just right. Many bathers progressed from one pool to the next. With no time limits, bathers could be as rushed or as leisurely as they wished. After soaking, Korean bathers scrubbed themselves again until their skin was bright red. The goal was to exfoliate all dead skin before rinsing a final time. When finished, our skin tingled, looking a bit like that of a freshly cooked lobster.

We loved using the bathhouse. It was warm and felt great after waking up in our unheated second-floor room during the winter months. Because we typically went only once a week, we didn't take bathing for granted; it was a treat. We always felt renewed on our short walk home. It didn't take long for us to realize our preferred duration times inside the bath were quite different. I was relatively quick, while Linda enjoyed visiting with other women and sharing back scrubbing responsibilities, and soaking longer. The men were not quite so friendly. Of the two of us, I was always first to leave.

Daily breakfasts with Mr. Lee were another treat and our favorite meal of the day. While many PCVs tired of the repetitious nature of the Korean diet, we never did. Our fare was the same for every meal we ate at home: soup and rice accompanied by side dishes of kimchi and other vegetables, some pickled and others spiced with hot pepper.

Samonim's soup was always a mildly spicy vegetable with bits of beef. The rice was sticky, and the sides varied from meal to meal. She was so concerned about our reaction to her food that she took a cooking class not long after we arrived. The course had Japanese influences, and as her class progressed, our sides began to vary. Our favorites included tempura lotus root, seasoned sesame leaves, fried potatoes, roasted grasshoppers, and dried seaweed. Most of those side dishes, always served on small plates family style, were foods new to us. We found them tasty, but we could not imagine that Korean cuisine would become popular in the States fifty years later.

The lone exception to our enjoyment of Samonim's meals was when Mr. Lee was absent at mealtime. Sometimes he had evening obligations, and we would end up eating by ourselves. Invariably, we were served a drastically different menu at those times. Usually, the meal consisted of a thin, bland bean sprout soup and fewer sides. We were not nearly as enthusiastic about those meals. When what we were served in Mr. Lee's absence became predictable, we learned to check his evening schedule. If he had to be elsewhere, Linda and I sometimes made plans to be elsewhere as well.

While not our favorite, the bean sprout soup confirmed for us another aspect of Korean culture. Women, we learned, were the keepers of the purse. Family finances were typically their responsibility. When we were served that thin, bland soup in Mr. Lee's absence, we assumed Samonim was cutting back on expenses. As our status as family members grew, she may have felt free to tighten purse strings when Mr. Lee was away.

Chapter 11

SEOUL INTRIGUE

In mid-January, with schools still on break, we boarded a train for Seoul. Peace Corps had arranged a two-week schedule of meetings and medical appointments for our K-III group. For part of that time our meetings took place at Academy House, a conference center in the hills on the northern outskirts of Seoul. The grounds, accommodations, and views were exceptional, equivalent to a four-star resort. We thoroughly enjoyed the Western style creature comforts, the cuisine, and the opportunity to reconnect with our friends from Blue Knob. The conference agenda included administrative and technical meetings focused on instructions for filing tax returns, medical information, travel guidelines, and expectations regarding our teaching responsibilities.

Two international incidents that unfolded around us made the conference even more memorable. First, on January 17, not long after we arrived at Academy House, a group of thirty-one North Korean commandos breached the border north of our location in the hills and headed to Seoul on a mission to assassinate South Korean President Park Chung Hee.

With abundant snow in the area, local villagers who were gathering firewood just south of the DMZ noticed the groups' tracks. Once discovered, the commandos split into small groups of two and three to make their way through the mountains. By January 21, most of the commandos had made it to the center of Seoul, where they reassembled at an historic palace. They changed into authentic looking South Korean army uniforms, formed up, and marched boldly toward

President Park's residence, the Blue House. They got within one hundred yards of the residence before being intercepted by an alert police commander. A firefight ensued with casualties on both sides. The surviving commandos fled. Ultimately, twenty-eight commandos died, one was captured, and two made it back to North Korea. The South Koreans lost twenty-six, including twenty-four civilians caught in the crossfire during the firefight in downtown Seoul. In addition, four American soldiers perished trying to block the returning commandos from crossing the DMZ.

During the South's attempt to capture the invaders, the North Koreans escalated the affair on January 23 by capturing the USS Pueblo, a U.S. spy ship posing as a technical research vessel. The capture of the Pueblo looked like an attempt to divert international attention away from the assassination plot.

As soon as the North Korean incursion became public information, our group at Academy House went into lockdown. One evening, we heard gunshots in the distance and saw flares lighting the night sky north of us. It turned out that the area around Academy House was on the route used by some of the would-be assassins as they tried to make their way back north. We heard an explosion nearby and learned the following day that a North Korean, preferring death to being captured, had blown himself up with a hand grenade just outside the Academy House gate.

By January 25, events had quieted down, but the search for commandos continued. We left Academy House on January 27. The last commandos weren't killed until January 29. We don't know how close we were to being evacuated, but we had been briefed on all the procedures if such orders came. As the incidents unfolded, Kevin O'Donnell, the Peace Corps Korea Director, briefed us on a cable he had received. Peace Corps headquarters in Washington, DC, was being flooded with calls from parents concerned about the status of the Korean PCVs. To relieve the growing pressure on the Peace Corps telephone switchboard, Kevin asked that we each quickly write a note to our parents, reassuring them of our safety and the precautions

Peace Corps and the American Embassy employed to protect us. We did so that day.

Since our arrival in Korea, we had known that South Korean troops were actively engaged in the Vietnam conflict. The ROK (Republic of Korea) army was notorious for its ferocity in battle. Predictably, most of our fellow PCVs had strong beliefs about the war, primarily unfavorable. Controversy within our ranks broke out at Academy House when a letter petitioning against the war, drafted by several members of our group, was circulated at the conference. It was suggested that those willing, sign the letter before it was sent off to elected officials in Washington DC.

When Kevin O'Donnell got wind of the brewing firestorm, he intervened. He wanted us to appreciate the potential fallout of taking such action and did it in a way that acknowledged all sides of the issue. While bitter division existed within our ranks, cooler heads prevailed, and no group action was taken. Despite Kevin's skill at defusing the situation, I was sure that some would continue to chafe at the group's decision.

The day before we departed the conference, something else of far less significance happened. Linda's favorite pair of avocado green leather loafers went missing. She was sure she knew exactly where she had placed them, but they were no longer there. An inquiry with housekeeping yielded nothing. She was disappointed. They were her favorite, most comfortable shoes, and she knew that ready-made shoes that fit her feet could not be found in Korea.

When we got back to Taegu, Linda consulted her co-teachers and was directed to a local cobbler who could make her a pair of shoes. Custom-made shoes were not cheap, and we had only a modest living allowance, so we wrote the Peace Corps fiscal officer in Seoul and requested reimbursement. The finance officer, Bruce Lawhead, known for his sense of humor and his unpredictable multi-national attire, did not respond right away. After some months, we received a letter that read:

"Dear Steve,

Your wife's shoes have touched a bureaucratic nerve. One of the hoops PC/W puts us through entails almost Ladybird's signature. (They also won't allow us to make an international phone call without PC/W's approval).

After checking the regulations, it becomes even more ludicrous because they would honor the claim if all your wife's possessions were stolen. Is there a chance you could get ahold of the slicky boy and ask him to make another run on your wife's snuggies, etc.? If not, maybe there is relief in knowing the loss is tax-deductible.

I hate to throw out one of the "When I was a Volunteer..." type stories, but I found that I could recover losses like this in Liberia by selling pencils on the street. Of course, Korea is different, but maybe you could start an "A" frame delivery service or something like that. I think part-time work by PCVs is a field untouched here in Korea.

Well, Steve, I'm sure you can work things out, but if not, you could borrow a little Hue Humphreyism and "Keep smiling."

Cheers,
Bruce"

When we received Bruce's reply, we thought the letter hilarious. We still chuckle about how it was "so Bruce!" He was one of those colorful, witty, creative, good-natured, and yet effective administrators who could set a limit and disarm you, all at the same time.

Shortly after receiving Bruce's letter, Kevin O'Donnell made a decision unique to all of Peace Corps—one that earned him additional respect and admiration from many of us. He knew individual PCV expenses varied by location and assignment. Urban Volunteers typically paid higher prices and had more social demands than those working in more remote villages. Complaints about insufficient living allowances crossed his desk with increasing frequency. They presented a time-consuming dilemma. As a result, Kevin came to a radical decision, one that tested the integrity of Korea's PCVs. He decided to give us the liberty to request a change in our living allowance.

The standard allowance at the time was 13,500 won per month per PCV. At the exchange rate of 270 won to the dollar, that meant we each received a monthly allowance equivalent to fifty dollars. Linda and I found we were able to manage with the standard allowance, even when we had unexpected expenses, like a new pair of shoes. Prices throughout Korea were relatively low at the time. For example, a bowl of ramen was thirty won, a bulgogi dinner was one hundred fifty won, a daily bus ride to school was ten *won*, and a night at a Korean inn was three hundred won. Our largest monthly expense was our room and board payment to the Lees, about 7,000 won for the two of us. Even with that, we usually could save a bit for the unexpected. Being trusted to set our income level was a source of pride for all of us.

Chapter 12

NEW ADVENTURES

February 1968 was a cold month. Waking up with ice on the inside of our single-pane windows made getting out of bed in the morning less than attractive. Our kerosene space heater did a great job warming the room once we braved the cold to strike a match and get it lit. We set our alarm early enough each day to allow me a quick exit from the warmth of the bed, light the heater, and then ease back under the covers to let the room warm before rising to start the day.

In the midst of winter we had a need for some warmer clothes, large enough to accommodate our layered approach to dressing during the cold weather. Since ready-made Western-style clothing didn't exist in Taegu, our co-teacher friends suggested we check out some downtown tailor shops known for both quality textiles and workmanship. We decide to give one a try and ordered a lined wool skirt for Linda and a corduroy sport coat for me. The tailor we selected not only crafted beautiful clothes, but the prices he charged also amazed us. The cost of the skirt and sport coat together came to less than ten U.S. dollars.

We subsequently discovered that all our fellow Korean teachers purchased custom-made clothes. The practice was common. Laundering practices used by local cleaning establishments were hard on our garments, and the clothes we brought with us just did not hold up to the harsh treatment. When a favorite Pendleton wool shirt of mine began to get thin in the collar and elbows, Linda took the old shirt to our tailor and asked if he could match it. He assured her he could. She was delighted with the result but wondered if it would fit like the old one. It fit perfectly. That shirt wore like iron and always looked great, all at a cost of less than two dollars. Those local tailors were a great find.

As the weeks passed the political tensions between North Korea, South Korea, and the United States over the assassination attempt on Korea's president and the capture of the Pueblo, began to subside, alleviating our fears about being evacuated. We looked forward to the new school year.

Following our six-week break, school resumed, and students had only a couple weeks of classes before final exams were scheduled. Then, after another short break, the new school year was to begin March 1. The seventh-graders would be starting at a new school with new teachers and new subjects. They were going to start learning English from scratch. We wanted to take advantage of what we assumed would be enthusiasm and a desire to get off to a positive start.

In preparation for the new school year, we began to build lesson plans and visual aids to complement the texts the students would use as they started their first year of English study. Lindsey, our friend who had accompanied us to Pusan after Christmas, and Judy, another K-I volunteer, offered to share ideas and collaborate on lesson plans. That collaboration with friends who had been teaching an entire year was an opportunity for us to learn and exchange ideas. None of us were formally trained as educators, but we all loved working with our students.

To cap our classroom preparations, the four of us put together plans for a short camping trip following final exams at the end of February. Lindsey and Judy wanted to hike into a mountain temple not too far away. We were game for some outdoor recreation, though we were a little hesitant since the daytime temperatures were not quite reaching fifty degrees. Still, we were curious to try camping in the Korean countryside.

Our objective was to visit a small practicing Buddhist temple in the mountains, approximately an hour's bus ride from Taegu. The four of us put together a list of supplies we would need for a three-day excursion, made a hasty visit to the neighborhood market, and packed sleeping bags and food in canvas knapsacks. Despite the cold mornings, we planned to sleep out under a canopy of stars.

On departure day, we gathered at Lindsey's place during a cloudburst. The ground was thoroughly soaked, and the near-term forecast was not good. We decided to wait a day and shorten the trip to two days. The plan was to bus to the village of Oakpo, hike five miles into the temple, camp nearby, do some hiking the following day, and then bus back to Taegu.

We departed Taegu that Saturday later than intended; it wasn't until mid-afternoon that we arrived at the trailhead. Our hike took us through some scrubby foothills before we started to ascend the mountain where the temple was located. The trees became bigger and denser as we climbed and the pine scent became stronger. We marveled at the dark green of the trees set against a brilliant blue sky. Much of the forested land in Korea had been harvested by Japan during the 1910–1945 annexation. Trees were preserved near the temples, but the lower hills were bare or had young stands of trees, most less than 20 years old. We relished being transported from the urban grit of Taegu to the tranquil beauty of an ancient mountain.

We arrived at the temple about five-thirty in the afternoon. The temperature had dropped but the crisp air felt good after the strenuous hike. Less than a dozen monks called the weathered temple home. The building's best days had come and gone. As the sun began to set, we quickly gathered what firewood we could find and started a campfire on a flat clearing not far from the temple. Because the small rural villages nearby used wood as their primary fuel for cooking and heat, and because Koreans were rebuilding their forests, firewood was nearly non-existent. We started a small fire to warm the canned spaghetti and beef stew we had scrounged in Taegu's black market. We combined those items with Korean canned peaches, some local apples and pears, and bread from a favorite Taegu bakery. The result was not gourmet, but we were hungry and looked forward to enjoying it together.

As our food was warming, one of the resident gray-clad monks came over to our campsite. He welcomed us in more than adequate English. The weather, he warned, was going to take a turn for the worse; with the sun going down, it would get cold and quite windy. He encouraged us to consider sleeping in a spare room at the temple. We were appreciative but were looking forward to sleeping under the stars. He said he understood and reassured us the invitation remained open and the room available should we decide to seek shelter and a warmer place to sleep.

Within the hour, we sat inside the cozy temple, opening our warmed canned goods. The monk's weather prediction had been spot-on. A bitterly cold wind had sent us scurrying for cover before we had a chance to eat anything. Our canned food, peeled fruit, and Kool-Aid never tasted better as the wind howled outside and we enjoyed the warmth of the ondol floor.

The large temple room we occupied was completely devoid of furnishings, save for a beautifully cast bronze Buddhist bell suspended from the ceiling at one end. About four feet in diameter, the bell nearly reached the floor. We resisted the urge to discover what sort of rich sound it might produce. After satisfying our hunger and enjoying a card game together, we spread our bedrolls across the ample floor space and settled in for a good night's sleep.

At four o'clock in the morning, we experienced one of the most unforgettable awakenings! The early rising monks commenced their daily morning worship ritual with slow rhythmic tapping on their wooden *mokugyo* ("clackers," as we called them). The instrument was actually a block of hollowed-out hardwood, tapered into a handle at one end. The shape was reminiscent of a small gourd, struck with a wooden mallet. The result was a deeply resonant sound that felt hypnotic as it echoed through the forest. Such a gentle, soothing, peaceful way to begin our day!

After a breakfast of bread and fruit, we hiked to the top of the mountain, passing by a rushing stream and picturesque waterfall. From a viewpoint on top, the surrounding countryside seemed to be awakening from winter. Even though fields and paddies weren't planted, new growth was beginning to show itself in the trees and grasses on the forest floor. We hated to leave the beauty of that place, but in the early afternoon, we thanked the monks for their hospitality, bade them farewell, and caught a bus from Oakpo back to the city.

Our little adventure, much like our New Year's trip to Pusan, whetted our appetites for seeing more of what was often referred to as "the land of the morning calm." That moniker was derived from the meaning of a beloved old name for Korea: *"Chosun."* Literally translated, the term means something close to "morning freshness," and refers to the tranquil beauty of the lush countryside that characterizes the Korean peninsula in all but the winter months.

Camping departure with Lindsey and Judy

Our warm temple accomodations

Chapter 13

DIFFERENT FACES OF ADJUSTMENT

Linda and I were anxious to get the new school year started. At her school, the new students dressed in colorful outfits; they were not required to wear uniforms. They wore their everyday clothes during the first term, saving parents the expense of buying lighter-weight uniforms that students might only wear for a few months. Parents could then purchase uniforms to start the fall term in a large enough size to accommodate warm winter layers.

My school was a different story. The boys started the year with their new high collared black jackets and pants, each with their name on a breast patch. While Linda's classrooms were kaleidoscopes of color, mine were monochromatic seas of black. The students' faces, however, were bright and eager.

Linda's enthusiasm for the new school year matched that of her students. She ambitiously decided to give each girl an American first name, one that sounded something like the girl's Korean name. Partway through that task, she began to wonder if it was truly possible; she had eight classes of sixty students each. We brainstormed long into the night. When, finally, she had a name for each student, she made a seating chart for each class and a separate chart to track their progress.

Not long after the term began it was full speed ahead. We noticed some of our fellow English teachers had begun paying attention to what Linda and I were doing; some even asked about the specific activities we used in the classroom. We wrote dialogs derived from the first-year textbooks, that students practiced with one another during class. Visual aids helped us teach vocabulary, and we did lots of pronunciation practice. The teachers noticed a buzz among the students, prompting questions about the large 3' x 4' thin plywood sheets we carried to each class. We displayed our visual aids on those flannel-covered boards. On the backside of the board we glued horizontal strips cut from old file folders into which we inserted flashcards for vocabulary practice. Linda made colorful construction paper masks her students wore when they practiced conversations at the front of the class. The girls seemed less embarrassed and more likely to speak loudly in front of their classmates when they covered their faces.

Students in my classes almost always behaved well. They knew what would happen if a teacher reported them to the disciplinary vice-principal. They tried to avoid that emotionally and sometimes physically painful experience at all costs. Students caught in some forms of transgression were ordered to report to the teacher's room, where they stood in front of the vice-principal's desk, received a loud tongue lashing and, at minimum, a rap on the knuckles. Often the punishment was even more physical.

Early in the term, one classroom incident seemed to loosen up the students in one of my classes. During the first class after lunch one day, I turned my back on the students to post a visual aid or write something on the chalkboard. The students were always restless when they didn't have eye contact with me, so I didn't think much of the noises emanating behind me. After only a few seconds, I turned around. All looked normal except two boys sitting next to each other near the front of the room were rubbing their heads. It was obvious something had happened.

I continued the lesson, choosing not to draw the class's attention to whatever was amiss. A short time later, I turned my back again for a moment. Upon re-facing the class, I noticed the same two boys were doing it again, rubbing their closely shaved heads. The same thing happened a total of three times during the period. After the third time, I couldn't hold back my smile. The two boys had such sad and painful expressions that I was reminded of a scene from *The*

Three Stooges. I started laughing and couldn't stop. Observing me, the students began to giggle too.

I knew I needed to keep the class from making so much noise that another teacher might feel compelled to investigate. But when I tried to resume the lesson, I couldn't contain my laughter. I just couldn't stop! My students didn't know what to make of the situation; Korean teachers never lose their composure in the classroom. If something or someone disrupted a class, Korean teachers delivered a threatening disciplinary lecture, and failing that, a referral to the vice-principal.

Finally, I regained my composure and continued the lesson. As the class broke up, I learned from a couple of the other students that the two boys in question were carrying on a dispute that had begun during lunch. I figured as much. The offenders, no doubt, wondered if they would hear from another teacher, or worse, the vice-principal about the disruption they had caused. When no negative repercussions occurred, something shifted in the atmosphere of that classroom. The students became less hesitant in subsequent lessons and more eager to participate. I'm not sure what precipitated the change. The students may have begun to see me as less of a threat and more a teacher whose classes could be interesting, or at least entertaining. For whatever reason, the students seemed more attentive in the days following that incident.

At home with the Lees, we gradually settled into a daily routine. The three kids typically finished their homework before dinner, allowing them time in the evening to play in our room or on the warm ondol floor downstairs. Mr. Lee was often away in the evening during those early spring days. He left after dinner three nights a week to attend an intensive English class at the local college. With dreams of continuing his religious studies overseas, he needed to improve his English to qualify for admission to a seminary in Japan or the United States. With Mr. Lee gone the young ones, Samonim, and the kitchen girls found themselves relatively free. We often played games with the kids while the women worked on sewing projects.

One key to our adjustment to life in Korea was our affection for the Lee children. Googi was bright, social, and full of ideas. Yooni, the middle sister, was shy and quiet but no less enthusiastic about joining us. Wani, the youngest, was always curious. He was cute and increasingly willing to engage us even when his older siblings weren't around. Those three always brightened our return home at the end of the day.

Not only did the kids warm to us quickly, they also served as mentors, helping us to improve our Korean and expand our vocabulary. They watched out for us, as well. During our first few months in Taegu, we sometimes went for a walk with one or more of the kids to do an errand for their mother or pick up something we needed at the neighborhood market. Most everywhere we walked we were taunted by shouts from other kids. We were such an oddity that they would holler, *"Hello-K!" "Ay, ki kuda!"* ("Whoa, so tall!") or *"Ay, kun ko ya!"* ("Wow, big nose!"). When they were with us, the Lee kids always intervened, telling the other kids to hush or stop being so rude. We appreciated their protectiveness, although we never took offense at those catcalls.

While Mr. Lee and Samonim seemed heartened by how we related to their children, we knew we were an additional burden to the household's workload. The women cooked our meals, did our laundry, answered our questions, and invited us to join them from time-to-time on family outings. Sensitive to those impacts, we hoped our presence would not become a hardship.

Two other circumstances influenced our life and work in Taegu. One was our status as relative newlyweds. Keenly aware of that fact, the teachers in our two schools were sensitive to our desire to do things together as a couple, even though Korean couples often seemed to live their lives separately. Men tended to engage in male activities, while women were responsible for maintaining the household and doing things outside the home with other women when time allowed. In our case, however, invitations were most often extended to both of us, whether for lunch, a trip to a tabang for drinks and a chat, or for dinner and a movie. *A Fist Full of Dollars* and *Cool Hand Luke,* in

English with Korean subtitles, were especially popular with the locals; we saw them more than once in the company of Korean friends.

A few of our colleagues seemed comfortable stepping outside the usual cultural boundaries; they were people who tended to reach out and invite us into their lives. One teacher at my school, Kwon Gi Suh, began to invite both Linda and I on hikes or out to community events with him and his wife. They gradually became our closest friends.

The other significant influence on our life and work in Taegu was the fact that we shared common values with our host family. Before applying to the Peace Corps, I had entertained thoughts of attending seminary, owing primarily to my positive experiences at the Presbyterian Church Linda and I attended during high school and college. Mr. Lee and I taught at Kei Sung, a private school affiliated with the Korean Presbyterian Church. Linda and I felt a kinship with both the school and the Lee family from the very beginning. The Lees enjoyed it when we joined them at Sunday worship services. They encouraged us to get involved with the local missionary community. Peace Corps had paired us with a family and schools that were a good fit for us.

Many of our single PCV friends had more significant adjustments to make. Living with a local family proved awkward for some of them. Hosting a volunteer was a challenge. Language, behavior, diet, and expenses all played a role. Korea struggled economically at that time. Average incomes were low, making an additional resident a potential burden despite the room and board payments we made. Some families were uncertain how their new guest would take to their diet. Most families lived in tiny homes where several members slept in a single room. Setting a room aside for a PCV could easily cramp a family's living space. Language was always a barrier, especially in the beginning. Being understood was a challenge in both directions, from family members to PCV and vice versa. Additionally, the individual differences between men and women, their habits and needs, made the fit with a PCV unpredictable.

The potential contamination of food and water concerned all of us. The Peace Corps doctors exhorted us to avoid all fresh, unpeeled fruits and vegetables, fish caught in rivers, and drinking water that had not been boiled. Human waste was commonly used as fertilizer, giving birth to our doctor's orientation lecture about every surface being covered with a "fine fecal veneer." The precautions that host families and restaurants used in meal preparation varied widely. If the water in a household was not boiled and the food not thoroughly cooked, PCVs risked exposure to bacteria, amoeba, or other sources of disease.

Given Linda's persistent vigilance, we usually suffered nothing more than minimal ill effects from eating out. At home, Samonim was careful about sanitation. We had total confidence in the meals she prepared. We were cautious, however, when asked into other people's homes. We avoided severe illness, but despite our best efforts, we still suffered intestinal upset from time to time. Other PCVs were often not as fortunate. Some contracted severe illnesses, sometimes requiring hospitalization. A few had to be evacuated back to the States for medical care.

We understood how fortunate we were and how difficult it was for some of our friends and the families they lived with to adjust. Our K-III group numbered eighty-eight when we arrived at Kimpo in October 1967. Over the course of two years, thirty members of our group ended up going home prematurely. A myriad of reasons contributed to the attrition. Some left for health reasons, others were unhappy in their work assignments, and some found their living circumstances untenable.

One woman's departure became legend. The speculation was that she left due to an experience in her outdoor latrine. Outhouses in rural areas were often perched atop the family pigsty. The floor typically had a simple rectangular opening over which occupants would squat, leaving them vulnerable to an unpleasant nudge from the four-legged occupant below. Apparently, as the story went, once was enough for that PCV.

Every one of us had a unique experience adjusting to life in Korea. No matter how unusual that experience, we could usually relate. Diet, housing, work assignments, harassment, theft, and the Korean way of life could all present uncomfortable realities with which we had to cope. Those experiences gave rise to a shared kinship among us, a bond that has remained strong and has kept most of us in touch with each other during the decades since.

Chapter 14

OPPORTUNITIES AND CHALLENGES

As the weather warmed in the spring of 1968, we entertained an increasing number of visitors at the Lee home. Students, co-teachers, and missionary friends dropped by with increasing frequency after school and on weekends. Thanks to the gracious nature of our family, the empty rooms on our upper floor became a popular place for Peace Corps friends from out of town to stay when visiting Taegu. To not infringe upon the use of the rooms downstairs, we usually invited visitors to join us upstairs in our room. As we did so, we began to consider making an adjustment to our space. The double bed, which we were never enthusiastic about, filled so much of the room that we could accommodate very few guests. Often, someone would have to sit on the bed above the others sitting on the floor. The arrangement was awkward.

We began to entertain the idea of replacing our bed with a *yo* – a foldable floor futon. As was the custom for almost all Koreans, we could sleep on the floor. During the day, the futon could be folded into a sitting area, making it possible to accommodate as many as six to eight visitors, all seated comfortably on floor cushions. Uncertain what lengths had been taken prior to our arrival to secure the bed for us, we decided to raise the issue with Mr. Lee.

When we spoke to Mr. Lee about replacing the bed, he didn't seem enthusiastic about the idea. We decided to let the idea go rather than push against what we imagined was resistance. We hoped we hadn't stepped over an invisible boundary. We knew the bed had been acquired out of a desire to help us feel comfortable. We did not want to seem ungrateful. However, less than two weeks later Mr. Lee raised the issue himself and suggested the switch. When Linda and Samonim had a grand time shopping for our new floor mattress and comforter, our concerns were put to rest.

Samonim was very supportive of us. Our relationship with her had grown close during our first six months, perhaps due to our improving ability to communicate and her increased comfort in having us in her household. Samonim even began to express an interest in learning to cook American dishes. She was, however, self-conscious about letting Linda into her stark and unheated kitchen. Instead, she sometimes brought a small, tin kerosene oven upstairs to the outdoor patio where she and Linda had a great time making simple dishes. The kids often joined them for the cooking lessons and enjoyed sampling the fare, which ranged from sautéed vegetables to applesauce. Those dishes, however, never showed up on our breakfast or dinner table downstairs. That wasn't a surprise; Koreans rarely departed from their traditional menu.

With the removal of our bed to one of the empty rooms down the hall, we needed a few more items to complete our little upstairs nest. A Saturday afternoon trip to the large market next to my school netted several floor cushions embroidered with colorful Korean designs and some baskets we could use for storage. The whole family seemed to agree that the new arrangement was much improved. Weighing how best to be culturally sensitive was sometimes a balancing act hard to gauge.

Our kerosene heater was an indispensable part of our room during the winter and early spring. It was about the size of a small television but light in weight until filled with kerosene. It could be easily moved and warmed the room quickly, especially on cold mornings and late afternoons at the end of the school day. Its top was flat enough to accommodate a teapot or a kettle, but it didn't get hot enough to boil water. To remedy that situation, we purchased a small electric heating coil that quickly boiled water when inserted into a cup or the small kettle we had selected at the December holiday party at my school.

That little coil nearly precipitated a disaster. At bedtime, Linda often liked to enjoy a cup of tea. One evening she filled our little brass-colored aluminum kettle and inserted the electric coil. I was already asleep, and as she waited for the coil to do its thing, she dozed off. I awoke sometime later to see Linda sound asleep. The kettle sitting atop our heater glowed red, the water having boiled away. In my sleepy fog, I pushed myself up. But instead of unplugging the coil, I hastily lifted it out of the kettle. As I held the coil, I was jolted out of my fog when the heating element melted before my eyes. The molten metal dropped between my legs as I sat on the floor.

Frightened back to my senses, I quickly replaced what remained of the coil in the kettle and unplugged it from the wall. By that time, Linda had come awake. Once we both calmed down, we began to understand the disaster we had narrowly avoided. The molten metal could have dropped on me rather than the floor, the entire pot could have melted, or the floor could have caught fire. After we took stock of the damage (no injuries, no fire, minor damage to the floor) we realized the consequences could have been much worse. It was a sobering lesson.

The timing of having more sitting space in our room coincided with a request we received from some neighborhood high school students. They expressed interest in having an evening English conversation class at the Lee home. The Lees were supportive, so we decided to give it a try. Before long, the group outgrew our upstairs space; we had nine students — a mix of five boys and four girls. We began to meet in the larger downstairs guest room.

Typically, boys and girls did not mix much during their high school years. Because schools were gender-separate, the teen students in our group were initially timid. Their interest in the class, however, grew to the point that we began to meet twice per week, Monday and Thursday evenings. As time went by, the boys and girls in the group became increasingly comfortable talking with each other. We thoroughly enjoyed facilitating their attempts to speak English, but we were pretty sure that wasn't what kept the group interested.

Those types of experiences captured the essence of what we were doing in Korea. We had an opportunity to teach something we knew. The students learned a bit and got to know us as Americans. We were a novelty, and while the students got to know us, we learned something about Korea. Some of Linda's middle school students even knocked on the Lee's gate occasionally with a bouquet of flowers for her. When they came in for a brief visit, they would often say things like, "You can't leave; you must stay!" We reassured them we weren't leaving any time soon.

Our students were curious and eager to learn. The drive and ambition we witnessed in Googi as he prepared for the middle school entrance exam at twelve years of age was not unique. Years later, when we noticed Korea's emergence as a nation on the move, we realized that the appetite for learning and willingness to work hard under difficult circumstances we witnessed in young people with whom we interacted was one factor that drove the country's future economic success.

That commitment to move forward was manifest in a project underway at my school. One of the buildings on the Kei Sung campus was being remodeled. When I inquired about the pounding I heard when I was out on the athletic field, the principal informed me that the school was investing in a language laboratory, complete with a master recording console and sixty listening stations. He asked if I would be willing to record the texts being used in the middle school to allow students to listen to the written material in the voice of a native English speaker. He proposed that I work closely with a co-teacher who would be responsible for the operation of the laboratory. It didn't take long for me to realize that when the installation was complete, the language lab project would likely keep me busy, along with my classroom teaching. I looked forward to the project, thinking it might be a legacy that would outlast my tenure at the school.

Legacy was an issue for many in our Peace Corps group. We wondered if the impact of teaching first-year English classes would quickly fade upon our departure, especially since most of our Korean counterparts did not show much interest in improving their speaking ability or adopting our oral-aural teaching methods in their classrooms. That desire to leave behind a tangible contribution began to fuel discontent within the group.

That spring, Linda faced a challenge of a different kind at her school. Her much-beloved co-teacher, Miss Sung, made the decision to join her husband in the United States, where he was a graduate student. Miss Sung expressed ambivalence about the move because her infant son had been born with a heart condition. Describing him as weak, she was anxious about what to do. She could take him and risk his health worsening, or she could leave him with her parents. It was a difficult decision for her. Ultimately, she decided he would be safest if left in Taegu.

Linda grieved the thought of losing her co-teacher. The two of them had become close during the short time they worked together. Miss Sung was a teacher unafraid of trying new things. She was a collaborator, freely sharing what might be helpful in the classroom, and motivated to become a better teacher herself. The two of them had hit it off, and Linda trusted and counted on her wise counsel. The school's farewell party was a tearful affair, with the two women exchanging gifts to express their fondness for each other.

As the new school year got underway, our friend Kathi, who had been part of our Christmas baking party at the Scholten's, dropped by for a visit in some distress. On a weekend trip to Pusan she had visited a couple of other single women friends who were thinking of going home early. We knew single women had it especially tough in Korea. Their host families were sometimes unsupportive, and they had a difficult time gaining respect at their schools. At times, they were the unfair targets of disparaging rumors in their communities.

Kathi shared with us the difficulties she was experiencing. Her host family had internal troubles and she received little support from them. More and more, she had to cook her own meals. She even discovered some of her possessions were missing from her room. At school, her teaching schedule kept changing. She seemed miserable;

so much was going wrong for her.

As we listened to Kathi's struggles, we began to fear she might decide to return home early. Fortunately, by the end of the month, she had better news. She had discussed her dilemma with Mel, who supported her interest in finding a different place to live. She had spoken with the Ministry of Education and requested permission to not report to her school on Saturdays. Often, PCVs had no teaching responsibilities on their school's half-day Saturday schedule but were, nonetheless, required to be in the teachers' room. When permission was granted to no longer work on Saturdays, Kathi began to feel encouraged. She enrolled in a calligraphy class and sought out other activities of interest in the community. We were much relieved.

Soon, however, we heard distressing news of a different type. Back home, on April 4, Martin Luther King Jr. had been assassinated in Memphis. We were shocked, saddened, and ashamed that such a thing could happen. Dr. King was a distant hero, a man whose work we followed and respected, but with whom we did not identify closely. We believed in his non-violent approach in advocating for the rights of Black Americans. Still, the Jim Crow practices of segregation, discrimination, denial of human rights, and violence against Blacks were alien to us. We had grown up in a conservative, predominantly white community where such things were not given much attention. While we were undergrads at UCSB, students of color were almost non-existent on campus. The plight of racial minorities in the US and violent clashes between racial groups there were distant to us, outside of our personal experience.

With Dr. King's death, we began to hear about violence across America. We read and heard about it but felt disconnected and powerless. Our Korean friends never talked about violence against Black people in America either. Of course, they knew of Dr. King, but Korean society was quite homogenous. In 1968 minority populations were almost non-existent there, and minority rights were not much in the consciousness of our Korean friends. We had, in fact, noticed that minorities of any kind received little recognition or respect within

Korean society.

Alarmed at our naivete regarding American racism, we made a commitment to increase our awareness. We read about the life of Malcolm X, learned the meaning of Jim Crow, and became more familiar with Dr. King's work. Our learning called our beliefs and faith into question, and those questions would become more pointed as we moved into spring and summer. We awoke to how sheltered our lives had been in America, with no friends and few acquaintances whose skin color or beliefs differed from our own.

Violence was not something we had ever experienced, but 1968 was becoming a volatile year at home, and we followed the events taking place from halfway around the globe. Our idyllic "settling in" to life as Peace Corps Volunteers in a foreign land was becoming unsettled.

While we wrestled with disturbing news from home, we met a couple newly arrived in Taegu. Our friend Helen, who we first met at Blue Knob when she presented a guest lecture on her experience living and working as a Mennonite in Korea, introduced us to Sharon and Gary. Their assignment intrigued us. They managed a demonstration farm and vocational school sponsored by the Mennonite Church. The farm, located just outside the city, provided young Koreans an opportunity to learn alternative farming, dairy, and construction practices. We wanted to learn more about their project, and they were interested in our work and what it was like living with a Korean family. Our friendship grew as we shared meals and explored the countryside together around Taegu. The Mennonites had their own vehicles, Land Rovers that could take us where local taxis couldn't. We hiked, picnicked, and discovered places we would otherwise never have seen. Over the spring and summer, we got together every few weeks or so to exchange stories, visit new sights, and often share food, including hand-cranked ice cream from the farm. Our new friendship offered us some respite from what was becoming an unsettled time for us.

Adding to the social unrest at home and unhappiness within the ranks of our PCV friends, Linda was coping with the loss of her trusted co-teacher, Miss Sung, and I was beginning to feel the pressure of helping create programs for the new language lab at my school. Changes, we could tell, were looming just around the corner.

Typical street vendor and market shops in Taegu

Chapter 15

RITES OF SPRING

Our friendship with Barrie and Jerry Raik, dubbed as fellow "honeymooners" by Taegu's newspaper, continued to develop. The Raiks lived with a caring family in Yechon, a rural town of about thirty thousand residents located several hours by either train or bus from Taegu. Coincidentally, the Raiks' host family had three small children, like ours, and Lee was the family name. The father was a teacher, and the mother operated a local dress shop. Since no one in the family spoke English, Barrie and Jerry were quickly becoming more proficient in Korean.

The Raiks told us about a springtime ritual known as "Stepping on the Coat." Hatched at their small college in New York, the ritual was a solemn spoof on the end of winter. A procession of participants, all wearing winter garb, paraded through town to an outdoor gathering spot where a ceremonial "priest" invited the celebrants to solemnly remove their winter coats, scarfs, caps, and gloves and present them to him for a "stepping on the coat" to commemorate the arrival of spring. The Raiks planned to reenact the event in Yechon and invited us to join them. We almost never turned down an opportunity to try something new.

So it was that on the first Saturday in May we met Mrs. Lee, the Raiks' Korean mother, in Taegu. She was in town to purchase fabric for her dress shop. When she finished shopping, we embarked with her on the four-hour bus ride to Yechon. The weather that day was warm and the countryside dazzlingly beautiful. Drab winter brown had turned to brilliant spring green. Along the route, we passed terraces of freshly planted rice patties, orchards where apple blossoms were in full glory, and small waterfalls that spilled over ridges above us as the bus negotiated the winding mountain road.

As we passed one village, we saw a couple being hoisted on a cot above the shoulders of what appeared to be at least fifty friends and relatives. Mrs. Lee believed we were witnessing a sixtieth birthday celebration, known as the *hwangap*; it was the most important of all Korean birthdays in adulthood. Traditionally, turning sixty signified two things — a celebration of longevity, and the conclusion of a sixty-year lunar calendar cycle. The revelers were engaged in singing, clapping, and lots of laughter as we passed by.

As our journey continued, more rural customs came into view. We noticed a group of women sitting in a circle in the shade of a large tree. Mrs. Lee guessed the women might have been gossiping about village happenings, a typical late afternoon tradition in the countryside. Men, too, would often gather at the end of the day. A hard day's work often closed with a social meet-up to discuss village events.

After a bumpy but thoroughly interesting ride through hills and valleys, our bus pulled into Yechon about seven o'clock that evening. We helped Mrs. Lee with her textile purchases, stowed our gear in Barrie and Jerry's room, and headed to a nearby Chinese restaurant for dinner.

While we had no desire to leave Taegu, we loved visiting Yechon. It was quiet, picturesque, personable, and respectful. Compared to Taegu, we found the pace of life there slower and more relaxed. The Raiks' host family was another attraction. Despite having little space in their tiny traditional country home, they were kind and welcoming. When we visited, we literally filled the house, especially when it came time to spread bedding out on the floor.

Sunday morning dawned clear and calm, promising to get warm closer to noon, the designated hour for Yechon's inaugural "Stepping on the Coat." First, after breakfast, Jerry and I challenged each other to a basketball game on the outdoor clay court at the school where he taught. Being 6'2", I had a distinct height advantage over Jerry, who had to stretch to reach 5'6". We had played regularly at Blue Knob and in Korea whenever a ball and court were nearby. Despite our difference in height, I had never bested Jerry in a 1:1 matchup. His quickness and great luck every time we took to the court became a challenge. Beating him was not quite an obsession, but a definite mission.

We took to the court that day and engaged in a spirited battle. By the end of the game, we had worked up a good sweat. The outcome, however, had not changed. Jerry somehow managed to squeak out a victory and then audaciously claim I would never beat him. He made up with confidence and guile what he lacked in physical stature. I promised him the outcome would be different next time.

After cooling off from our game, time for the big event arrived. As the only person in Korea "authorized" to lead the "Stepping on the Coat" ceremony, Jerry served as "high priest" and leader of the procession. Barrie, Linda, and I followed behind. We were about to retire our winter garb, not to be worn again until the weather cooled in autumn. The Raiks' host family was in on the spoof, but they declined to join us as celebrants as the four of us donned all our winter gear in the late morning. The temperature had warmed considerably, and there was not a cloud in the sky. Jerry was almost unrecognizable in his scarf, cap, and glasses, but his short stature undoubtedly gave him away to any villager who took notice.

We hummed a slow dirge from the Lee home, walking in single file behind Priest Jerry, through the town toward the river and the bridge that would take us to the far side and up nearby *Nam San* hill. By the time we arrived at the bridge, we had quite a gathering of onlookers, all adopting our solemn, sober, non-smiling countenance. We could see curious glances and hear questions uttered in low tones. "Just what," they no doubt were asking, "were these foreigners up to?"

The ceremony commenced as we reached the hilltop, with the Lees trailing behind the somber-faced villagers. First, we lined up facing the Priest, who beckoned all to pay attention. Then, one by one, we each bowed deeply to the onlookers and then deeply again to the Priest. Finally, we each took our turn stepping forward to slowly remove all our winter gear. Holding it out as an offering, we knelt before the Priest, who then made a pronouncement about the end of winter, slipped off a shoe, and placed his foot upon the outstretched clothes. We each then returned to our spot, much relieved to have shed our heavy coats and scarves on what turned out to be a hot Yechon day. Our procession then made its way slowly down the hill as we hummed a more light-hearted tune.

We had no idea what the townspeople who had accompanied us to the hilltop thought about that odd ceremony. Coincidentally, our friends had unknowingly chosen Buddha's birthday for the event. We wondered if the villagers thought there might be a connection between the two. We were curious, too, about what the Lees thought. No doubt, a discussion took place between them with Barrie and Jerry later in the day. If the spoof were clear, the villagers at least got a glimpse of American (maybe New Yorker) humor.

For our ride home that afternoon, we decided to take the train, giving ourselves some relief from the bouncy wash-boarded dirt track we had endured the day before. That train trip, which took about the same amount of time as the bus, proved interesting. We had third-class tickets; therefore, no reserved seats. Being a local, the train stopped at most villages and towns along the route. Fortunately, the third-class car wasn't full when we boarded at the Yechon station, so we got seats on the bench installed around the perimeter. At one stop, a group of young men boarded. We learned their induction into required military service was happening the very next day. They were in a celebratory mood, and it was obvious they had been drinking. Flushed faces, bellowing singing voices, and glazed eyes gave away their inebriated state. They serenaded us with raucous song and laughter as we rolled along the tracks at a casual pace. As they departed several stops later, those sitting around us looked our way and shrugged as if to say, "Boys will be boys."

As spring established a solid foothold, new patterns in daily Korean life began to reveal themselves. Walking to school along the river,

Linda noticed older women squatting low on their haunches at the river's edge, washing clothes in large rubber tubs. She knew how strong and agile those women had to be to do that kind of work for hours at a time. Their knees stuck straight up on either side of their bodies as they leaned forward, scrubbing their wash on the river rocks with their heads nearly touching the ground.

Agriculture and construction began to pick up. I noticed how wiry-strong were the men who carried heavy loads on crude wooden A-frame backpacks, and the women who hoisted heavy tubs and carried them on their heads. Two-wheeled carts, filled with rocks, gravel, or produce, were pulled manually through the streets, loads that I could not even budge. When the Lees had some repair work done to their ondol heating system, supplies did not arrive by truck. Instead, lumber, nails, oilpaper, and other supplies arrived on the back of a heavy-duty bicycle or an ox-pulled cart. Unless the job was too great, all the work was done by muscle, without gas or electricity.

Spring brought a realization that Linda needed some additions to her wardrobe. The summer outfits she had packed in her trunk at Blue Knob were much too casual for teaching at her school. Her options were to send for what she needed from California or seek out a tailor in town. Since the cost of custom-made clothing was manageable on our modest living allowance and the quality excellent, Linda decided to have several dresses and skirts made at a shop recommended by a fellow teacher, one we had not used previously.

To her dismay, after three fittings, the dresses she had commissioned were not quite right. The combination of Linda's size in contrast with the proportions of Korean bodies, and the fact that Korean women didn't wear much in the way of undergarments made it difficult for the seamstress to deliver a good fit. Linda accepted the finished products, not wanting to return to the shop a fourth time. She wore what she bought, and the outfits looked great, but they were never as comfortable as she had hoped.

While Linda dealt with her dressmaker, I had an uncomfortable situation of my own. A teacher I met invited me to teach classes on

Saturday afternoons at a private school where he worked. I initially declined; I had my own teaching responsibilities on Saturday mornings. Despite my hesitance the teacher persisted. He asked that I visit the school before I made a final decision. I agreed to a visit and was invited to sit in on classes on a Saturday afternoon, followed by dinner and a movie. Not wanting to offend him, I accepted.

The "visit" turned out to be an afternoon of co-teaching, accompanied by a sales pitch to commit to an ongoing slate of Saturday afternoon classes. I sensed that if I accepted the teacher's invitation to an evening of entertainment afterward, I would feel obligated and expected to reciprocate by accepting his offer. As graciously as I could, I thanked him for the opportunity and declined the invitation to go out that evening. Linda and I were both relieved and recognized the need to be clearer about our limits in the future.

Toward the end of the month, we made a weekend overnight visit to Haeinsa, a Buddhist temple that had been recommended by a host of Korean friends. They described the temple and its grounds as a picturesque complex high in the mountains, about a three-hour bus ride from Taegu. Located within Kayasan National Park, Haeinsa turned out to be a magical place.

Moss hung from ancient fir trees in the dense forest where the temple and a small adjacent tourist village occupied a steep hillside. The weather that weekend made the experience even more special. Low clouds hung over the mountains and drifted throughout the temple grounds. The scene resembled brush paintings of misty ancient villages with traditionally dressed peasants toiling in rice paddies or walking along forested paths.

As we strolled, a young monk approached. In flawless English, he offered to accompany us and share the history of the temple. In his quiet manner he told us that since the year 1398 the temple had housed the Tripitaka Koreana, Buddhist scriptures carved onto over 81,000 wood print blocks. A quiet reverence permeated the temple's terraces as we moved through the grounds and looked on with amazement at the carefully shelved woodblock carvings of Buddhist scripture.

That monk's kind gesture made our day. He helped us understand the importance of what we were seeing, and gave us a sense of the pride Koreans feel toward their antiquities.

The next afternoon, we witnessed another rite of spring. A group of women old enough to be grandmothers assembled on the picnic ground adjacent to the temple. In a circle, they danced to the beat of traditional drums. We noticed a number of the women were decidedly intoxicated. Later, we learned such celebrations were not unusual. The practice of drinking, singing, and dancing on special occasions was very Korean. We wondered if those women might have been doing things they would never have dreamed of doing in their home village.

A festive atmosphere pervaded the temple grounds on that Sunday, and we thoroughly enjoyed being part of the fun. I learned that when grandmotherly partiers felt no pain, they sometimes invited me, or literally dragged me, into the celebration. With their inhibitions loosened, I became a target, maybe because of my height, my status as a foreigner, my big nose, or my goofy grin. For whatever reason, there was no escaping those moments. The invitation sometimes came in the form of a forceful yank of my arm. I just rolled with it and considered it a part of being a young American on a festive weekend in Korea.

Jerry and Steve on Yechon Basketball Court

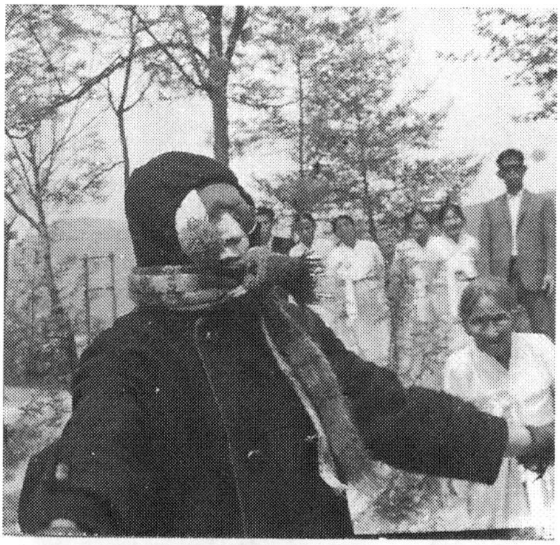

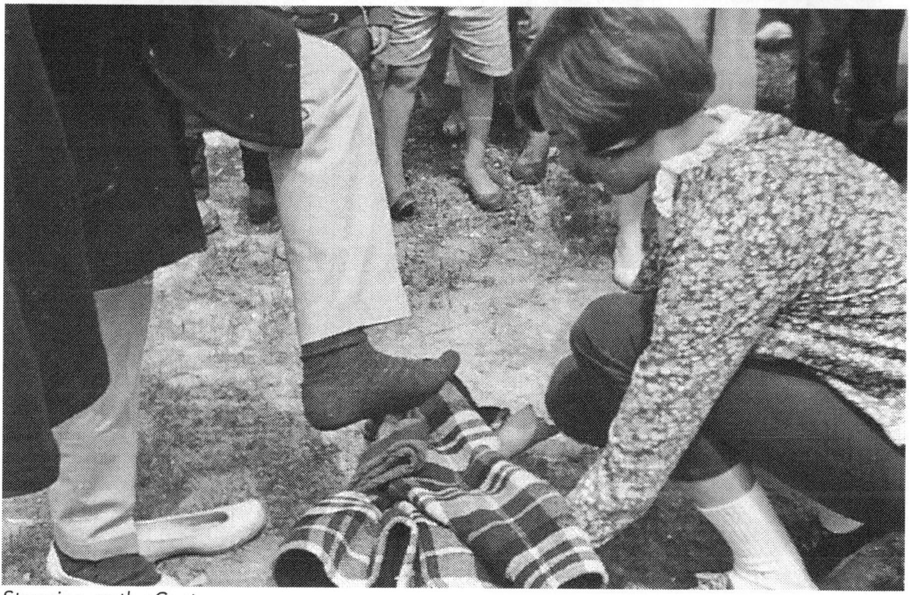

Stepping on the Coat.

Spring Laborers.

Haeinsa on a Misty Day

Chapter 16

MORE UNSETTLING EVENTS

A week after returning from Haeinsa, Linda and I were shocked to learn that Robert F. Kennedy had been shot and killed on June 6th in Los Angeles. That news rocked our foundation again! We couldn't believe it. So many disturbing events were unfolding at home. Protests targeting the war in Viet Nam had escalated to the point that President Johnson withdrew his candidacy from the presidential election campaign at the end of March. Riots in cities across the United States had followed the assassination of Dr. King in April. The Kennedy tragedy hit us hard. Linda and I were confused, anguished, and ashamed by everything that was happening. We had a difficult time talking with our Korean friends about it. They didn't understand how such terrible things could be happening in the United States. We wondered the same thing. The year 1968 was becoming the most eventful and turbulent year of the decade.

With Kennedy's death, we began to question ourselves. It seemed that what we were attempting to do as Peace Corps Volunteers was being undermined. It felt personal. Peace Corps had begun during John Kennedy's administration, directed by Sargent Shriver, whose wife was President Kennedy's sister. Linda and I identified with the Kennedy clan. The loss of JFK was like a wound that had never fully healed. He had been a beacon of hope, a Progressive with a "can do" attitude, a sense of humor, and a grace that captured young and old alike. The killings of Martin Luther King Jr. and Robert Kennedy seemed like assaults on those ideals. We were confused and upset. We thought, "How can this be? What's happening to our country?"

Our faith in what we were doing was shaken. Korean friends asked us questions we couldn't answer. Some wanted us to justify our volunteer work considering what was transpiring at home. We were angry and sad at the same time. In retrospect, the tragedies that occurred during that time in the United States drove home an appreciation of our vulnerability, the fragility of our world, the uncertainty of what lay ahead, and the reality of injustice.

While we struggled with our rattled feelings, the Lee family was again there for us. They could tell we were upset. The family expressed their concern and gave us space. On the day we heard the Kennedy news, we were scheduled to host a class that evening for the neighborhood high school students. Without our asking, Samonim greeted the students when they arrived and told them we would not be holding class that night. That was such a considerate thing for her to do. She intuited that we needed some time to ourselves.

A two-day meeting of all PCVs in our Kyungsangpookdo province was on the calendar for the second week of June. The meeting's purpose was to review how the English teaching program was progressing with representatives of both the Peace Corps and the Korean Ministry of Education. We were thankful for the opportunity to get together with our friends at such a troubling time.

Emotions ran high at the meeting. Fueled in part, no doubt, by the recent troubling events at home, many of our fellow PCVs questioned the value of the TESL (Teaching English as a Second Language) Program. They expressed pessimism about the lack of impact they were having on their fellow Korean English teachers, and the questionable long-term benefit of teaching just first-year students. They felt frustrated in the face of what they considered futility. Some complained that school administrators and teachers did not value or respect the work of inexperienced PCV instructors. Korean teachers, they said, often showed no interest in improving either their ability to speak English or their teaching methods. We weren't sure whether that disinterest stemmed from a fear of being seen as deficient, an unwillingness to consider alternative teaching methods, or something else.

Whatever the reason, many of our friends had begun to believe their efforts to promote improvement in English instruction would fail.

Despite our angst about events at home, Linda and I felt more positive about the work we were doing at our schools. Our students were responsive, and our fellow teachers had begun to show at least modest interest in our efforts. My school was investing in a language lab, and Linda's classes and after-school conversation club were going well. In addition, we had successful teaching projects at the U.S. Information Service (USIS) and with high school students in our neighborhood. So, while events back home disturbed us, we were not as discouraged as others.

Still, that mini conference left us with some uneasy feelings. We knew a significant number of our friends were unhappy. Possible causes of their distress crossed our minds: troubling living arrangements, discouragement with work assignments, unrealistic expectations, homesickness, physical illness, social upheaval back home, and more. Based on what we observed at the meeting, we braced ourselves for change. It seemed likely that some in our group would be seeking to alter their assignments, while others might decide to return home. Time would tell.

Chapter 17

GETTING OUTDOORS

In mid-June, we learned that a picnic field trip was on the schedule at each of our schools. Beyond recreation, those events performed an important public service. Secondary schools throughout the country had springtime outings at which students helped eradicate pests that harmed young forests.

While forests on the Korean peninsula had suffered annual infestations of pine caterpillars for centuries, they had also been sustainably harvested as a primary fuel for heating and cooking. During the Japanese occupation, however, forests were over-harvested. Much of what remained at the close of World War II was decimated during the civil war of the early 1950s. Since that war, with coal the preferred household fuel, the few remaining trees were carefully protected and new ones planted in an attempt to restore formerly forested land. Much of that work remained. With that realization we understood why the hills were so brown when we arrived in October. Stands of evergreen trees were sparse and still lacking in height.

In spring, fat green caterpillars regularly attacked pines to gorge on their needles. They threatened the health of those trees. One strategy undertaken by the government to control the caterpillar population was to task secondary schools with their removal. On Chae Il's picnic day, the entire student body of two thousand middle and high school girls traveled into the foothills. Teachers organized students into teams and assigned each group to a stand of young trees. Their task was to find and remove caterpillars from small and mid-sized trees. Supplied with plastic bags and long tweezers or sticks that could be used like chopsticks, the teams scoured their assigned areas. The girls plucked the corpulent, easy-to-spot, greenish crawlers off branches of and dropped them into their bags. When the bags were heavy with wriggly caterpillars, students dumped the contents into a designated nearby shallow ravine.

Linda was surprised and more than a bit bewildered by how the day unfolded. First, each teacher gathered their class together and provided instructions for removing, sacking, and disposing of the caterpillars. Then, after providing instructions, the teachers sat in small groups to visit and enjoy the boxed lunches each had brought from home. Meanwhile, with little attention from their teachers, the hordes of students headed off through the trees to hunt their prey.

Curious, Linda wanted to observe her students. She imagined middle school girls might be a bit shy about plucking three-inch-long caterpillars from tree branches and depositing them into plastic bags about the size of a lunch sack. She was right. The girls screamed each time they plucked a wriggly creature from a branch. If they happened to drop one before getting it into a bag, more squealing ensued as the girls rushed to see who would capture it and get it sacked. When the girls spotted a caterpillar beyond their reach, they called out to Linda, who was taller than most, to come pluck it for them.

It was quite a sight. Shouts and giggles drifted throughout the small stands of trees as the girls engaged in the hunt. Due to the plentiful caterpillar population, the girls' bags soon began to fill. Once sufficiently loaded, the girls shook the contents of their bags into the designated ravine and headed off to eat their lunch and play games.

The most puzzling thing about the exercise occurred when the girls emptied their bags. Linda was amazed to discover nothing further was done as the number of dumped caterpillars grew to the thousands. Although the caterpillars immediately began moving up the sides of the shallow ravine, the teachers took no action. It seemed odd that no strategy had been devised for ridding the area of the creatures once the girls had removed them from the trees. Apparently, no one had considered a next step.

As a postscript, the pine caterpillar continued to be a significant pest in South Korea until the 1970s, when the government established a national forest service. Reforestation and pest eradication became a science-based priority, and the caterpillar population was brought under control.

With warmer weather, we began searching for other things to do outdoors. The teachers at Kei Sung drafted me to play on their volleyball team. I had a definite height advantage, but despite having grown up in Southern California where volleyball was popular, I was a novice. The team practiced a few times before we started having contests with faculty from other schools. What our team lacked in skill was made up for with spirited play. Spectators, including Linda, cheered enthusiastically on the sidelines. Those outdoor clay court games were great fun. I was disappointed when the season ended after just a few matches.

As we traveled the streets of the city, we discovered outdoor tennis courts we had not noticed previously. Tennis had been one of our diversions during college; we were curious to give those courts a try. After finding a couple of rackets at Taegu's big outdoor market downtown, we invited another Peace Corps couple to play on weekends. I soon discovered that playing on packed dirt was hard on shoes. Mine, already well used before I packed them in a trunk at Blue Knob, quickly gave out. When I went hunting for a replacement pair, the largest shoe I could find was a full size too small. My Korean friends confirmed that size eleven was the largest available. Despite my feet being size twelve, I bought a pair and endured the discomfort.

I had a chance to test those shoes out on the basketball court when we made a spur-of-the-moment decision to visit the Raiks one weekend. We had planned an overnight camping trip with my friend Gi Suh and his wife. On the Saturday morning of our departure, however, the four of us met up at the bus station in the middle of a cloudburst. We were thoroughly drenched, and the clouds looked as if they weren't going anywhere soon. We decided to postpone the camping trip. It wasn't the first time we had been rained out.

Internally, I found myself wondering if rainouts of our adventures were becoming a pattern.

Still at the bus station, we considered what to do when I noticed the posted schedule of departures indicated a bus was about to leave for Yechon. Linda and I spontaneously had the same idea. With a change of clothes and toiletries packed in our knapsacks and no other plans for the weekend, we looked at each other and said, "What the heck, let's go!"

We had no way to check if the Raiks would be home, and we had only enough cash with us to cover the bus fare one-way. Without a great deal of thought we gambled, trusting things would work out. Gi Suh and Duk Hee were headed back to their home and volunteered to let the Lees know where we would be.

Barrie and Jerry were delighted by our surprise visit. During the weekend, as we picnicked overlooking the nearby river, the Raiks raised an idea for us to consider. They both had a history of attending summer camps in their youth and wondered if we would be interested in helping them lead a day camp in Yechon. They had already found operators of a local orphanage interested in hosting a camp. After brainstorming what a weeklong camp might include, we committed to moving forward, thinking that the August school break would be a good time.

Before heading back to Taegu, I challenged Jerry to another basketball game. Once again, I went away defeated, but I had a new excuse. I blamed the loss on my ill-fitting shoes, claiming that a larger pair would have resulted in a more competitive, less painful effort on my part. As usual, Jerry wasn't convinced.

Chae Il Caterpillar Picnic

Springtime Volleyball Match

Chapter 18

A COUNTRY HOME

One of the unique gifts that the Peace Corps experience presented us was an opportunity to see and be seen in a way that enhanced people on both sides of a cultural divide. That lesson was driven home when a new friend of ours, Nak Kyung, invited us to visit his ancestral home in a small village outside Taegu. Nak Kyung was a college student who was working on improving his English. We had become friends during the winter and, with the weather warming, he wanted to introduce us to his family. Initially, we weren't sure what was driving his invitation. We thought maybe it was a way to help us understand another side of Korea, or perhaps it was to introduce his new American friends respectfully to his family. We weren't sure but looked forward to the day.

The visit started one morning with an hour-long bus ride to the home of Nak Kyung's cousin, who had joined us for the day. After introductions and a brief walking tour of his village, we enjoyed a small feast of baked goods, sliced apples, and tea. Since it was almost midday, we assumed that might be lunch, so we didn't hold back in accepting their hospitality. Then, after visiting a short while, we all said good-bye and piled into a small taxi to continue our journey, still at least a half-hour's drive to Nak Kyung's village.

Our taxi driver was quite a daredevil. He literally assaulted the country road, filled with chuckholes, as if he were escaping a wildfire. As my fear for our safety increased, I began to think he might be trying to impress us with his driving skill. To our collective relief, after a few miles he had to slow when we came upon an outdoor market in a large clearing adjacent to a small village. Festive and colorful, mobile markets like that traveled around to rural villages, setting up in a designated area every five days or so. Customers from other nearby villages flocked to those markets. All manner of goods was available: food, housewares, clothing, even livestock. As our driver negotiated the narrow road, dodging cows, goats, and village chickens, we took in the scene. After passing by the market, the road narrowed to become more like a dike between rice paddies, just wide enough for a car. Because the lane was so narrow, our risk-taking driver had to slow to avoid slipping off the causeway into a watery paddy.

After about forty-five minutes Nak Kyung's village finally came into view. More akin to a hamlet, it consisted of a tiny collection of houses bordering rice paddies and an apple orchard. We parked and made our way to the family home, a U-shaped house with a thatched roof and small courtyard where the family cow was tethered, all behind a high earthen wall. Nak Kyung introduced us to his parents and his two older brothers. The oldest brother and his wife lived with the parents, a common practice in Korea, as the firstborn son or daughter often shouldered responsibility for aging parents.

Another custom that was becoming familiar was the way in which Koreans treated guests. Whenever we were invited for a meal, our hosts most often said in Korean, "Outside of a little bit, we have nothing, but please eat a lot." Then, spread before us would be a carefully prepared feast, far more than a small army could eat. Nak Kyung's mother used that exact phrase when she invited us to partake in refreshments. Clearly, a great deal of effort had gone into preparing for our visit. Nak Kyung, however, quickly tipped us off that the elaborate table before us was just an appetizer. The actual meal, even grander, would come later.

After refreshments, the family invited us to another part of the home. Nak Kyung shared that his paternal grandfather had passed away three months prior. We entered a room where his father lived in mourning. Pictures of the deceased, the funeral, the coffin, and the whole family were hung about the room. As Nak Kyung translated, each photo was described, and the tradition of mourning elders was explained in detail for us.

Tradition dictated that the deceased's eldest son not enter any of the other rooms in the house for three years, during which he would wear only traditional white mourning clothes and sackcloth cap. His obligation was to maintain a small adjoining room in honor of his father. That room contained some of his father's possessions, his photograph on a small table, and most importantly, his spirit. It was customary for all family guests to visit that room, pay the deceased their respects, and sign a registry that was maintained from generation to generation. Because we were the first Americans to visit the home, we were told our entry would be remembered forever.

Across the courtyard, we met Nak Kyung's eighty-two-year-old grandmother. Nak Kyung had coached us on how to greet her. We knelt with both hands and feet on the floor, bowed deeply, and each said in our best honorific Korean, "I know nothing, please guide me." She was a vibrant lady who seemed delighted to meet us, shaking and holding our hands for the longest time. We believed the opportunity to pay our respects to Grandfather's room and to meet Grandmother were the real reason for our visit. Nak Kyung showed his respect to the family by introducing and sharing his new friends from America. Our meeting with the grandmother concluded with an invitation to a visually opulent feast of traditional foods. The trouble the family had taken to welcome us and prepare such a lavish spread was humbling.

After eating and learning more about the family, we had the honor of meeting and paying respects to Nak Kyung's maternal grandfather and grandmother. After a short visit with them and posing for a family photo, we toured the village's narrow paths and were shown the hamlet's ancestor worship hall. It was a special place that relatives coming to the village could visit and show respect for their ancestors. Owing to their Confucian heritage, all Koreans regularly paid homage to their ancestors, even practicing Christians. Consistent with that respect, we were taken to a hillside where multiple mounds protruded from its slope. Those were burial mounds. Nak Kyung's recently deceased grandfather lay beneath the freshest of the mounds. No doubt, other members of Nak Kyung's family would be laid to rest on that hillside in the future.

As we departed the village, many residents come out to wave us goodbye. It was an experience Linda and I have never forgotten. We felt so grateful to Nak Kyung for inviting us. It cemented a friendship that continued until he left Taegu to fulfill his military obligation and then resumed years later with a memorable reunion when we returned to Korea for a visit forty years later, in 2009.

Traveling Market

Nak Kyung (on right) with his cousin

Nak Kyung's Maternal Grandparents

Nak Kyung's father shares his calligraphy

Chung Nak Kyung's Family

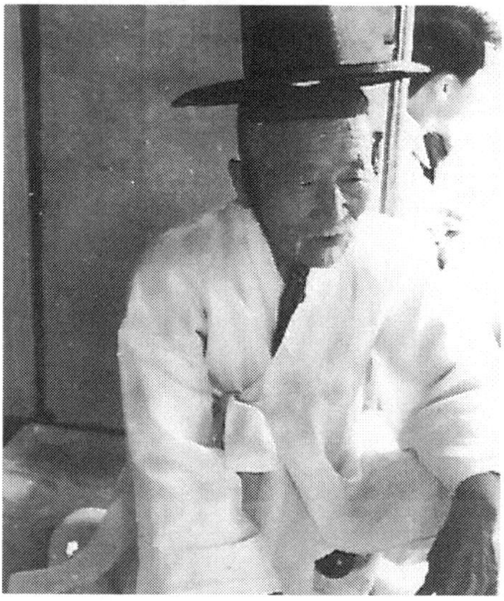

Nak Kyung's Grandfather

A feast

Chapter 19

SURPRISES, DISCOMFORT AND LOSS

Taegu's reputation for extreme weather was validated in July. Temperatures were in the 90s and the humidity was high. Spring rain had been far less than average, so much so that water rationing had begun. Public bathhouses opened only one day per week, and pumping water at home was allowed only every other day until mid-July, when it changed to every third day. Everyone felt sticky and uncomfortable.

The Lees decided to remove all the items stored in their bathtub to allow all of us to take cold-water showers, meaning we could fill a bucket with water, wash, and then upend the bucket on ourselves. We had to be careful not to ingest any of that water, but it did feel great.

The heat didn't stop the construction business. All over town, streets were being paved and old buildings torn down and replaced. It seemed we couldn't go more than a block or two without encountering another building either coming down or going up. We sensed a real push to modernize the city.

A casualty of those efforts in our neighborhood was the loss of several low-income families that Linda encountered on her walk to school each day. Along one of the alleys on her route, a small number of shanties had been pieced together along a wall that separated the dirt alley from the houses behind. Several families had taken up residence there. Each day, as Linda passed, they greeted her in the most polite and friendly way. She felt a connection to them.

One Monday morning the shanties had been removed. The families were gone. We weren't sure how much warning they'd received, if any. They'd had no heat and no running water, barely a roof over their heads, yet they had always been kind and respectful as they acknowledged Linda on her daily walk. She missed their friendly greetings and worried about what had become of them. All had left, except one elderly gentleman who returned to his spot along the wall to sit, perhaps finding it familiar or emotionally comforting. Soon, however, he was gone as well. As far as we knew, no social services were available to step in and assist those families. They were simply gone.

A few weeks later, Linda encountered a rather funny scene on that same walk to and from school. One afternoon, in the same alley from which the families had been removed, she came upon three young girls, maybe four years old, playing together. At once, they stopped what they were doing, backed up to the wall, dropped their panties at the same time, and squatted in unison to urinate, sending three trickles down the dirt. Peeing in the street by both children and adults was not unusual, but the synchrony of the act by all three girls was a complete surprise. Whether it had been planned or was spontaneous, Linda was not sure, and if they intended to make a statement, the meaning was not clear. But the memory stuck.

While the distress of Robert Kennedy's murder and the unhappiness of our PCV friends had not abated, our summer calendar began to fill. The USIS Director planned a July 4th celebration at his residence, our own first wedding anniversary was July 8, and sometime around the middle of the month our K-I friends were due to complete their tour. Following those events, a three-day Peace Corps medical meeting was scheduled in Seoul for annual physicals and booster vaccinations. Then, beginning the last week of the month, our schools were to start a five-week break. At the beginning of that break, my school scheduled a three-day teacher excursion to an offshore island in the Sea of Japan. While I was to be gone, Linda was invited to care for the children of our missionary friends, the Grubbs, at Taechon, a beach community on the country's west coast. July would be full of activities; we had only a few open days the entire month.

Koreans often notified us of scheduled events at the last minute. I remember being informed one afternoon that the English teachers at my school planned a meeting after classes that day. After the meeting, we all went out to a nearby restaurant for dinner. I had no way to notify the family that I wouldn't be home until late. When last minute notifications became a pattern, we learned to be flexible and tried not to worry when one or the other of us didn't show up when expected.

The Ministry of Education surprised us one day at the end of June, calling on both Linda and I at our respective schools and asking that we come to the Ministry after classes that very afternoon. A farewell banquet for all K-I PCVs in the province was planned for early that evening, and our presence was requested. The late notice was a bit bewildering, but the event held other surprises we could not have anticipated.

First, some of the K-I volunteers looked transformed. Gone were the beards and shaggy hair. Talk was not of their worksites or host families but of what lay ahead, life beyond Korea. Second, the banquet, attended by numerous officials and special guests, included a personal hostess for each male K-I. Those women were *Kisaeng*, elegantly dressed and coiffed, and trained to entertain men of elite status. It was the Korean way of honoring and showing respect to male guests. Women, however, were never afforded such treatment. Thus, the outgoing female K-I volunteers had no escorts. We were all aware that women were not granted the same respect or recognition as the men. Still, we felt empathy and some discomfort at the situation. The K-I men were uncomfortable as well; the presence of Kisaeng acted as a familiar reminder to both male and female volunteers that women held second-class status in traditional Korean society.

In stark contrast to the last-minute invitations that we sometimes received from Korean officials, the July 4th American Independence Day celebration at the home of the USIS Director was organized and announced well in advance. A big crowd attended the outdoor garden party, an elaborate affair at the director's residence that included an open bar, buffet dinner, and fireworks. Acknowledged again, the K-I volunteers received congratulations from a diverse group of partiers, including local Korean officials, U.S. military brass, missionaries, and other PCVs. Our hostess, the Director's pregnant wife, looked as if she could deliver at any moment, but there she was, making the rounds and welcoming all.

Several of our K-I friends were leaving within the week. They were a special group, true pioneers in our eyes. They paved the way for the rest of us and set a high bar in the way they handled their responsibilities. We were closest to our friend Lindsey who was returning to his home in Hawai'i. He had been a mentor and guide, a friend and fellow explorer. We would miss his sensitive ways and cheerful, confident optimism. We would try to emulate the understanding and kindness he showed us as new volunteers when we welcomed and got to know new groups that would arrive in our second year.

Our first wedding anniversary followed on the heels of the July 4th celebration. Samonim prepared a special dinner that we enjoyed with the whole family. Their thoughtfulness was touching. Leading up to that dinner, cards and letters had arrived from family and friends back home. My mom, known for her fun-loving bodacious spirit and creativity, sent Linda a card at her school, one we still chuckle about to this day. It arrived mid-day in the teacher's room, and when Linda opened it, she couldn't help giggling. When her fellow women teachers asked what was so funny, Linda showed them the card. The cover read: "*Confucius say: When celebrating anniversary be like a girl without bra...*" Inside it said: "*Bust Loose!*" Linda had a grand time translating that.

A week later, we rode the train to Seoul for our medical review. To avoid missing much school, our appointments took place over a three-day weekend. Physical exams included a total of seven injections that hit us hard with short-term fever and soreness. The Peace Corps put us up in a yogwan with real showers — our saving grace. The heat wave we endured in Taegu engulfed the entire Korean peninsula, so the showers were a godsend; we enjoyed them every day, although we were mindful to conserve water.

Despite feeling like swollen pin cushions, we took advantage of free time between medical appointments. Seoul was a great city to explore. We perused small shops, admiring watercolor paintings, furniture, and Chinese calligraphy. We enjoyed looking at the brush paintings of Chinese characters, a popular art form. Scrolls and framed quotes, poems, and ancient Chinese expressions were mysterious, a challenge for us to decipher; most of the time we failed, but we still found the calligraphy striking.

Chinese characters were not only seen in calligraphic art, but they were also everywhere in print. Our middle school students really didn't like learning Chinese. Googi often complained about having to memorize hundreds of Chinese characters at school. Students much preferred the Korean alphabet. Relatively simple, it was consistent and phonetic, with an easy-to-read combination of fourteen consonants and ten vowels. The characters looked odd to us, but we learned them quickly at Blue Knob. Because of the phonetic alphabet, we could pronounce any Korean word we saw. Unlike English, there were only rare exceptions in spelling or pronunciation. Still, we often didn't understand the meaning behind what was written. Most often, our limited vocabulary prevented us from fully understanding the printed word.

Written Chinese was different. Rather than being based on an alphabet, Chinese consisted of individual unique characters, each based on an ancient artistic representation of the character's meaning. Sometimes a word or concept would encompass several characters. Hundreds of Chinese characters had to be memorized to make sense of what was on a printed page of the newspaper. Fluency in reading Chinese required knowledge of several thousand characters. In addition, the spoken sound represented by a character was not phonetic. It had to be memorized; there were no clues to its sound in the written form.

Chinese characters were ubiquitous in Korea in the 1960s, painted on storefronts, printed in newspapers, and on packages at the market. We managed to learn a few of the most common characters, but for the most part, we were clueless. In more recent years, the use of Chinese characters in both print and on storefronts has declined significantly, in favor of the Korean alphabet. Today's students are, no doubt, grateful.

Although always interesting to visit, Seoul's urban sprawl could be overwhelming. A city of several million in the mid-1960s, Seoul was radically different from Taegu. Despite having a population of over a half-million, Taegu felt like a small town in comparison to Seoul. When it came to commerce, restaurants, theaters, and the number of people on the streets, Taegu seemed more manageable, finding our way around more straightforward.

When Linda and I look back on our life during that July, we recall a jumbled combination of surprises, discomfort, and loss. The changes on Linda's walk to school, the drought and rationing of water, the celebrations for our departing K-I friends, the number of vaccinations during our physical exams, and coping with the heat and humidity — all on the heels of the assassinations in the United States and our friends' discontent — had an emotional impact. The Seoul trip confirmed what we feared. Several of our Blue Knob friends were returning to the States, some for physical health reasons, others because they were unhappy, and still others because of urgent family issues. Our friend David, who spent Christmas with us after his carbon monoxide poisoning, was one who decided to leave; he simply wasn't happy with his life in Korea.

Acutely aware of our departing friends, Linda and I sensed an unraveling of our tight-knit group from Blue Knob. Fortunately, we had a solid circle of friends in Taegu, and the Lee family remained our rock of steadiness. The Presbyterian and Mennonite missionaries were steadfast friends as well. They introduced us to Korean churches in nearby rural villages and invited us for social visits to their homes. My fellow teacher Gi Suh, and his wife Duk Hee, had become close friends as well. We shared mutual interests in hiking, going to the movies, visiting temples, and participating in holiday celebrations. As Gi Suh and Duk Hee introduced us to some of their friends, we felt increasingly connected with the community.

We arrived back in Taegu for ten days of teaching before our schools began the five-week summer break. Brutally hot temperatures made teaching and learning a challenge. Despite stifling classrooms, my students still wore their high collared black jackets. Their discomfort likely contributed to their difficulty in attending to classroom activities. All my fellow teachers agreed that the students were ready for a break.

During that third week of July, we suffered yet another loss. Our friend Kathi was medically evacuated to a hospital back in the States. Her situation seemed incredibly unjust. Her earlier family and school difficulties had finally started to resolve. With the support of Mel, she had planned to change both her living and work settings. She was engaged in calligraphy lessons and had plans for involvement in other community activities. Sadly, she became acutely ill with a bacterial infection just after our banquet that recognized the K-I volunteers. Hospitalized first in Taegu, she was transferred to a U.S. Army hospital in Seoul. Doctors there determined that the severity of her bacterial infection required care back in the U.S. Kathi returned to Taegu to pack up her trunk for storage and say goodbye. She assumed she would return once her infection was resolved. However, some weeks later, we received a letter from her explaining she would not be returning. It seemed so unfair, given what Kathi had already endured. We were going to miss her.

Chapter 20

ESCAPES FROM THE HEAT

The five-week summer vacation came at a good time. We needed a break from both the losses we felt and the uncomfortable heat. The day after classes ended, I was to travel with my fellow teachers on a school-sponsored island trip as Linda headed to the west coast to care for three young boys while their parents attended a conference in Seoul. She planned to be at the family's beach cabin for nine days; I would join them there after my school trip. Then, after returning to Taegu for a day, we would travel to Yechon, where we were to co-lead a children's day camp with the Raiks, the camp we had discussed earlier in June. Those were the plans, but we had already learned that plans didn't always play out the way we expected.

Everything started as envisioned. Linda's beach cabin, part of a missionary resort, was located within the equivalent of a gated community along a beautiful section of the coast. There was a lodge for guests, several individual cabins, tennis courts, a commissary, and bakery. Built on a cliff, the cabin had stair access down to the beach, a vast expanse of white sand that stretched far into the distance, with several small islands just offshore. A forest of evergreens wrapped around the entire place, right down to the beach. Western in style, the cabin came with two housekeeper cooks — a real treat. Their presence allowed Linda to spend the entirety of each day with the Grubbs' three boys. Taking advantage of the sunny, warm weather, they played tennis, Frisbee on the beach, hiked, swam, and sailed a small boat with other missionary families. She loved the boys; they had a grand time together.

My trip to the offshore island got off to a promising start. In the company of thirty-five other teachers from my school, we traveled by bus and ship to Ulungdo, seventy-five miles off the east coast of the peninsula. The excursion was a reward from the school for all the work done by the faculty during the year. It was an opportunity to relax, unwind, have some fun together, and enjoy a part of Korea that most in the group had never seen. Our schedule called for spending two full days on the island, where we could hike, swim, and learn about village life. We lodged at a rustic inn, dined on island seafood, inhaled the salty air, and enjoyed the ocean breeze — such a relief from the heat in Taegu.

Some teachers complained about the all-night boat trip, during which several became seasick as the boat plowed its way through high swells and deep troughs. At one point during the night, I awoke and saw water pouring through a porthole, like it was coming out of a fire hose. Then, as the ship climbed out of a swell, a big wave struck us broadside. I was out of harm's way, but some of my fellow teachers got wet. That porthole was secured; we never took on more water, but the ride was up and down the entire night.

Within the group, objections also surfaced about the inn's primitive quality. It was old, built during the Japanese occupation before WWII. Most Koreans felt no love for the Japanese, who had imposed their will over the Korean people for decades in the first half of the century. Despite the grousing, I thought the inn was terrific. We were all in a big room on the second floor with many windows cut low on the wall. When we lounged on the tatami mat floor, we could easily see out across a narrow valley to the ocean. We all slept in that same room, making for a soft chorus of snores throughout the night.

What I valued most about the trip was the opportunity to visit with some of the other teachers in a less formal setting. While we lounged indoors we chatted, and I learned to play the traditional game of *Paduk*, known as "Go" in other parts of the world. Outdoors, we took a few organized hikes, but mostly we had free time to do what we wished. I loved wandering the trails along the grassy hillsides and taking photos, sometimes with another teacher and sometimes on my own.

Ulungdo was larger than I expected. Home to a population of twenty-four thousand residents, fishing provided the primary commerce. Several villages dotted the coastline. The tiny houses looked like those on the mainland, earth-colored single-story dwellings roofed with grass thatch. Nearly every small yard had drying racks constructed with long poles over which were draped drying squid, often called cuttlefish. Dried squid was a popular snack everywhere in Korea. We often took it on hikes and kept some in our room at the Lee's. It was tough, stringy, and salty.

Warm, crystal-clear water surrounded the island. While swimming, I could easily see thirty feet down to the ocean floor. The clarity of the water made for an enchanting boat ride around the island. The ocean appeared turquoise as we floated over stretches of sandy bottom on a sunny day. The weather was glorious…until the last day.

Our return was scheduled for the morning of the trip's third day, July 28th. We awoke that morning to the sound of torrential rain; it came down in proverbial buckets. Tropical Storm Mary prevented us from traveling anywhere that day. The ship scheduled to pick us up could not leave port back on the Korean mainland.

We spent two additional days on the island, mostly holed up in the inn as the rain continued. I wrote letters, played Paduk, and braved the elements to send a telegram each day to Linda at her cabin on the beach at Taechon, not knowing if they would get through to her. We finally boarded our return vessel on the evening of July 31st. The return passage was rough. With the ocean unsettled following the storm, the ride was not unlike that of a roller coaster. The ship dipped and swayed from side-to-side most of the night. A good number of my fellow travelers became seasick again. Fortunately, I felt only a little queasy. Relieved to be back in port the next morning, we boarded a bus for Taegu.

I arrived at the Lee's in the late afternoon on August 1st. After sharing some Ulungdo stories with the family, I climbed the stairs to our room for a much-needed rest. I had not slept much the night before on the ship. I repacked my bag the following day, bid the family adieu, and headed to the train station.

The trip to the beach where Linda had been for the week took seven hours. Her charges and I knew each other from our visits to their home in Taegu. They were eager to hear about my adventure, so we all swapped stories late into the evening. After getting them settled down for the night, Linda and I finally had a chance to talk. I was relieved to hear that my telegrams had found her each day. They left her with only minor worries about the safety of our ocean voyage back from the island.

I had just one full day at the beach before Linda and I had to depart. Our tight schedule had us due in Yechon on August 4th, where we were to co-lead what turned out to be the second of a two-week summer camp for children at the local orphanage. We rode the train back to Taegu in beastly hot weather. The previous ten days had been a welcome respite for both of us. Temperatures on and near the ocean were warm but far more moderate than what felt like an inland oven. We spent a quick overnight at the Lees for the second time in just a few days, with just enough time to check in with them, sleep, repack and catch a bus the following day.

We marvel now, as we look back on that summer, at the tight choreography of our activities. It wasn't our preference, but simply how the opportunities and our obligations fell together. We didn't want to miss anything, and we were willing to tolerate some hurried trips in exchange for new adventures. We wondered what the Lee family thought as we rushed off.

After our short stopover in Taegu, we took the increasingly familiar bumpy bus ride to Yechon on Saturday, August 3. On Monday, we were to begin helping with the second week of the summer camp. Earlier in the spring, when the Raiks proposed doing a day camp at a Yechon orphanage, the idea was so enthusiastically received the original plan expanded to two weeks. The first week had gone well. With about sixty campers, we were going to relieve some PCV friends who had helped during week one.

The campers were all residents of Sang Hae Won orphanage. We had never visited the orphanage and had some reservations about what we would find, based on the poor condition of orphanages we had visited in and around Taegu. Sang Hae Won turned out to be an exceptional place in a beautiful setting alongside a river. The campus had several buildings, a meeting hall large enough to hold eighty-five resident children, and lots of space for outdoor play. Most important, the staff seemed devoted to the children. The director and his wife, a young couple with four children of their own, had diversified the operation. The grounds included a flock of seventeen hundred chickens, apple and pear orchards, and a garden full of melons. Farm produce subsidized their income and provided nutrition for the kids.

While we found Sang Hae Won refreshing, we wondered why so many orphanages existed in Korea when relatively few existed back in the States. We came to understand at least three ways children ended up in a Korean orphanage:

1. Some babies were born out of wedlock, unacceptable in Korean society. Those children tended to be rejected by the population, as were their mothers.
2. Some were of mixed racial heritage. As many as sixty thousand American military personnel resided in the country. Children with American fathers and Korean mothers had no place in mainstream culture; often, they were abandoned by their mother.
3. Some families were so poor they could not support additional children. In those families, new arrivals were sometimes not welcomed, especially girls. Boys were seen as assets in low-income families, girls as liabilities. In Korean society, having a traceable bloodline was critically important. Abandoned children had no traceable heritage, thus no place in society.

We found the campers, aged six to seventeen, a real treat. Most orphanages, including Sang Hae Won, were short-staffed, meaning the children had only a modest amount of day-to-day contact with adults. They were essentially starved for attention. With the camp staffed by volunteers, the campers threw themselves wholeheartedly into every activity. Indoor games, outdoor sports, dancing, singing, and crafts — they engaged in all of them with gusto. Enthusiastic and very supportive of one another, their appreciation for what we were doing made the whole week rewarding.

Swimming in the river, where there were deep pools and rocks to climb for diving, was most popular. The continuing heat wave made the cool water especially attractive. Despite the warnings we had received from our doctor about the potential contamination of river water, we joined in. Relief from the heat was worth the risk of encountering invisible disease-causing organisms that might be present. We just had to avoid ingesting the water.

At camp, we divided the children into two groups, older and younger. Activities for the secondary school-age youth took place in the morning, those for the elementary kids in the afternoon. We kept the morning group busy with basketball, soccer, tennis, swimming, and an English class. The younger kids enjoyed singing, having relays of all types, playing games like capture the flag and dodge ball, and swimming in the afternoon heat. A bonus for us was a chance to practice our Korean. The kids loved interacting with us, so Linda and I had to quickly get up to speed with some new phrases and camp vocabulary.

During the week, we ate breakfast and lunch at the orphanage with the kids. Dinners with the Raiks included a review of plans for the following day. We lodged at the home of a man who helped in the camp's afternoon sessions. An elder in the local church, he and his wife had three children and lived in a traditional Korean home, one maintained with great pride. It was landscaped with vegetable and flower gardens and populated by a flock of healthy-looking chickens. Their two giant pigs, housed in a pen right next to the outhouse, greeted us with friendly grunts each morning.

With the river nearby, mosquitos were a constant summertime annoyance in Yechon. We slept under a mosquito tent and kept ourselves slathered with repellant during the day. The continuing heat made the situation worse, but the fun we had with the kids more than made up for whatever physical discomfort we felt.

A welcome relief from the heat arrived on Thursday, the fourth day of the camp's second week. Buckets of rain poured down, washing out our outdoor activities that day. As an alternative, the orphanage director suggested that the camp staff go on a mid-day picnic to check out a spot for future activities with the kids. The place he had in mind was near a pavilion that would shelter us from the rain. After a bus ride and a short hike along a hillside above the river, we came upon a picturesque scene: four tiny earthen homes with thatched roofs. The cluster of houses sat among green shade trees and colorful flower gardens. We heard a gurgling stream nearby as we took in the view of the river below. The tranquility and beauty were striking.

A gentle rain fell as we walked further, by a waterfall and near a small building where several farmers threshed barley with hand tools. Witnessing such physical work, I wondered how long it would be before that way of life would change forever by the adoption of more modern farming methods. Something special, I thought, might be lost in the name of progress.

Blue skies returned the following day. We rode in a bus with the campers about fifteen miles to a different photogenic mountainous spot for a picnic they had been looking forward to all week. Both morning and afternoon groups were combined that day as we hiked to the picnic area, accessible only via a long suspension bridge high above a rushing river. We wondered about the bridge's safety; it looked old and rickety. Crossing proved a bit scary as the bridge swayed under our weight while we looked down to a river far below. While we had our reservations, the children were not the least bit intimidated. They loved it!

On the far side of the bridge, we wound our way down to the canyon floor, passing terraces of lush green rice paddies brimming with water set off by a brilliant blue sky. As we neared the river at the canyon floor, we found an ideal place to swim. A waterfall poured into a deep clear pool between rock cliffs in a narrow gorge. Nearby, a grove of trees shaded an area large enough for the picnic. For natural beauty, the setting rivaled Haeinsa, the ancient temple we admired in the mountains near Taegu.

Saturday, the final day of camp, was crowned with an intramural track meet. We divided the campers into two teams, as equally matched as we could guess, based on what we had observed during the week. Boys and girls of all ages were blended into the teams. Events gradually became more challenging during the afternoon as the ages of the competitors increased. We planned a whole range of running, jumping, and Frisbee-throwing events. Most impressive was the spirit among the kids. As their teammates competed, the kids on the sidelines performed songs and yells, led by spontaneous cheerleaders. Everyone enjoyed the day, and the competition was close. Final score: 114-111!

Before we departed for Taegu, the camp and orphanage staffs gathered for breakfast to review the two-week experiment. All agreed it had been a big success. As we boarded our bus, Linda and I were sad to leave the kids, but happy knowing Barrie and Jerry would maintain their connection with them in subsequent months.

After a long, dusty bus ride, and despite the continuing heat wave, it was great to be home. Not long after we arrived, the Lees invited us to join them on a mid-week excursion to Pohang, a popular beach on the east coast. We knew we needed a couple of days to recoup our energy from the constant activities of the camp, so the timing was perfect. We had a lifelong love of the beach and wondered how the Lee family would choose to spend their time there.

On one of the days before our beach trip, I dropped by my school to see how the language lab was coming along. I was disappointed to learn it was not ready. Construction delays caused by the heat and the complexity of installing audio equipment pushed the completion date forward. The delay meant we would not start putting lessons together and making recordings until school resumed in September, primarily due to a two-week sightseeing trip we had planned for ourselves during the last two weeks of August.

Our plans for that trip included traveling by train, bus and ferry along the coast from west of Pusan, across the broad southern tip of the peninsula, and then up the east coast, ending in Seoul. We didn't want to sacrifice that vacation. I was concerned the Kei Sung administrators might be disappointed about the delay in building lessons for the lab, but they didn't seem bothered; at least they didn't let it show.

What I had seen of the lab layout went beyond my expectations. The equipment and the design of the physical space all looked terrific. Linda had agreed to work with me on making the initial set of recordings. Since we both still had our normal obligations at school, we knew we would have to work with the equipment after regular school hours. Though the time commitment would be considerable, we thought the project worthwhile, a tangible contribution that would have a life beyond my tenure at the school.

The beach trip that week found the Lee kids in high spirits on what turned out to be yet another scorcher of a day. Yooni, the middle sister, had a new haircut, what Linda called a pixie-cut. It looked cute, but on the bus ride, her brothers insisted she looked like a boy. We assured her we disagreed; she seemed to take the teasing in stride. The beach that day was crowded. We all got wet playing in the ocean, all but Mr. Lee. Dressed in slacks and sport shirt, he avoided the water. We tossed a Frisbee, took pictures, and enjoyed the picnic lunch Samonim had prepared.

Cart vendors and little makeshift booths fronted the Pohang beach. The vendors sold toys, snacks, and rented tire tubes. The kids coaxed us into trying one of their favorite treats, a fresh raw sea cucumber. I could handle only one bite! Definitely an acquired taste, I didn't plan to adopt it anytime soon. That harrowing experience aside, we had a grand day. We were all relieved to get away from the furnace that Taegu had become.

Scenes from Ulongdo.

Raiks and Friends at Yechon Day Camp

Lee Family at Pohang Beach

Chapter 21

VACATION TREK

The day after the beach trip to Pohang, we packed for our two-week tour of coastal Korea. The plan was to first travel south to Kwangju, to find a particular orphanage where friends from home sponsored a child. We wanted to meet the little girl and send back photos. From there, we planned to continue south to the coast, then take a ferry east across the broad base of the peninsula to Pusan before heading north up the coast, with stops along the way, as far as Kangnung. From there we would cross over to Seoul for a Peace Corps conference before returning to Taegu. The trip would be a big circle and keep us close to the ocean, allowing us to take in popular attractions while enjoying cooler temperatures.

The trip got off to a soggy start. As we boarded for the six-hour train ride to Kwangju, a welcome rain began to fall. In Kwangju we made our way on foot under clearing skies to a yogwan that Dr. Scholten had recommended. As it was Friday and the end of the workweek, we expected weekend revelers to make it a livelier place than usual. Yogwans, notorious for thin walls and sliding paper doors, had little soundproofing. Sure enough, singing and shouts, fueled no doubt by considerable drinking, lasted long into the night. We slept intermittently, at best.

Up early the next morning, we grabbed some breakfast at a nearby bakery and sought directions to Changsong, a village on the outskirts of Kwangju where we would find the orphanage we wanted to visit. Reaching Changsong required an hour-long bus ride from Kwangju station, after which we still had a mile-and-a-half hike in the heat from the bus stop to the orphanage.

A Changsong villager directed us to follow a well-traveled walking track instead of the dirt road used by vehicles. After about a half-mile, we came to a train trestle that crossed a wide river – the only access to the other side and the orphanage. Koreans commonly took the shortest route to wherever they might be going, and crossing a trestle was not unusual. For us, it was a new experience.

About forty feet above the water and one hundred yards long, the trestle had no pedestrian walkway and no guardrail. If we were to get across the river, the railroad ties — spaced about two feet apart with nothing but the river below — would have to be our pathway. Linda and I were both apprehensive about negotiating the trestle with no proverbial safety net. Our biggest fear was that a train would come along while we were mid-span. We had no time to retrace our steps and take the road. While I kept my misgivings to myself, the words of my high school baseball coach came to mind, reminding me to be careful. He once commented after I returned to the dugout, "Gallon, you're no gazelle."

As we began what felt like a high wire act, Linda refused to focus on the water below. Instead, she focused on planting one foot squarely on each railroad tie. We watched every step and made it across without incident. My letter home described the episode as "fun!" That's not how we recall it fifty years later. "Terrifying" seems a more apt description.

After crossing the river, finding the orphanage was easy. From Taegu, Linda had sent the director a letter about our intended visit, so she was expecting us. We met our friends' sponsored child, a tiny, shy four-year-old girl, named Ae Ran. She sat by quietly as we chatted with the director and shared refreshments. Eventually, Ae Ran became comfortable enough to interact with us. With some coaxing, she even sang us a song. I wasn't sure she understood who we were or our reason for wanting to meet her. However, she did seem to relax as we ate lunch and then agreed to pose for a picture.

We couldn't help but wonder about Ae Ran's future. We knew orphans had no place within Korean society. Would she be adopted? Would she stay in Korea? Would she marry? With those questions weighing on us, we bid Ae Ran farewell in the early afternoon. Our goal that afternoon was to bus back to Kwangju and catch a train to Yosu, a port city on the south coast. The director kindly offered to drive us back to the bus stop; neither of us looked forward to dealing with the train trestle again.

The late afternoon train ride to Yosu was visually spectacular. In my letter home, I wrote, "*You can't imagine the beauty of mountains terraced with green rice paddies overlooking valleys blanketed with fields of all shapes, filled with young rice seedlings and other crops. The valley floor was so lush it looked like a patchwork quilt in shades of green and gold. All that, against a dark blue sky and puffy white clouds.*" We loved pastoral scenes like that, colorfully sculpted landscapes hewn over centuries. In the summer, Korea was a beautiful country, a far cry from the bleak winter landscape that gave rise to our first impressions.

After a noisy Saturday night in a Yosu yogwan, we rose early and found our way to the docks. Our friends, the ones we partied with on New Year's Eve, had told us about a daylong ferry that cruised through picturesque, sparsely populated coastal islands. The boat took us from Yosu on the southwest coast to Pusan in the southeast, across the base of the Korean peninsula. Warm and calm, the ocean that day was like glass. While we stood at the rail on the top deck of the ferry, a gentle ocean breeze cooled us as we drank in the sights. Tiny hamlets dotted island shorelines as fishing boats and sea-going junks plied the waterway. As we gazed upon the tranquil beauty, our thoughts drifted back to the shy little girl we'd met the day before and wondered what her future held.

In Pusan, we connected with some of our PCV buddies, saw some different parts of the city, visited the foreigners' commissary, and made another trip to the famous seafood buffet at the Seamen's Club. After two days we were anxious to move on. We caught a morning train to Kyungju, two hours north and just inland from the coast. Kyungju, home to multiple historic treasures, was the ancient capital of the Silla kingdom (57 BC – 935 AD). Of primary interest to us was Pulgooksa, a much-celebrated Buddhist temple complex on the city's outskirts.

Constructed in the mid-700s, Pulgooksa (Temple of the Buddha Land) was known for its multiple landscaped terraces, stone stairways, large colorfully painted pavilions, unusual pagodas, and two large statues of the Buddha. Historians considered the temple complex a masterpiece of the golden age of Buddhist architecture.

As we exited the train at Pulgooksa station we were immediately surrounded by a gaggle of "guides," young men who assertively represented different yogwans in the area. Their sales pitches assaulted us as we walked in the direction of the temple, just over a mile away. Our intention was to find a yogwan where we could park our gear before heading off to explore, but we trusted our eyes more than our ears. We wanted to see the prospective inns before we expressed any interest. As we walked, those pitchmen began to drop away until only one persistent salesman remained. We decided to ask him a few questions about the inn he represented. We enjoyed negotiating with him until his asking price seemed reasonable and then inquired about taking a look. The inn was actually quite nice and in a good location. We thanked him for his persistence and agreed to stay. It was just noontime; we had the whole afternoon to explore.

Despite being a national treasure, Pulgooksa had only a handful of visitors that Tuesday afternoon. As we approached, we were struck by the grandeur of both the setting and the entrance. The entire site was above us as we walked, terraced up the hillside and accessed thru a gate atop a steeply sloping set of stairs, elegantly hewn from large granite blocks. The wooden entrance gate supported an elaborately painted horizontal pagoda, providing a majestic entry to the whole temple complex. As we climbed the high rises of the granite stairs, we sensed we were approaching something special. Initially we missed the symbolism. We learned later that the staircase contained 33 steps, corresponding with the 33 steps to Buddhist enlightenment.

As we passed through the entrance gate, the temple grounds spread before us, dominated by two prominent granite pagodas, one simple and one more ornate. Both pagodas dated back to 751 and stood on either side of the main pavillion, which housed a golden, seated Buddha. We stopped to soak it all in. Up the gently sloping hillside were additional terraced courtyards containing large single story tile roofed sanctuaries. Other smaller terraces graced the grounds, all beautifully landscaped and dotted with shade trees that provided welcome relief from the hot, cloudless summer afternoon.

As impressive as the temple grounds were, we found an equally stunning site further up the mountain. With a commanding view of the East Sea, Sokguram Grotto was a deep cavern carved into the mountainside. We made our way up to the colorfully painted entrance and entered through a simple, unassuming door. Inside, we found ourselves in a dimly lit anteroom that contained the statues of four great Silla kings. Through another door we entered a larger room filled with life-sized painted wooden statues of eight fearsome warriors, guarding the entrance to a softly lit central hall, where under a carefully crafted dome of stone blocks, sat a flawless pure granite Buddha. Over ten feet tall, the Buddha sat cross-legged on a five-foot high lotus petal throne, attended by statues of twelve saints in niches along the surrounding circular wall. It would be difficult to exaggerate the impact on us as we gazed upon the softly lit Buddha just a few feet away. Never had we seen such a statue. "Peaceful," "Perfect," "Serene," and "Majestic" were the only words that suffice to describe its appearance. We were stopped in our tracks, overcome by a spiritual calm so powerful I can still vividly envision the scene.

We exited the grotto in a sublime state, moving slowly so as not to disturb our reverie. Then, as we were about to hail a jitney for a ride down the mountain, we were caught off guard and jolted back to our senses. Off to the side of the grotto exit, in the nearby forest, we heard a loud physical altercation taking place between two older women who had been selling cold drinks and snacks from the large rubber tubs they carried on their heads. The tubs were in the dirt, as were the women. Dressed in t-shirts and long skirts they were sprawled on the ground, wrestling, scratching, yanking each other's hair, and shouting words we could not understand, but about which we could make an educated guess. A dispute had erupted, with neither woman backing down. Finally, two young men managed to get them separated, followed by assistance from a monk and a police officer. As we departed the area, the fight had stopped, but the women still sat glaring at one another. The experience left us shaking our heads. The juxtaposition between the serenity within the nearby sacred Buddhist sanctuary and the explosive conflict we had just witnessed was stark.

At our yogwan that afternoon, we had another powerful experience. Just as the sun was about to set, a thunderstorm came out of nowhere. Rain poured down in sheets. Then, just as quickly, the clouds broke up. From our room we saw the drenched temple complex on the hillside in the distance, bathed in sunlight. The sight was picture-postcard perfect, replete with a rainbow. Later that evening, we shared how the whole day seemed a metaphor. The train ride, vocal pitchmen, spiritual tranquility, volatile emotions, and natural beauty all seemed to be pieces of the complex puzzle that was Korea. We knew that day was one we would never forget.

Next morning, we were off again. A sunny summer day presented us with views from our bus of a rocky coastline where agricultural terraces were carved out of the hillside all the way down to the ocean's edge. Yonghae, our destination for the day, turned out to be much smaller than it appeared on the map. We caught one of the town's two taxis for a short ride out to the beach where we had planned to meet our friends, the Raiks.

We found Barrie and Jerry at the only yogwan on the beach. We were surprised to see them in the company of the orphanage director from Yechon, together with two of her children. When the director heard the Raiks planned to meet us on the coast, she offered to drive them and give her kids an opportunity to play at the beach. It was great to see them all again so soon after the summer camp.

Sadly, our plans to travel north together with the Raiks didn't materialize. At the yogwan, we found Jerry in acute intestinal pain. His agony was so great we all decided he needed to seek out a doctor. We minded their belongings as the director drove the Raiks back to town. They found a Korean doctor who was so concerned about Jerry's condition that he administered a dose of morphine to quiet the pain. Barrie, knowing that decision carried some risk, had tried without success to contact Dr. Scholten in Taegu. She finally got through the next morning.

Dr. Scholten expressed alarm that Jerry had received an injection from a local physician. Fearing infection or worse, he ordered both Jerry and Barrie to Taegu as soon as possible. Jerry felt better by then, but he was exhausted, and the rain had returned. They decided to take a rest day in Yonghae before departing for Taegu. By next morning Jerry was almost back to normal, but both he and Barrie were anxious to keep their appointment with Dr. Scholten. We saw them off at the bus station and decided to move on ourselves. We boarded a bus for Ulchin, another four-hour ride north along the coast.

Our sightseeing destination near Ulchin was the Songyugul Caverns, the most extensive limestone cave system in Korea and one of the largest in all of Asia. With the entrance to the caverns about a ninety-minute hike from town, we decided to spend the afternoon exploring. We found a brand new yogwan, spotlessly clean, with a seventy-six-year-old grandfather in residence, looking very much the part with a gray beard and smoking a traditional long, skinny pipe. We sat with him for a while, chatted about his family, and answered his questions about our work and what we thought of Korea. He seemed pleased that we had good things to say.

On a walk later that afternoon, we found Ulchin to be charming. We wandered quaint well-kept streets, found a new cultural center and noted what appeared to be nicely maintained schools. A group of elementary-aged children, who no doubt saw us as a novelty, spontaneously offered to show us around, guiding us to some of their favorite spots. They seemed proud of Ulchin. Nobody taunted or gawked at us, though we were no doubt an unusual sight. We found the town and our reception there to be different from what we had grown to expect. It seemed unspoiled and refreshing.

Our morning walk, under cloudy skies, to the caverns took us along a clear sparkling river with lush rice paddies and vegetable patches right down to the water's edge. We arrived at the cavern entrance just as it started to rain again. We joined a group of about thirty people preparing to enter and were amazed at what we found inside. According to the literature, the cavern extended over three miles into the mountain; tourists had access to only a small portion of what appeared to be a natural wonder.

Inside, water dripped everywhere from the high ceilings. Walking paths were muddy, lighting was poor, and crude wooden bridges spanned pools of water along the path. Bare light bulbs hung from a wire a couple of feet above our heads. Our friends had encouraged us to take a flashlight, and we were glad to have it with us, both for safety and to see the limestone formations more clearly. We had to squeeze through some tight spaces, but despite the physical challenges and lack of improvements, the place was a fantastic display of color and calcium formations. Stalactites were everywhere: red, white, yellow, purple, and all shades in between. We had to be careful to stay on the paths to avoid running into them as they hung from overhead. Soaking wet and muddy, we emerged from the cavern after exploring for over an hour. Our impression was that with better lighting and improved pathways the caverns could be made safer and even more stunning. That is exactly what has happened. Now known as Hwanseongul, the tourist brochure states the cavern attracts over a million visitors per year.

The wind blew as we departed the cavern entrance, and rain still pelted down. The flimsy bamboo and plastic umbrellas we had brought along, sold everywhere for a pittance, quickly broke apart as we made our way out to the road. We tried to cover our heads with what remained of the umbrellas, but the rest of our bodies got a good soaking from the rain. A hospitable country family invited us to wait out the cloudburst under their shelter. We appreciated that sort of thoughtful gesture from the Korean people we met, especially when they perceived we might be having difficulty, physically or emotionally.

After all the rain, we were ready for some beach time. Pukpyong, a town further up the coast, was known for white sand and clear ocean water. That was our next destination. My letter home painted a picture of what we saw from the bus, *"...beautiful beaches, huge rocks upon which waves crashed, dashing spray high in the air...thatch-roofed villages built next to the beach...chickens, oxen, and hogs penned right on the rocky shore."*

Reminders of Korea's spy consciousness were also present along the coast. Small military bunkers, whose tops were just above ground level amid the rocks and along open stretches of beach, were positioned as lookout posts. Staffed at night to watch for landings by North Korean insurgents, those lookouts were testimony to the country's vigilance. On all our bus trips, especially along the coast, army personnel or national police stopped and boarded at least once each morning and afternoon as they checked the identification cards of the local Koreans. The threat was real, and those precautionary actions were so frequent we didn't give them much thought. They were an expected part of daily life.

In Pukpyong, once again under sunny skies, we discovered the beach to be about a mile from town. We preferred to stay near the surf, but we remembered there had been only one yogwan at the beach in Yonghae. Uncertain of what we might find, we set off in a taxi to explore our options. Surprised, we found a half-dozen inns right on the beach. We had no trouble finding a room. In fact, we were the only guests at the yogwan we selected.

Despite the recent rains, Korea was still in the midst of a heat wave. Why we wondered, were there not more people at a place known for its attractive beach? The answer was rooted in custom and tradition. At that time, Korea had a prescribed beach season — July 15 to August 15. Before or after those dates, even the most popular beaches saw only a tiny handful of sunbathers and swimmers. During "beach season," it could be difficult to find a place to spread your towel on the sand, let alone find a room at a nearby inn. Knowing that, we still found it hard to believe Pukpyong was nearly deserted. The days were sweltering. It was the weekend, but it was after August 15. Almost no one was on the beach. Together with just a small handful of unconventional Koreans, we had it to ourselves. For two days, Linda and I soaked up the sun, swam in the beautifully clear water, and recharged our batteries.

We had a few more days before we had to be in Seoul for a mid-service conference of all our K-III Blue Knob alums, and we had one more place we wanted to see. Monday morning, we were up and traveling again, this time to Kangnung, a town further north where our friend Tom was stationed. He boarded in a yogwan, so his residence was not difficult to find. We had made informal plans to stop by but when we arrived we discovered he had not yet returned from a vacation trip to Japan. We decided to stay at his yogwan, hoping he might get back before we left for Seoul.

That afternoon we made airplane reservations. Seoul was a full day's journey by either bus or train from Kangnung. Instead, we decided to try Korean Air Lines; flying was not expensive and would shorten the trip to just an hour. After securing our reservations for two days hence, we had time to explore the town. During our walk we met an American missionary. While we chatted, we discovered he was from the same mountainous area of Southern California where my family had lived during my early childhood. After visiting awhile, he insisted we come to his home that evening to meet his family and have dinner.

When we arrived at their home, the minister's wife and Linda recognized each other immediately. They had both been at the missionary resort at Taechon earlier in July. They had not met formally but had seen each other there, another small world coincidence. We thoroughly enjoyed reminiscing about my childhood home and sharing impressions of Korea. The meal was something to behold as well. It was authentic comfort food: fried chicken, mashed potatoes, green beans, and lemon meringue pie. We were stuffed!

Tom had still not returned the next morning. We weren't worried; we assumed he'd had a change of plans and we would see him at our conference in Seoul. Our goal that day was to see Soraksan (Mount Sorak), reputed to be one of the more striking mountainous regions in all of Korea. We were curious to see it, having been impressed with Haeinsa near Taegu, the Yechon area, and Pulgooksa near Kyungju. We wondered how Soraksan, an area best known for its scenic hiking trails, would compare.

We started the day with a bus ride to Sokcho, a small port city not far up the coast. From there, we planned to take another bus into the mountains. While we waited in Sokcho, we took a walk along the harbor fishing docks. Everywhere we saw racks of drying *ohjingoh*, the squid-like cuttlefish so loved as a salty snack. Harvested offshore at night from boats equipped with powerful overhead lights, the fish apparently were plentiful, given the ubiquity of full drying racks we saw all along the shore.

Mid-morning, we caught the bus to Soraksan, which deposited us at a tourist village near Shinheysa, a Buddhist Temple. We skipped a tour of the temple in favor of seeking out a trailhead. Finding one quickly we set off. Our goal was to hike a distance up the mountain and return in time to catch the last bus back to Kangnung. In short order, we found ourselves dwarfed by rocky peaks that encircled us. A trail marker pointed in several different directions. Based on the distances noted on the sign, we calculated we had just enough time to hike to Bison Dae (Twin Peaks). We had no idea what to expect but decided to give it a go.

The trail turned out to be an arduous climb. The terminus was a cavern high up on a granite rock face. As we neared the top, we found ourselves climbing up steps gouged out of the sloping granite wall. The last six hundred meters, however, were nearly straight up. A metal staircase bolted to the sheer rock marked the final pitch to the cavern entrance. It appeared sturdy and well anchored, so we moved on up, holding tight to the handrail as sweat poured off us.

Upon reaching the top, our legs felt like rubber. Turning around at the cavern entrance, we were greeted with a breathtaking view. In the bright sunlight, we gazed out at a jagged range of granite peaks atop wooded mountains—a tiny ribbon of white water coursed through the narrow valley far below. We noticed water dripping from the ceiling into a cauldron on the floor. Assuming it was for drinking, we helped ourselves. That was the sweetest water we had tasted in a long time.

We couldn't linger long in the cavern; we needed to head back down to catch our bus. The descent was just as beautiful and challenging as the climb up. We made it to the bus stop just in time and were in Kangnung by seven o'clock that evening, the end of a truly memorable twelve-hour day. Tom had still not returned. We hoped he was safe.

Due at the Kangnung airport the next morning, it was time to catch our flight to Seoul. The airport was little more than a narrow, paved strip in the countryside. When we saw the nose of the little DC-3 airplane pointed steeply into the air outside the small one-room terminal, we began to wonder about the wisdom of flying KAL. We still had vivid memories of our flights from Los Angeles to Altoona. It turned out we had nothing to worry about. Despite the deafening engine noise, the flight was smooth and quick, much better than the alternative six-hour train ride.

Our two-week excursion had revealed to us a Korea very different from the big cities of Seoul, Taegu, and Pusan. We witnessed beautiful landscapes, had positive experiences with locals, marveled at natural wonders, and were enchanted by historic treasures. Our affection for the country and its people grew; we looked forward to more discoveries.

Ae Ran and Orphanage Director

Terraced Rice Paddies

Communal Work

Preparing to Transplant Rice Seedlings

Sailing Junk

Pulgooksa's Granite Staircase

Island Waterfront Village

Pulgooksa Temple

Sokguram Entrance

Hiking Trail to Bison Dae

Bison Dae Cavern

Coastal Village

DC-3 Flight to Seoul

Chapter 22

MID-SERVICE

We weren't expecting what we found at Kimpo Airport on Wednesday afternoon, August 27. The terminal had been attractively remodeled, and the parking lot and road into Seoul totally paved. Downtown had changed as well. Modern buildings were going up, traffic signals introduced, and a Coca-Cola bottling plant had opened. We were in awe of the city's transformation.

With our conference not scheduled to start until Friday, we had a free day in Seoul. One of our goals was to investigate the possibility of scheduling an international trip for the winter holiday break. Peace Corps encouraged us to take a mid-service vacation and while many of our friends chose to explore Japan, we had fantasized about traveling south to see more of Asia.

To help us consider the feasibility of a trip, we had been referred to Eve, the spouse of a government diplomat who worked as a part-time travel consultant. Accepting Eve's invitation to her home for a luncheon meeting, we shared our ideas over soup and sandwiches. With Eve's help, we began to outline a three-week itinerary that included Hong Kong, Thailand, Cambodia, and Malaysia. Eve pledged to research flights, accommodations, and estimated costs. The potential for actually taking such a trip seemed better than we had expected. We left feeling optimistic.

Our conference started the following day. Billed as a mid-service review of our first year, it provided an opportunity to discuss what was going well, what was not, and what recommendations we had for the future. The conference turned out to be a stark contrast to our meeting with Eve. As the meeting began, we were reminded that our tour of service would end sometime in late July or August of 1969, coinciding with the summer break at our schools. Just one year remained. For us, that fact had just begun to sink in; one year seemed like such a short time. We weren't sure we wanted to finish quite that soon.

While we hesitated to think about completing our service, the mood in the room quickly turned negative. From our previous meeting in Taegu, we knew some in our group were disenchanted. That sentiment began to emerge from all parts of the country. Many of our fellow Volunteers expressed skepticism about the impact they were having in their schools. They felt impotent to effect change or improve English teaching methods. Some expressed doubt about the value of spending another year toiling in the face of futility, believing their Korean colleagues had little interest in change or improvement.

As the discussion progressed, Peace Corps staff tried to shed light on the predicament we faced. The Korean school system, they reported, was notorious for poor vertical communication. At the top of the decision-making ladder, the Ministry of Education wanted to improve the quality of English instruction in secondary schools. Often, however, the word did not get sent much lower than the provincial boards of education, and the boards made the assignments of PCVs to schools. The consequence being that many schools knew nothing about our mission. They had little to no knowledge of the teaching methods we promoted or how best to utilize us. Kevin O'Donnell acknowledged the frustrations and reported his staff was in the process of scheduling regional meetings with school principals to discuss the TESL program.

Linda and I understood the skepticism voiced at the meeting, but we did not share the same degree of unhappiness. Buoyed by the support of our host family and an evolving circle of friendships, we had a more positive outlook. Linda had found some of the women teachers open to new ideas. Teachers at both our schools seemed motivated to enhance the quality of education they offered to students. For that reason, the language lab at Kei Sung was in development.

Beyond our work assignments, day-to-day living in Korea had its challenges. We were all aware of stares and insensitive shouts when getting around on the streets, especially in urban areas. Our presence was unusual, and most Koreans had no idea why we were there. Many were suspicious about our presence in their country; historically, Korea had not had pleasant experiences with outsiders. In the twentieth century alone, the country had been forcibly occupied and taken advantage of by the Japanese annexation for several decades. Also, the peninsula became a battlefield for a bloody war that ended with both a divided homeland and continuous incursions from north of the DMZ.

In the 1960s, over sixty thousand United States military personnel were stationed on bases throughout the country. The populace was continually warned about the threat of communism and told to be on the lookout for spies. Signs to that effect were posted in every city and village. Knowing of the country's preoccupation with infiltration, we understood that we might be targets for disdain or suspicion. For a whole variety of reasons, Koreans often responded to foreigners in unpleasant ways. A few of us had had experiences that went well beyond name-calling and rudeness. Some volunteers described situations in which they had been spat upon, had objects thrown at them, or worse. Others just said they were tired of being abused and disrespected.

A crucial point made during the meeting was that our Blue Knob training focused on the importance of not offending Koreans. We had been advised about being respectful, but nothing was said about what we might face as foreigners in Korea and how we might cope with what we encountered. In Linda's and my experience, offensive treatment tended to be limited to urban areas and places close to military installations. Without fail, we received gracious treatment in the countryside.

In response to the grievances so passionately shared by some, others summarized a variety of coping strategies we had found effective. Linda and I joined others in sharing our experience in dealing with taunts and how we searched for activities outside our school assignments that provided a sense of fulfillment. Peace Corps Korea staff encouraged us all to take the long view, to consider our role in Korea and the fact that Peace Corps was just starting to consider ways to improve English teaching in the context of Korea's traditional approach to education. They pointed out that change takes time, and new methods were seldom adopted when first introduced. The group supported the idea of moving Peace Corps efforts to the college level, to help prepare new teachers rather than continuing to encourage change among established, more traditionally trained educators.

Peace Corps staff appeared to understand and expressed commitment to taking supportive action in response to what we told them. Those volunteers who considered their schools inflexible and closed to the idea of change or improvement were encouraged to negotiate their schedules, to allow participation in alternative activities consistent with the Peace Corps goal of furthering mutual understanding. They could also request changes in their assignment, including full-time college teaching.

As the meeting wrapped up, we sensed that some members of our group were rethinking their skepticism. The open discussions, sharing of feelings, and staff willingness to listen went a long way toward clearing the air and enhancing the bonds we felt with one another. The group seemed comforted by the awareness that many of us had experienced the same challenges and frustrations. Linda and I felt encouraged by the softening tenor of the mood. We knew some would choose to opt out and return home, but the majority seemed committed to making the most of their situations.

Peace Corps leadership impressed us as being entirely behind the group's desire to make a positive difference in the lives of both PCVs and our Korean hosts. They complimented us on our response to the policy that gave us the opportunity to set our own living allowances. That experiment had been successful in several ways. First, PCVs felt trusted by the staff. Second, the staff saw how responsibly we handled the opportunity. Third, the policy liberated administrators from fielding complaints about insufficient allowances. The policy shift became a source of pride for staff and PCVs alike.

Before heading back to Taegu, we had another more light-hearted and trivial experience that gave voice to the challenges we faced. As the conference concluded, a small group of us decided to try a new Italian restaurant. Our experience with Korean versions of western cuisine had been disappointing, but we were curious to see how Italian food might be interpreted in Seoul. Here is how I described the experience in my letter home:

"The prices were outrageous by Korean standards. The cheapest thing on the menu was spaghetti and meatballs, accompanied by soup, salad, rolls, and butter. We all thought that combination might be enough to satisfy us, so we ordered. First came the spaghetti, then the salad. Both were fine — not great, but good. Then came nothing. After a while, we inquired with the waiter. He had no awareness of the soup, the rolls or butter. We once again laughed at our own failure to clarify what the meal included before we ordered...Sometimes the menus in such places were the most interesting part of eating out."

As Linda and I rode the train south for our reunion with the Lee family, we debriefed the conference. Linda felt encouraged to negotiate a release from Saturday teaching and secure permission to leave school during the week when her teaching day was done. My school never had restrictions, so I had the freedom to take a day off or leave early anytime as long as I covered my responsibilities and didn't make such requests too frequently. We made plans to pursue calligraphy lessons from a local teacher and to accept an invitation to teach a couple of English conversation classes at the local university. We looked forward to what lay ahead in the second half of our Peace Corps adventure.

Chapter 23

BACK IN THE FLOW

We arrived back at the Lee home mid-day on Sunday, September 1. Mr. Lee and Samonim had not yet returned from church, but we enjoyed a hug-filled reunion with the kids. We had been away most of August with our trips to Taechon and Ulungdo early in the month, our week in Yechon for the summer camp, our two-week excursion along Korea's coast, and the conference in Seoul. Samonim confided later that Yooni, the eleven-year-old girl, had rushed out to greet them in the alley as they returned home and announced, jumping up and down, that we were back.

The previous Friday had been Wani's ninth birthday. Except for a baby's first birthday and an elder's sixtieth, birthdays were not much celebrated in Korea. We decided to prepare a little party to introduce the family to how we often celebrated birthdays at home. That afternoon, we decorated one of the empty second floor rooms across the hall from ours with some orange and purple balloons and crepe paper streamers that my mom had sent us in an earlier care package. We fired up the little tin stove on the upstairs outdoor patio. Despite being unable to control the oven's temperature, Linda managed to bake a delicious orange cake from a mix we had acquired at the foreigner's commissary in Pusan. For a party game, I drew a large equine creature on butcher paper, and on a separate piece, a big tail. I taped the donkey to the wall and saved the tail for later.

The whole family ate together that night. We shared stories about our trip and the Lees surprised us with news of Shinja's wedding. Shinja, who was in her twenties, had been a friend and mentor during the early months of our stay when she worked as Samonim's household assistant. We suspected Shinja was Samonim's niece. She might have been recruited to help Samonim with household tasks while the younger girl, Kihyun, learned her role.

In late spring, Shinja had departed Taegu to return to her rural home. We knew wedding plans were in the works for her, but not when the event was to take place. Consistent with Korean tradition, the marriage had been arranged by Shinja's parents. On a visit earlier in the summer, Shinja confided to Linda that her betrothed was shorter than she in stature. He was slender and she a little on the stout side. She feared they might make an odd-looking couple. Everyone in the family, however, reassured her the match was a good one. We regretted missing the wedding. It would have been a treat to be with Shinja on her special day and witness a traditional wedding. As she told the story, Samonim couldn't stop predicting, with a twinkle in her eye, that Shinja would soon be a mother.

After dinner that evening, we invited the whole family upstairs to the streamer-festooned room where we described how we celebrate birthdays at home. We feted Wani with the cake, complete with candles, a "Happy Birthday" serenade, and a game of pin-the-tail-on-the-donkey. Laughter and shouts of encouragement accompanied the kids' blindfolded attempts to stick the tail on the donkey's behind. Afterward, we shared small gifts for everyone, souvenirs from our trip. Good spirits abounded.

At school the next day, Linda found a little surprise of her own. The teacher's room had been unoccupied during the August break… all but her desk. When Linda sat down, she noticed a pungent disagreeable odor. Opening the drawers, she found evidence that some uninvited guests had discovered a package of partially consumed margarine and left behind a smelly mess. All the teaching materials she had stored inside the desk went into the trash, followed by her washing every nook and cranny. The other teachers pitched in to help, and the custodian promised to spray the entire desk with a disinfectant chemical after school that day.

During that first week back at school, Linda raised her concerns about her workday schedule. She successfully negotiated her departure time and attendance requirements. No longer did she have to teach Saturday classes, and the option to leave after completing her daily teaching responsibilities was granted as well. Linda had a sense of freedom she had not had before. A bonus came when she was invited to meet regularly with the other English teachers in her building. Curious about her teaching methods, they wanted to learn more. Several of them began visiting her classes and practicing some of the methods they observed during their weekly after-school departmental meetings. The whole group enjoyed spending time together. Lunchtime often included sharing take-out from a nearby Chinese restaurant, sometimes making an entire meal of *saguatang* (sweetened apples), one of Linda's favorites.

Another surprising thing happened that first week after the summer break. As Linda walked to school along her usual route one morning, three young girls, elementary school students, ran to intercept her. Prepared to hear the usual taunts, she saw them cross in front of her, stop, bow, and say in unison, "*Songsengnim!*" (Honorific form for "Teacher"). They then hurried off without another peep. Linda knew that most people along her walking route knew she was a Chae Il teacher. The girls' unexpected show of respect touched her. Although a small thing, on the heels of hearing how some of our friends were being treated elsewhere in the country, it was a memorable moment.

With college classes back in session the second week of September, Linda and I began teaching two afternoons a week at Young Nam University. We each taught a separate class, and both were scheduled in the late afternoon, so our middle school schedules were only minimally disrupted. Those university classes were a real treat for us. Teaching older students who had been exposed previously to some English instruction in their high school years meant we could teach more challenging material and engage the students in conversation. At least, those were our expectations as we began.

We discovered quickly that while some college students could recite phrases and sentences, they had little idea how to use them in a conversation. They had difficulty using simple sentence patterns to express a thought or action. In addition, given the considerable differences in the production of sounds in Korean and English, their pronunciation made it sometimes difficult to comprehend what they were saying, even when using technically correct words and phrases. We ended up using many of the same drills we used with our seventh-graders to improve pronunciation. Still, we loved the challenge of working with the older students.

As our university students struggled with English, we struggled with Korean. We could communicate at least minimally with our fellow teachers, transact purchases at the market, make plans with our family, provide instructions to taxi drivers, and make inquiries when we needed directions. However, beyond daily survival, our communication abilities had plateaued. Clear evidence of our limitations came in the form of a Foreign Service Institute test of speaking ability. FSI tests were administered to all PCVs three times: at the completion of training, at mid-service, and at the end of service. In FSI terms, Korean was a Category IV language, defined as "super hard," and exceptionally difficult for native English speakers. An FSI examiner arrived in Taegu at the beginning of the month. It was time for us to be tested.

A Korean examiner spent a brief fifteen minutes evaluating our comprehension, grammar, pronunciation, vocabulary, and fluency. The result was a score that ranged from 0 (no proficiency whatsoever) to 5 (completely fluent). Linda and I had a goal score of 2 (limited working ability). We didn't quite make our goal; we were both assigned 1+, meaning more than elementary proficiency but not quite up to a level 2. The fact that we relied on English with each other and with Mr. Lee had limited our progress. We didn't want that to be an excuse, so we committed to working on both increasing our understanding and our ability to speak Korean.

I especially wanted to grasp more of what was being said at our daily faculty meetings in the teachers' room at Kei Sung. The head teacher and vice-principal made announcements every morning, and I could decipher none of what they said. They spoke rapidly and used vocabulary that was beyond mine. I often had to ask a fellow teacher after the meeting whether there had been any announcements of which I needed to be aware. Even then, I struggled; my Korean-English dictionary became dog-eared.

The opportunity to take calligraphy lessons from an elderly teacher who lived not far from us both taxed and helped Linda and I to expand our Korean. We heard about him from Helen, our missionary friend who was a student of his. She offered to introduce us, explaining that he wanted to meet us before accepting us as students. To prepare for that first visit we went to Helen's house to practice some basics. She showed us the correct way to hold a brush and watched us practice making the Chinese character for the number "1," a simple straight line painted horizontally, left to right. It wasn't, we learned, quite that easy. The practice of Korean calligraphy had prescribed elements. Learning correct posture, how the brush was held, and how the tip of the brush was used to begin and end a stroke, were just the beginning. As well, the art had to be done only with the right hand, not easy for someone left hand dominant, like me. The fact I had become semi-proficient with chopsticks helped.

With Helen's coaching and a little practice under our belts, we went for our interview the next day. The elderly teacher had a *hanyak* (Chinese herb medicines) shop within our neighborhood outdoor market. His residence was attached to the shop, which made the experience of going into his home for lessons both convenient and a wonderful olfactory experience; so many aromas mingled in a pungent earthy potion. At the conclusion of our meeting, which included some brief practice, he invited us to come to his hanyak shop anytime for a lesson; no schedule or appointment was necessary, but practice was mandatory. That calligraphy lessons could be spontaneous was a good thing. We knew we couldn't always predict how each day would unfold.

One Saturday evening that week we had a surprise visit from

my friend Gi Suh and his wife, Duk Hee. They had a favor to ask. Duk Hee was soon to begin a new job as receptionist at Dong San Presbyterian Hospital. Some of the foreign-born hospital patrons did not speak Korean. Duk Hee would sometimes need to use English when answering the phone or greeting visitors at the reception desk. We role-played telephone conversations and brainstormed various ways Duk Hee could respond to information requests. We sensed her insecurity and made a date to visit their home for more practice the following week.

In the middle of the month our schedule hit a logjam. Lesson planning for our middle school and university classes, Korean language lessons, calligraphy practice, and dinner invitations were all predictable events on our calendar. What made the month unusual was the opening of the Kei Sung language lab, scheduled for September 28. Another teacher, Mr. Yi, and I were responsible for preparing the lab for the grand opening public demonstration. We had just three weeks. When fully operational, the school's English teachers would eventually hold class in the lab once each week. Each of those weekly lessons, we decided, needed to include a script timed to fill an hour of instruction, a simply illustrated student workbook, and recordings that would serve as the instructional medium. Additionally, Mr. Yi and I wanted to practice with the equipment to become proficient enough to avoid appearing like total rookies during the grand opening demonstration.

With that deadline before us, we planned to produce two written lesson plans, workbooks, and instructional tapes in English. Ten days before the open house, we had lesson plans and workbooks ready to go. However, no recordings had yet been made to accompany those lessons. With Linda's help and the deadline looming, we began recording. We created master tapes during the late afternoons. Then, Mr. Yi and I practiced using the equipment with the recordings and workbooks the following day.

During the hectic week before the open house, Linda and I decided to take a day off on the weekend. Sharon and Gary, our Mennonite friends, had invited us to join them on their first visit to Pulgooksa, the extraordinary historic temple we had seen on our summer excursion along the coast. We had never paid much attention to the proximity of Taegu to Kyungju, where the temple was located. I assumed it was quite a distance but had never looked at a map. Surprised, we learned Kyungju was only thirty-five miles away, just over an hour by car. The day we chose for the trip dawned cool and cloudy, not the best for enjoying the temple's exquisite grounds and natural surroundings. Nonetheless, we enjoyed sharing the experience with our friends and found it a welcome break from the pressure we were feeling in Taegu.

The day after our trip to Pulgooksa, we had a dinner date at the home of Mr. Kwon Oh Suk, Kei Sung's head teacher. He wanted us to meet two of his friends who had returned recently from studying at an American university. We had a great time discussing the contrasts between life in Korea and their experience in the States. Their English was more limited than we expected, but we managed. As we talked, Mr. Kwon's wife presented us with an impressive dinner. However, as was Korean custom, she did not join us for the meal.

The next evening, we met for dinner with Gi Suh and Duk Hee. In contrast with the previous night, Duk Hee joined us for the meal. Only a few years older than us, Gi Suh and Duk Hee weren't as bound to tradition as were some of our more senior colleagues and friends. After we ate, we did more practice to help Duk Hee prepare for her new receptionist job. We made recordings of typical receptionist situations that Duk Hee could practice as she prepared for her first day of work.

The following three evenings included lessons with our Korean tutor, calligraphy practice, and a Friday visit to our teacher at his hanyak shop. That week we started to feel over committed. Our obligations seemed reminiscent of the Kingston Trio's popular folk song about Charlie not being able to exit his MTA commuter train for lack of funds. Our problem, however, was short lived. The next Saturday was show time: the grand opening for Kei Sung's new language laboratory.

During the week prior to the big day, Mr. Yi and I planned

and rehearsed our demonstration lessons each day. We knew a large crowd was expected. Kei Sung administrators had invited the provincial minister of education, the president of the local university, several principals of local high schools, and English teachers from throughout the city.

Thanks to our daily practice, the event went off without a hitch. Mr. Yi did a great job introducing our ideas about how the lab would be used. He explained how the students would have classes in the lab and how it would be open after school for students to practice listening and speaking on their own. The demonstration lessons we had prepared were well received, and the equipment performed flawlessly. For the first time, I thought my colleagues at Kei Sung understood why a lesson plan and workbook were needed for each classroom hour in the lab. They seemed to understand that a simple recording of the student text was not a sufficient lesson.

Afterward, Mr. Kwon, our head teacher, invited Mr. Yi, Linda, and me for a sukiyaki dinner at a downtown restaurant. Relieved at how the day had gone, we ate and visited for a good three hours. My letter home that week noted, "*The evening was one of the most enjoyable we've spent here.*"

Following the successful rollout, I continued to be challenged by the lab. We had begun putting lessons together for less than a month. A mountain of work yet remained before the lab would be ready for regular use. We determined if students had one lesson per week in the lab, a total of approximately forty lessons would be needed to cover an academic year — a tall order for the two of us. The other teachers seemed hesitant to get involved. I thought they might be holding back to assess the lab's success before they risked helping. I hoped to involve them to assure they would continue to develop new lessons and programs after I left the school. For the time being, however, our task was to produce demonstration lessons that would be helpful to students and stimulate teacher interest. Fortunately, we had help. Linda and another Peace Corps couple often joined me for weekly late afternoon recording sessions.

Kwon Gi Suh and Duk Hee

Gi Suh and Kwon Oh Suk, Kei Sung's Head Teacher

Chapter 24

CHUSEOK

October was one of the most anticipated months of the year in Korea. Locals boasted of their "beautiful high skies." The weather was often crisp and clear, leaves on the trees in the mountains took on the colors of the sunset, and the calendar was rich with holidays.

Gaecheionjeol (National Foundation Day) on October 3 commemorated the beginnings of Korean culture and the legendary first Korean state in 2333 BC. *Hangulnal* (Korean Language Day) on October 9 celebrated the creation of Korean script by the 15th-century king, Sejong the Great. Both holidays acknowledged the glory of Korea's lengthy history and its unique alphabet, sources of great national pride. The season's most anticipated holiday, however, was *Chuseok* (Autumn Eve), a three-day harvest festival akin to our Thanksgiving.

Chuseok always occurred during a full moon on the fifteenth day of the eighth month of the lunar calendar, typically falling on a weekend in early October. Special foods, family gatherings, feasts, and Confucian ancestral remembrances were all part of Chuseok. Kids loved the Chuseok tradition of receiving gifts of new clothes and having lots of sweet *duk*, soft rice cake.

For Chuseok in 1968 the summer drought and heat wave had given way to cooler temperatures. We had a few rainy days, but for the most part, the skies were clear and sunny, just as the travel brochures predicted. Policemen, bus girls, and even the honey bucket guys began to wear warmer clothes. The rice and pepper harvests were well underway. Just across the river from our neighborhood, we saw golden sheaths of rice straw propped up like little teepees in the dry paddies, and woven straw mats appeared everywhere on the roadsides where rice, barley, and bright red peppers dried in the sun.

Chuseok that year was the second weekend in October. My friend Gi Suh was an avid hiker and outdoorsman. He invited Linda and me to join him and two of his friends on an overnight hike and camping trip during the three-day Chuseok holiday. The plan was to start at the base of Gayasan Mountain, hike to the top, and then down the other side to Haeinsa temple. We had visited that temple earlier in the year and thought it was one of the most beautiful spots in Korea. We were anxious to see the colorful fall foliage and loved the idea of more hiking and camping.

On the weekend before we were to depart, Gi Suh and I went to the outdoor market to shop for a larger backpack than the one Linda and I used on our summer trip. As usual, I had difficulty finding gear big enough to fit my frame. We finally found a canvas pack that could work with its straps fully extended. Although uncomfortable, it would hold our two sleeping bags and a small tent. That evening Gi Suh took Linda and me to meet the other two hikers, Mr. Hwang and Mr. Pak. We met at Mr. Hwang's house and were not prepared for what we found. Never had we seen such a finely crafted, tasteful Korean home.

Located not far from our neighborhood on the outskirts of town, the beautifully decorated and lit home was a traditional design. Mr. Hwang, a man of means, owned a lumber company with retail yards in Taegu and Pusan. Short, athletic, spirited, and outgoing, he had a twinkle in his eye that suggested a real passion for life. We liked him immediately. He brimmed with enthusiasm for the adventure. Our fellow hiker, Mr. Pak, was a construction engineer contracted to the local United States Army base. More reserved and slight, he impressed us as steady, and an experienced hiker and camper. Both men spoke excellent English; communication would not be a problem.

We spent that evening getting to know each other and creating lists of what we wanted to take on the hike. We planned to carry supplies to do our own cooking, tents and gear warm enough to keep us comfortable during the cool nighttime and early morning hours. We all departed that evening with assignments to accomplish during the following week. The plan was to meet the next Saturday afternoon at Mr. Hwang's, ride out to the trailhead, and hike partway up the mountain. After finding a place to camp, we would rise early Sunday, continue to the top, pause for lunch, then head down to Haeinsa to catch the last bus for Taegu in the late afternoon. To us, it sounded like a tight schedule. Having had experience with plans that sometimes went awry, we were curious to see how the adventure would unfold.

We all met at Mr. Hwang's at three o'clock Saturday afternoon. Linda and I had speculated about how the five of us would get to the trailhead. Taxis in Korea were small, sub-compact. They usually held only the driver and three or four passengers if three squeezed into the tiny back seat. That afternoon we found a large green 1950 Plymouth parked in Mr. Hwang's drive—a huge car by Korean standards. Except for some surplus Jeeps, the only vehicles we saw in those days were small Korean-made Shinjin taxis. We had never seen anything like that Plymouth on the streets of Taegu. Mr. Hwang had connections.

After stuffing our gear into a very full trunk, Mr. Hwang, Mr. Pak, and the driver slid into the front seat while Gi Suh, Linda, and I folded into the back. With the car sagging low to the ground, we headed off. I wasn't sure how far we needed to go, but I knew we would have a bit of a hike before we would be pitching our camp. By the time we departed, it was already close to four o'clock.

The trip quickly became hair-raising. Our driver piloted that old Plymouth down the gravel road as if he were competing in a cross-country race. I wondered if Mr. Hwang, knowing how far we had to go, had told him to step on it; the guy was a terror behind the wheel. We went so fast on the rough road that poor Mr. Pak lost his lunch out the passenger window. When that happened, I thought the driver might slow the pace. Instead, it seemed to spur him to push the accelerator even harder. Rather than slowing down, the ride became even wilder until, mercifully, one of the tires blew out.

After putting on the spare, which had bare cord showing through the tread, the driver became more cautious. The road gradually narrowed to something more akin to a single-track goat trail. When we had gone as far as we could, a very carsick Mr. Pak was happy to bid the driver farewell. While we unpacked the trunk, Mr. Hwang approached a farmer working in an adjacent field to ask for directions. He was told the trailhead we sought was near a small hamlet a couple of miles back down the road; we had come too far! By the time Mr. Hwang returned to tell us the news, the driver and the Plymouth were long gone.

We retraced our route on foot and found the hamlet at about seven o'clock that evening. Skirting a cluster of houses, we located a path that appeared to head up the mountain. Since it was getting late, we began searching for a suitable camp spot just past the tiny village. We soon came to a small, harvested cabbage patch where we made camp, surrounded by terraced rice paddies that climbed up the mountain's flank.

Linda and Mr. Pak, who had quickly recovered from his stomach upset, were busy right away preparing a dinner of soup and rice supplemented, of course, with kimchi. The rest of us pitched our small tents, scrounged firewood in the nearby forest, and prepared a campfire. The sky was clear and the moon full and bright as we settled around the fire for a delicious hot meal and talk of plans for the next day. The campfire attracted a couple of men from the hamlet who approached and bid us a hearty Chuseok welcome with some locally brewed rice wine. They joined us around the fire, asked about our plans, and shared stories of what we would see as we climbed the following day.

We wanted to be on the trail by eight the next morning. However, despite being up before seven, breakfast and breaking camp took longer than planned. Linda and Mr. Pak had a traditional breakfast of rice and soup quickly underway as soon as we dressed. The rest of us stowed tents and sleeping bags into our backpacks. After breakfast, just as we were preparing to break camp, the gentlemen who visited us the night before arrived with thoughtful Chuseok gifts of duk and a bottle of homemade wine for a toast after our climb. Since the trail had several unmarked forks for the first mile or so, they volunteered one of their sons to keep us on the right path. Such thoughtful gestures, typical of folks who lived in tiny hamlets and villages, touched all of us. After brushing our teeth where a clear stream of water fell from a terraced rice patty, and a final check of our campsite, we departed, waving goodbye to our new friends. It was ten o'clock.

We knew we had to make up for our late start. The climb to the mountaintop was predicted to take over three hours. The descent to Haeinsa, after an essential lunch break, would take another hour. The last bus to Taegu was scheduled to depart the temple grounds at half-past four that afternoon. It was essential to make that bus because Mr. Pak and Linda were expected at work the following day. The rest of us had planned to take Monday off, but we all felt committed to making it to the bus on time.

At about two o'clock, we arrived at a military lookout on the mountain's crest. The lone soldier on duty offered to let us use his facilities to prepare lunch, which naturally would include cooked rice, soup, and kimchi; our hiking partners never considered having anything less. The preparation of Korean food takes a fair amount of time, so by the time we were ready to hit the trail again, it was half-past three. We still had three miles to go, all downhill. Our goal was to arrive at the bus stop at least fifteen minutes before departure to purchase tickets and refresh for the long ride back to Taegu. Time was going to be tight.

We set off briskly, and our pace accelerated to a run as we descended. Despite our cumbersome backpacks and the twisting downhill trail and rocky footing, we made excellent time and managed to avoid injury along the way. The predicted hour-long descent to the temple took us just thirty-five minutes. Our rubbery legs barely held us up as we reached the bus loading area, only to be greeted by a big surprise.

We were taken aback to see no bus. Not only was there no bus, but there were also no prospective passengers waiting to board. Rushing to the ticket booth, the attendant told us the bus had been totally full and departed early, about fifteen minutes before our arrival. It quickly dawned on us that we had made a serious miscalculation. We had planned to return to Taegu on the Sunday afternoon of Chuseok, the most popular holiday of the year, when the temple would be overflowing with celebrants. We had one of those forehead-slapping realizations as we exclaimed, "What were we thinking?"

The next bus was not scheduled until early the following morning. We searched the area for a taxi. No luck. Our only alternative was to overnight in one of the yogwans near the temple. By nine that night Linda and I were bedded down, when a knock sounded at our door. Two taxis had just arrived. Mr. Pak, desperately wanting to get home, was first to get his pants zipped and fly downstairs to commandeer both cabs. The rest of us quickly got ourselves together, settled up with the innkeeper, and headed for Taegu in a downpour.

The ride back lacked the drama of our get-away ride the day before. Linda and I arrived at the Lees just before the midnight curfew. We feared our rap on the gate would awaken the family. Mr. Lee greeted us with a sleepy look on his face and a smile that said he was glad we had made it home safely. We slept well that night.

So many memories have stayed with us from that trip. The wild ride, the fellowship with our new friends, the friendliness of the locals, the fall colors, the sharing of camping and cooking responsibilities, the problem-solving, and our brief visit to Haeinsa all made for an unforgettable Chuseok holiday.

Harvest time in the countryside.

Chuseok campers

Chapter 25

AUTUMN SURPRISES

Further into October, our middle school students came to school wearing their heavier winter uniforms. I wasn't sure why, but my students seemed less attentive and more restless than usual. Possibly, their growing awareness of impending cold weather caused the change in them. More likely, their restlessness stemmed from the school's annual intramural athletic competitions that would soon take place. October was set aside not only for national holidays, but also for sports festivals held throughout the province. At the middle school level, there were no athletic teams or sports competitions between schools during the year. Instead, classes at Kei Sung competed in afternoon contests, similar to track and field meets. For the faculty, however, October was volleyball time.

Kei Sung was well known for its faculty volleyball team. I had played for the team earlier in the summer. At that time, we had practiced very little and didn't fare well in the few matches we played. I came to understand that those games were just a warm-up—a tryout of sorts for me. The real competition, a citywide tournament, was scheduled for the last Saturday in October.

At the beginning of the month, I learned that after-school volleyball practice would soon begin. The fact that we'd be practicing from three to six every afternoon, for the two weeks before the tournament, indicated that volleyball held more importance than I had previously thought. Unbeknownst to me until the first practice, the Kei Sung team was the defending city champion. That upped the ante a bit. Our no-nonsense head teacher, Mr. Kwon, who had the physical appearance of a chiseled military officer, acted as team manager. He held well-organized, spirited practices. Everyone took those practices seriously. I relished the regular exercise and thoroughly enjoyed being part of the team. As the tournament approached, expectations were high that we could retain the championship trophy.

Tournament day brought cool temperatures and an overcast, gray sky. At a local college, six chalk-lined courts were arrayed on a broad, hard-packed dirt field. Matches were scheduled back-to-back throughout the day. By mid-afternoon, our Kei Sung team had made it to the semi-finals, but not without a fair amount of drama. Officials, I learned, did not always have the last say. When someone disputed a call, protests could break out on both sides. Umpires could get offended and sometimes threatened to quit. A negotiated settlement had to be reached before the match could continue. During those disputes, my teammates and I stood around until things were settled between the coaches, team captains, and officials.

Our semi-final match was hotly contested; the opponent was the best we had faced all day. As we played, the lead changed back and forth. Ultimately, Kei Sung came out on the losing end, much to everyone's disappointment on our side. Then, shortly after the match ended, Mr. Kwon lodged a protest. He claimed the winning team had a player who was not a faculty member, a clear violation of the rules. A big argument ensued. After a lengthy dispute, Mr. Kwon prevailed, and our opponent was disqualified. However, that ruling did not mean we would move forward into the championship match. Instead, in what to me was a mysterious decision, the other finalist team became tournament champions, while our team was awarded third place. We accepted the decision, but I was left scratching my head. It did not seem logical, but my teammates thought the decision to be correct.

Such was life in Korea. We didn't always understand the behind-the-scenes issues at play. There was "face" to be considered. Maintaining respectful working relationships was often paramount, with accord being reached by mutually acceptable compromise, not always consistent with what the rules might suggest.

Vollleyball Tournament

The puzzling officiating of volleyball games wasn't a total surprise. I had had a similar experience earlier in the year. Knowing I had been a baseball player, Mr. Lee invited Linda and me to take in a high school baseball game in the spring. In the middle of the game, one team disputed an umpire's ruling and refused to play for half an hour. The game ended tied at 0-0, which resulted in another debate over whether to continue. Umpires and the rules were not always the final authorities when it came to disputes.

Back at school, Peace Corps presented me with another situation I did not fully understand. Many PCVs had voiced complaints about how the TESL program functioned in the schools. As a result, a consultant was commissioned to gather impressions and make recommendations to the Ministry of Education and Peace Corps administrators. The consultant arrived at Kei Sung to observe one of my classes, meet with the Korean English teachers to discuss the TESL approach, and answer their questions. The lesson I taught that day had gone well, although a stranger's presence in the classroom no doubt kept the students on their toes. Back in the *kyomushil* (teacher's room) my Korean colleagues seemed receptive to the consultant's comments. I wasn't sure they weren't simply being polite. From my experience, most of the Korean English teachers felt threatened by the idea of adopting a different approach in the classroom.

Afterward, in private, the consultant encouraged me to focus more on my classroom teaching and not devote as much time to developing the language lab. His emphasis seemed to be on the importance of the in-person TESL approach to language learning. The message I received was, "Go slow, be a resource, and try not to push too hard." I was not exactly sure about the origin of that advice. As I have mentioned previously, Koreans typically employed a third party to impart information hard for the receiver to hear. They avoided direct messages to preserve "face" and maintain positive relationships. I asked myself, "Did the consultant's encouragement to take it easy come from the school administration, from the other English teachers, from Peace Corps, or was it purely the consultant's impression of what might be the best approach for me to take?" I wasn't sure.

I couldn't imagine the school wanted me to reduce my emphasis on developing the lab. Clearly, the Peace Corps and the Korean Ministry of Education had an investment in improving the quality of English instruction, especially in the classroom. Most schools, however, did not have the resources for a language lab like the one being developed at Kei Sung. I decided to continue dividing my effort between the classroom and the lab, thinking my most significant contribution would be to help create a program that would live on beyond my presence at the school.

In the second half of October, Linda and I had another surprise. Friends of our parents were coming to Taegu to visit the Presbyterian mission and see Dong San Hospital, the Presbyterian-affiliated medical center where our friend Duk Hee was the new receptionist. That couple was going to be hosted by the missionary family for whom Linda had provided childcare at Taechon earlier in the summer. It amazed us that our parents' friends had a connection and interest in Taegu. Before departing from home, those friends had pledged to provide our parents with a report on how we were doing.

We had never heard of any other Peace Corps volunteers in Korea being visited by friends or family from home. The missionary family, knowing how special that visit would be, included us in planning their guests' four-day itinerary. Among other things, they would tour our schools, have dinner with us at the Lee home, and take a day trip to Haeinsa. At the end of their trip, we all planned to travel to Seoul to see them off.

Introducing that couple from home to our life in Korea thrilled us. Our folks would get a firsthand account about our physical health, where we lived, and some of our experiences. They would be able to see pictures of the Lee family, learn about our schools, and hear what our principals said about our work. They were going to sample Korean food, be introduced to tearooms, and develop impressions of Taegu and the Korean countryside. We wished our families could have had an opportunity for such a visit.

Our daily lives were so different from life in the United States. Living in Korea had evoked shifts in how we viewed ourselves—changes that would be life-long. We did not fully understand at the time, but we were learning important lessons: the acceptance of situations we did not fully understand, coping with the unexpected, broadening our limits of acceptance for unfamiliar ideas and behaviors, and the value of patience when things didn't go as planned. Our parents' friends took back physical descriptions of us and their own observations of our life in Korea. But what they could not see was how our Peace Corps experience was impacting our beliefs, feelings, behaviors, and visions of the future.

One more surprise awaited us as October transitioned to November. Our friend Helen, who had introduced us to our calligraphy teacher, came by to tell us he had suddenly become ill, and his family planned to close his hanyak shop. She did not know his plans or the seriousness of his illness. The news upset and saddened us. We had only visited his shop for lessons a few times and had found him to be a gentle, patient soul and his lessons something of a meditation for us. Since his shop was on our route to the outdoor market, we asked his neighbors often about his health. Sadly, he never recovered sufficiently to re-open his shop, at least not while we were in Taegu. Our calligraphy lessons never restarted, and we never had a chance to thank him for his kindness.

Chapter 26

STUDENT COMPETITION

Every year the Ministry of Education hosted a provincial English competition for middle school students in which the contestants recited a memorized passage that judges scored for fluency, pronunciation, and appropriate emotional inflection. Each school in the province was invited to hold an internal contest, with winners from those events advanced to the regional event in Taegu. As first year learners, our seventh-grade students were not eligible to participate. Linda and I coached the eighth and ninth grade winners in our respective in-school contests. Chae Il selected five students, and Kei Sung three, for the provincial event.

Controversy erupted at Chae Il when one student, Pong Sook, was left off the team. From Linda's perspective, she excelled at pronunciation and delivery. Faculty members charged with the selection decisions thought Pong Sook had failed to memorize the full text. Linda reasoned that plenty of time remained before the competition for her to commit the passage to memory. She lobbied hard for Pong Sook's inclusion. Finally, after considerable discussion, the Chae Il decision-makers relented and included Pong Sook on their roster of contestants.

Linda and I coached our teams separately after school for several days. Then, to mix it up and give the students a chance to present in front of people they did not know, we decided to invite both teams to the Lee home for an evening practice two days before the provincial event. At first, the girls were so shy they chose to go down the short hallway on the second floor to one of the empty unheated rooms to practice, while the boys stayed in our much warmer room. Linda reminded the girls they would be speaking in front of judges, other competitors, their parents and teachers at the actual competition. When she encouraged them to work at overcoming their shyness, they responded to the challenge. As the girls' confidence grew, they agreed to practice with the boys, and by the conclusion of our session, we thought they were ready to compete.

The Friday preliminary rounds, an all-day affair, brought teams from throughout the province, many accompanied by their school's PCV. In all, 130 middle school students were entered in the competition. Each recited the same passage for four judges: two Koreans and two Americans. Those judges earned our admiration. They attended carefully to each competitor, and by the end of the day, they had listened to 130 recitations of the same passage. Without trying, everyone in the audience had the entire passage memorized.

Our students all did their best. One student from Kei Sung and one from Chae Il made it onto the list of sixteen finalists that would compete the next afternoon in another round of presentations. Pong Sook, the eighth-grade girl for whom Linda had advocated in the face of faculty resistance, made the cut. My school's finalist, Byong Ho, was a ninth-grader.

Earlier in the day, midway through the preliminary rounds, the Education Ministry provided a buffet luncheon for everyone attending the competition. Since English was the featured activity, the Ministry provided Western utensils—knives and forks. Several of Linda's students had never eaten with anything but chopsticks and spoons. In response to the girls' confused looks, Linda used the opportunity to lead a short tutorial on the use of Western flatware. We enjoyed watching the girls manage their shyness and giggles as they experimented with the utensils. They learned more than they expected that day!

That evening, Linda and I met with our two students still in the competition to do some additional coaching before the finals the following afternoon. Afterward, Pong Sook asked to meet Linda again the next morning for still more practice. Linda thought she was ready but agreed to meet later in the morning. Byong Ho and I made plans to meet at the auditorium the next day, just before the beginning of the final recitations.

The finals began at one o'clock and proceeded to fill the entire afternoon, ending at half-past six that evening. Family members, teachers, and students were all experiencing nervous anxiety. While no one expected our students to win the competition, finishing in the top three would be an outstanding achievement. As the contest ended, we felt certain that both our students had done well. We were all on the edges of our seats as the judges prepared to announce the winners at the awards ceremony.

Everyone in attendance had an investment in the competition results. Families had pride in their child and an understanding that placing high in the competition might lead to further educational opportunities. For the schools, high placement would bring recognition of their excellence. Kei Sung already had the community's respect as a quality private school. For Chae Il, a public girls school not ranked among the better ones in the province, the results meant something different. Despite its name, which translated as "First Rank" or "Number One," Chae Il was considered a second-tier school. A good showing by a Chae Il student would boost the school's reputation in the province and potentially lead to more applicants for admission.

The judges began the award ceremonies by explaining the criteria they used in judging the students. Following that, the boys' awards were announced. Byong Ho placed third. His parents and the faculty members from Kei Sung were thrilled as he took his place on the winners' podium. Next were the announcements of the girl winners. Pong Sook did not make the top three. As the winners made their way to the podium, Linda was in disbelief. She thought Pong Sook deserved higher placement.

Finally, the last award was announced, one for the overall champion of the entire competition. The judges described the qualities of the winning recitation and then announced the winner: Pong

Sook from Chae Il Girls Middle School! With her hands covering her face, Pong Sook, the only eighth grade student on the podium, made her way to the top tier. Her rooting section in the audience erupted with joy – a celebration so loud we suspected people passing by outside might wonder what was going on inside the auditorium. Pong Sook's parents and siblings hugged, and the Chae Il **teachers** smiled and shook hands. As she joined the Chae Il delegation, Pong Sook, with her head down and hands over her mouth, tried to hide her excitement in the face of her recognition. To be the overall winner was a high honor, indeed!

Soon the group's attention turned to Linda. First, everyone expressed their appreciation for all her effort in coaching Pong Sook and the other Chae Il students. Then, in true Linda fashion, she turned the attention back to Pong Sook, complimenting her in English on her hard work and the excellent job she did. As the celebration ended, Linda and I accepted invitations from our respective schools to join the winners for dinner. We headed off in different directions, she with the Chae Il contingent and I with Byong Ho's family and Kei Sung faculty members.

The following morning, Sunday, Pong Sook knocked on the Lees' gate just after breakfast. She presented Linda with a beautiful pearl-inlaid red lacquer vase and matching serving tray, gifts from her parents. Gifting others for favors was a cultural tradition that extended to all manner of good deeds, from dinner invitations to special favors.

Around noon that day, we received an invitation to join the Ministry of Education, the Chae Il principal, and Linda's co-teacher, Miss Moon, for a congratulatory dinner that evening. The next day, at an all-school assembly, the principal presented Pong Sook with her winner's certificate and two books befitting a first-place finisher in the provincial contest: a Webster's Collegiate English Dictionary and the Complete Works of William Shakespeare. That evening we were invited to still another dinner, courtesy of Pong Sook's parents, with Ministry of Education representatives and several Chae Il faculty members.

We had never witnessed such celebrations of appreciation and respect...three nights in a row! Our sense was that Pong Sook's parents felt obligated to the ministry, the teachers at Chae Il, and Linda for bestowing honor on their family. Showing appreciation and respect was crucial in so many aspects of Korean life.

Celebrations of a different kind continued throughout the remainder of November. Linda's birthday was at the end of the month. In a reversal of Korean tradition, her co-teachers took her out to dinner. Typically, the celebrant took responsibility for any birthday festivities; in Linda's case, her colleagues totally disregarded tradition. The lone exception occurred when Samonim allowed Linda to bake a cake in the little tin oven in her kitchen and share it with the rest of us on her birthday. That was a true honor...the first time Linda had been allowed in Samonim's kitchen!

American Thanksgiving weekend was capped with an invitation for the two of us to attend a community gathering sponsored by the Korean International Women's Friendship Association. We were asked to share reflections on our first year in Korea. About thirty PCVs and seventy Korean women attended to honor the work of Peace Corps Volunteers in the province. The evening included several speakers and entertainment that featured traditional music and dance. During our talk we shared stories, some humorous and some that incorporated lessons we had learned while in Korea. The gathering was a true intercultural event.

Chapter 27

YEAR'S END

In early December of 1968, with just over seven months left in our Peace Corps assignment, our thoughts turned toward our return home. The annual middle school entrance exams gave us a few days off from our usual teaching duties. As we prepared for Christmas, we put together a holiday letter for friends and relatives. It was another opportunity for us to reflect on our experience in Korea.

Drafting that letter prompted us to begin thinking about what we might want to do following Peace Corps service. Before joining Peace Corps, I had considered a career in the Christian ministry. I had applied and been admitted to seminary, an admission put on hold when our Peace Corps invitation arrived. After nearly two years, I found my career interests shifting. What I saw of missionary work in Korea spawned in me some hesitancy. Nearly the entire missionary community in Taegu was sequestered behind a wall in a large compound. Most lived in Western-style homes, very different from those inhabited by Koreans. To me, that seemed inconsistent with the goal of mission work. I thought it more appropriate for clergy and their families to integrate into the community, rather than segregate themselves into a conclave. As I examined that values conflict, I realized my initial interest in the ministry stemmed not so much from my faith in Christian doctrine, but more from the support and influence of the charismatic pastor who guided our church youth group. I began to think about other vocational paths.

Teaching was turning out to be a creative outlet for me. I enjoyed the challenge of crafting learning experiences and making a connection with students. My undergraduate degree in psychology seemed a natural step to a degree in counseling and guidance. After exchanging letters with my UCSB advisor, I sent inquiries to several graduate programs and found I was too late to apply for the fall 1969 term. Deadlines for application submission were fast approaching, and I was just getting started. It looked like we would have a year to fill following our Peace Corps tour before I could begin graduate school.

Linda enjoyed teaching, but her priorities were always on her relationships with students and colleagues. In the year following her graduation and before our wedding, she loved her medical social work position. She suspected there would be employment opportunities for her at home without a graduate degree; her optimism always buffered my anxiety.

Peace Corps staff in Seoul shared several post-service possibilities for us to consider. They mentioned extending for an additional year in Korea. We liked that option, but we were also tempted to consider a new two-year Peace Corps assignment in another country. Stateside, we could apply to become Peace Corps recruiters, positions that typically lasted one year but were quite competitive. That seemed a long shot. One more possibility was a Peace Corps training position, helping prepare recruits for service in Korea or some other country. We were advised to think about what we would most like to do and then revisit the issue in spring when opportunities would become clearer.

While we considered our future, we had other pressing near-term obligations that demanded our attention. We began to hear our names on the local Armed Forces Korea Network (AFKN) radio station, our daily connection to the outside world. Regular announcements were being made about the NCO Wives luncheon at which we were to be the featured speakers. That invitation came not long after the talk we gave at the Korean International Women's Association. We suspected there might be a connection.

Those radio announcements precipitated inquiries from some of our Taegu-based PCV friends. They were curious about what we planned to say. Since most of the NCO wives who would be in attendance at the luncheon resided either on the base or in a military housing area off the base, we decided to talk about our experience living in the local economy, our lives with the Lee family, and our roles as teachers in local middle schools. We wanted to share some of what we were learning about ourselves, how life in Korea gave us insights into the way we lived in the United States, and how those in the audience could engage in some cultural discoveries on their own.

For the Lee family, early December meant the time had come to make kimchi again. As she prepared, Samonim did something unexpected, but very welcome; she thrilled Linda by inviting her to participate in the daylong kimchi making process. By doing so we learned even more about the ingredients in Korea's most traditional dish.

Samonim, Kihyun, and Linda first mixed the bright red chunky paste that was added between the leaves of each cabbage head. Red pepper powder, barley tea, apple and pear pieces, carrots, onions, turnips, small bits of shrimp, garlic, salt, and a few other "secret" ingredients went into the mix. They coated each leaf with the paste, folded the pasted leaves back in place on each cabbage head, then cut the heads into smaller pieces and placed them into deep ceramic jars for gradual fermentation throughout the winter. Spicy hot and crunchy when fresh, a bit softer and sour later in the year, we never tired of the kimchi served at every meal. As an ancillary benefit, three daily doses of kimchi turned out to be a great way to keep my sinuses clear.

Mid-month, with the year's supply of kimchi in the pots, we were off to administer final exams for our classes at the university. Those duties carried some ambivalence for us because we did not plan to resume teaching those classes in the upcoming winter term. A new group of PCVs was scheduled to arrive, all of them assigned to work in colleges and universities. Young Nam University, where we taught, expected to receive at least one of those volunteers. Linda and I would miss the opportunity to work with older students. Saying goodbye to them felt like a loss, but that cloud had a silver lining. A little breathing room might find its way into our calendar.

Christmas week started with baking for the Lee family at our doctor's house. We knew the kids loved chocolate chip cookies, so we decided to make some for their Christmas morning stockings, supplemented with brownies, gingerbread, and sugar cookies from mixes we had picked up at the international commissary in Pusan. While Linda baked, I graded final exams from our university classes. Our plan for the week included the annual faculty party at my school, Christmas Eve with friends at the Mennonite farm, and Christmas day with the Lees.

As those events approached, we became acutely aware that it was our last holiday season with our extended Peace Corps family, both Korean and American. We didn't know if we'd be getting together again with some of our friends who lived in remote villages before we all began to scatter when summer arrived. We wanted to squeeze as many visits as we could into the week.

To start, the party at my school included a riotous combination of games and special performances. Linda and I had everyone howling at our version of "The Twist" and we cracked up watching the wives feeding milk to their blindfolded husbands. Christmas eve with Sharon, Gary, and others at the Mennonite farm gave us flashbacks to a traditional North American celebration. We sang carols, played games, opened gifts, and enjoyed a feast of homemade western style cooking. Thoughtful and generous, Sharon even baked fresh cinnamon rolls for us to share with the Lees the next day.

On Christmas morning, after breakfast and a church service, we gathered with the family in our upstairs room to open stockings from Santa. We prayed, sang a carol, and the kids opened their gifts while we all enjoyed Sharon's cinnamon rolls. We had presents for each family member, made even more special by the inclusion of gifts our parents had sent for the Lee family. The warmth we felt in our room that morning came from more than just the sunlight streaming through the windows.

Later that day, we visited Gi Suh and Duk Hee, exchanged gifts, and shared a tasty Korean Christmas dinner that Duk Hee had prepared. When we bid them goodnight, we still had one more stop; we gathered with PCV friends at a local yogwan to wrap up our holiday celebrations. It had been another event-filled, heartwarming Christmas.

The next day found us packing for the Asia trip we initially discussed with Eve, our travel consultant, back in August. The adventure we imagined then was about to happen. We were scheduled to fly from Seoul on Monday, December 30, but we still had some outstanding issues to attend to before departing. We were funding the trip with an advance of funds from our Peace Corps resettlement allowance. However, neither those funds nor our travel documents had arrived in Taegu. Calls to both the Peace Corps office and Eve reassured us that all was in order, but for security reasons we would have to pick up the documents in Seoul. To do so, we decided to depart Taegu at the end of the week. That gave us a couple of days to collect everything before our departure.

Chapter 28

A DIFFERENT ASIA

We awakened on the morning of Friday, December 27, in a panic. We had slept right through our alarm! In scramble mode we dressed hurriedly, said quick good-byes to the family, grabbed our luggage, and dashed out of the house. At the train station we boarded at the last possible moment. Breathless, we collapsed into our seats. By the time we arrived in Seoul, fully recovered from our near calamity, we were prepared to tackle a long list of weekend errands.

Our upcoming trip on Monday morning would take us to multiple destinations: Thailand and Malaysia, countries served by Peace Corps; Hong Kong, an international and economic hub; and Cambodia, home to historic wonders. Because we planned to pick up important documents and cash for the trip, we booked a room at the World Vision Guesthouse, which provided greater security than our usual yogwan. The Guesthouse was a large Western style brick home with multiple creature comforts: steam heat, hot showers, delicious meals, and a cozy fireplace. It seemed like the Ritz to us.

Friday afternoon and Saturday included trips to the Peace Corps office, a bank, our travel planner, and the Malay and Thai embassies. By Saturday evening, everything on our list was checked off: air tickets, hotel bookings, traveler's checks, health cards, and visa documents. With an unscheduled Sunday, we took up residence in the US Army library to read about the places we would be visiting. That night, with new adventures at our doorstep, sleep was fitful. Our itinerary looked like this:

Dec	30-31	Hong Kong
Jan	1-7	Bangkok
	7-10	Penang Island
	10-13	Kuala Lumpur
	14-17	Siem Reap
	17-21	Hong Kong
	21	Seoul

Earlier in the fall, while putting the trip together, we had reviewed our destinations with Mel, our supportive regional rep. He reminded us that going to Siem Reap could be risky. Our government had no diplomatic relations with the Kingdom of Cambodia. If something untoward happened, we would be on our own with no supportive embassy nearby. Being young and naive, we didn't worry much about any danger we might face. The temples of Angkor and the ancient Khmer civilization held a fascination for us; we wanted to see the antiquities firsthand. With his duty to warn done, Mel conveyed his approval with a wink and a nod.

After fifteen months in Korea, we were accustomed to a lack of development: dirt streets, open sewers, aging buildings, and an economy that primarily operated on the backs of manual laborers. Pockets of prosperity and economic signs of progress were emerging; new construction was on the rise and new businesses were popping up in the cities. Urban infrastructure, however, and life in rural villages contained few conveniences. Most people had little, and their lives were harsh. Per capita GDP in Korea at the time was less than $200 per year. Living conditions for most of the population could not be described as dire, but they were far from comfortable. We were curious to see how other parts of Asia compared.

HONG KONG

We quickly became aware that other parts of Asia enjoyed different standards of living. New discoveries began with our flight to Hong Kong; Thai International Airways' "Orchid Flight" lived up to its attractive moniker. Cabin appointments, professionalism of the crew, gourmet food, and luxuriant legroom were all first-class despite the fact we sat near the back of the plane. In Hong Kong, on the less expensive Kowloon side of the harbor, our hotel was comfortable, affordable and the very definition of quality. A change in air temperature was dramatic, too. In Seoul, we had bundled against the sub-freezing temperature. In Hong Kong, we needed only shirtsleeves. We sensed that we were about to experience places quite different from any with which we were familiar in Korea.

Before we left our Kowloon hotel to start exploring, we called Evey and Ira, Mennonite colleagues of our Taegu friends Sharon and Gary. Eager to meet us, they suggested we rendezvous that afternoon at a nearby café. Hong Kong was a cosmopolitan crossroads. Chinese at its cultural core, the city offered food and goods from all over the world. The café where we met Evey and Ira on that first afternoon served iconic American favorites. We chatted over juicy hamburgers and scoops of ice cream, satisfying cravings that had gnawed at us for months.

As darkness set in, Ira suggested we take a ferry across the harbor to get our first glimpse of Hong Kong Island, the territory's center of commerce. The weather was still warm and the sky full of stars as we docked near the downtown business district. Cheerful Christmas decorations and lights still adorned the streets as we departed the ferry. We were struck by how clean and modern the high-rise buildings were, a sharp contrast to the grime and developing nature of Taegu and even Seoul. The sights became even more dazzling as we ascended Victoria Peak on the funicular. The view from the peak to downtown, the harbor, and Kowloon was breathtaking. Bright lights seemed to spread for miles.

The following day, New Year's Eve day, we joined Evey and Ira as they transported gift bundles from the Mennonite mission to a government school on a small nearby island within the expansive harbor, accessible only by ferry. There, as we walked along the dirt path from the ferry dock, we passed colorful gardens and well-tended rice paddies. In contrast to that pastoral beauty, the concrete single-room school building sat on a rock-strewn dirt field. Class was not in session that day, but we guessed the room, furnished with long tables, would hold around a hundred students. Education in Hong Kong was not publicly funded. The number of schools and the availability of teachers were both insufficient to meet the need. Moreover, the required tuition made the cost of education prohibitive for poorer families. For children in those families there was no formal education at all.

After dropping off the gift bundles, we made our way to the home of a Mennonite elder on the island. In his sparsely furnished concrete home near the water, we partook in a luncheon feast, Chinese style. The food differed from the Chinese fare we were served in Korea and was drastically different from Chinese dishes we were familiar with back home in the States. Served family-style, the menu included whole crab, unshelled shrimp, whole baked fish, fried bone-in chicken chunks, rice, and soup – simple hearty food without sauces of any kind. Different, too, was the lack of utensils, save for chopsticks. Eating was a tactile experience.

Back in Kowloon, Linda and I were on our own for New Year's Eve. Curious to check out our options for ringing in the New Year we went exploring. We found a steakhouse far nicer than any restaurant we had seen in Korea and decided to give it a try. We both had the same reaction; we were uncomfortable in an establishment so tastefully elegant it seemed almost decadent. After dinner, we wandered into a nightclub to check out the music, but that place was also too glitzy for our taste. We didn't stay long and wondered if our basic, straightforward life in Taegu had impacted our tolerance for flashiness.

We returned to our hotel well before midnight and were greeted with another surprise. Firecrackers sounded like staccato gunfire as the loud pops echoed off the high rise buildings that surrounded us. Those sounds came from all directions and continued long into the early morning hours, making sleep difficult. Linda and I weren't altogether sure we liked Hong Kong.

Scheduled to fly to Bangkok the following afternoon, we had the morning hours to explore. We ferried back to Hong Kong Island and climbed aboard a double-decker bus for a low-budget tour. Sitting in the open on the upper deck, we developed a different impression of the city. The cool morning air refreshed us as we drank in the sights. We skirted the island's shore as far as Aberdeen, a picturesque bay filled with junks and floating restaurants.

Beyond the central business district, Hong Kong juxtaposed old and new. Steel and glass high-rises intermingled with older apartment houses festooned with bamboo poles supporting laundry drying in the humid air. The streets teemed with people and small shops of all kinds. Realizing Hong Kong had much more to offer, we looked forward to spending three more days there at the end of our trip. We planned more time with Evey and Ira again, too. They had graciously offered to care for our winter clothes as we continued our travels south. Upon our return we would reclaim our belongings and pick up some auto parts to take to Gary in Taegu.

THAILAND

The afternoon of New Year's Day was even warmer and more humid in Bangkok. After checking into our downtown hotel, we decided to go out for an early dinner and catch up on the sleep we had missed the night before. Returning to our room after dinner, we were met with an unexpected situation. We found several lizards seeming to defy gravity on walls and ceiling, mainly near the neon overhead lights. The hotel receptionist told us they were harmless geckoes, valued for their ability to limit the population of insects that thrive in warm, humid climates. Linda did not like lizards and feared the little creatures would fall in the night as we slept. "Freaked out" would be an apt phrase to describe her reaction to sharing our room with those cute little quadrupeds.

It took a couple of hours of reassuring talk before Linda began to accept the idea that geckoes were not likely to fall and, once the lights were turned off, more likely to migrate to other sources of light to which their prey might be attracted. Geckoes, we found, were commonplace during our entire trip. It wasn't long before Linda grew accustomed to their presence in our accommodations and even appreciated their efficiency at keeping the mosquito population in check.

Bangkok seemed far more crowded than Seoul. People, buses, cars, motorbikes, and tuk-tuk taxis jammed the streets from curb-to-curb. The tuk-tuks looked like colorfully painted recycled overgrown three-wheeled golf carts. Collectively, the traffic noise was deafening, and all the vehicles were being driven as if they were late and trying to make up time.

Making our way through what seemed like constant rush hour traffic, we found our way to the Presbyterian Mission the following morning; we had heard it was an excellent place to gather tourist information. There we met Gene, a former Thailand PCV. After exchanging Peace Corps stories, he volunteered to help us get oriented by giving us a brief driving tour of the city. Meeting Gene was a stroke of luck. He introduced us to government buildings, temples, universities, museums, and the train station. Then, at our request, he dropped us at the United States Overseas Mission (USOM) office, where we hoped to connect with my father's cousin, a USOM engineer. Before heading into the Mission, we exchanged contact information with Gene and agreed to meet up again later in the week.

At USOM, we contacted cousin Ted who invited us to his home that evening. He, his wife, and three teenaged daughters lived in a beautiful two-story home finished almost entirely in deliciously fragrant teak. We resisted their overtures to make their home our headquarters for our week in Bangkok. We had no intention of imposing on their hospitality. However, later in the evening, when friends of theirs dropped in, we were cajoled into staying. The friends insisted we would be crazy not to accept Ted's invitation. It became a humorous situation, with Ted's friends raving about the family's desire to have company. Finally, convinced of the sincerity of the invitation, we accepted and agreed to return the following day.

At dawn the next morning, we toured Bangkok's famous floating market, where we learned the entire city had once been a city of *klongs* (canals). In times past, transportation within the city was either by foot or canal boat. As the city grew, many klongs in the older sections of the city were backfilled, but the watery substrate remained underneath the streets. Stopped at an intersection not far from the market, we could sense a subtle rocking of our taxi.

The floating market filled the klongs during the early morning hours. Boatloads of colorful produce and flowers crowded the waterways. Our tour boat joined the congestion, traversing business and residential areas amidst towering trees. We witnessed many transactions as sellers sold to customers in other boats and pedestrians along the bank. Over the next few days, we found klongs still existed throughout the city.

Following the market tour, we decided to take one of the tuk-tuk taxis to move our luggage to Ted's home. Reputed to be faster than conventional taxis because they could use the narrower "gutter ball" lane next to the curb, we found riding in one to first be a thrill, quickly followed by mounting anxiety as our driver showed more fondness for the accelerator than the brake. Those three-wheelers were open-air, with just an awning overhead as protection from sun and rain. They darted through traffic, taking risks left and right. Our overly aggressive driver that afternoon reminded us of the daredevil drivers we'd encountered in Korea. I wondered why it was that we gravitated to so many risk-prone drivers.

As we traveled swiftly that morning in the gutter lane, our tuk-tuk was cut-off by a larger taxi turning directly in front of us. Instead of braking, our driver t-boned the taxi on the passenger side, bringing us to an abrupt, jarring stop. There were no seat belts, just skinny railings on each side of the vehicle by which we braced ourselves. While we tried to recover our senses in the moments following the collision, an argument ensued between the two drivers over who was at fault for the dent in the larger taxi's door. After taking personal inventories for injuries and finding only minor bumps, Linda on her shin and I on my forehead, we abandoned the drivers as they argued and walked our gear over to a bus stop. We took a bus the rest of the way to Ted's house. That was our first and last adventure with the eye-catching three-wheeled gutter-balling tuk-tuks.

During our brief city tour the day before, we had mentioned to Gene our interest in taking a day trip to Ayudhya, Thailand's ancient capital. He generously offered to be our guide, and we set a date for mid-week. From the train, we glimpsed people fishing in the klongs with big nets, men farming with yoked oxen, and water buffalo emerging from a lake with green plants hanging from their horns. In Ayudhya, Gene took us to the home of a Thai friend of his, the owner of a local distillery, who graciously suggested we take his car and chauffeur for the day. On that hot dry day, we took in ancient Buddhist temples, an open-air market, and the old capitol city that looked like it was in decline. We were disappointed to see such a historic part of the country neglected. Ayudhya had definitely seen better days.

One scene that fascinated us was of several men skillfully playing something akin to a game of hacky sack with a rattan ball. We were captivated watching them pass the ball without ever touching it with their hands. They could bump it over one player's head, and then that player deftly kicked it or bumped it with an elbow or foot to another player. We observed them for several minutes, during which they never made an error; the ball stayed in motion the entire time.

During that whole week, cousin Ted's family, Gene, and another minister we met at the Presbyterian mission served as our guides. They were all generous with their time. We visited famous Buddhist temples, browsed at a large weekend market, snapped photos of the stunning buildings at Chulalongkorn University, prowled the national museum, took in a traditional dance performance at an outdoor theater, and toured the Grand Palace. Surrounding all that, we fell in love with Thai cuisine. It was quite a week.

MALAYSIA

After five active days of touring Bangkok, we were ready for a more relaxed pace. We found it on Penang Island. Located south of Bangkok and not far off the northwest coast of Malaysia, the island was a tropical paradise. White sandy beaches, warm ocean water, lush flora, and a cultural mix of Malay, Indian, and Chinese people, made Penang an isle of enchantment. We stayed in a family-owned boutique hotel right on the beach. "Sea view, great food, warm service, and retro charm" is how the Lone Pine Hotel describes itself on the web today, and that's precisely how it was in 1969. Their meals were so excellent we went nowhere else. Elaborate four-course breakfasts were included in the six dollar per night rate, and five-course dinners were available for an additional dollar and a half. To complement the delicious fare, we sat at linen-draped tables outdoors on the grass, beneath shade trees adjacent to the beach. We felt like royalty.

During our days on Penang, we sunbathed, swam, purchased watercolor paintings from a strolling beach vendor and watched a team of fisherman, some in turbans, pull in heavy nets that teemed with fish and a few poisonous sea snakes. We actually enjoyed getting drenched in a warm afternoon squall on a bike ride along the coastal island road. In Georgetown, the island's urban center, we found a rich multi-cultural atmosphere, great for absorbing exotic sights, sounds, and aromas. As we explored, we found a Peace Corps office, and on a nearby street, we met Connie, the wife of the local regional Peace Corps rep. Fifteen years later we serendipitously met up again with Connie and her husband Vern in Oregon, where Vern and I worked together for several years at the same government agency. We remain friends to this day.

Our island visit was too brief. We loved the beauty, tropical breezes, cultural diversity, relaxed pace, and extraordinary hospitality at the Lone Pine Hotel. We would have been happy to spend more time there. Kuala Lumpur (KL), our next stop, turned out to be quite a contrast to the tranquility of Penang Island.

On the flight to the mainland, we were fascinated by the rolling terrain, planted in groves of large trees as far as our eyes could see. The trees, planted close together, were arranged in symmetric circles circumscribing sloping hillsides. They appeared meticulously maintained. Those groves were rubber tree plantations, important contributors to Malaysia's economy.

Saturday afternoon in Kuala Lumpur was market day. After getting settled into our room at the YMCA, we set out for the outdoor market, thinking it might be an excellent place to try some local fare. The street vendors did not disappoint. Fried bananas, chicken satay, baked coconut surprise, and other goodies turned into dinner for us at a total cost of less than one dollar each. The crafts caught our attention as well. Linda found a woven shoulder bag for sixty cents that became one of her favorites. What fun it was to shop when quality was high and prices low.

Another unexpected meeting happened as we shopped. We met Jack, a current Malaysia PCV. We felt a definite connection with the PCVs we met in our travels. Jack was in KL for the weekend and invited us to accompany him on his return bus ride home the next day, a trip of about 60 miles. We jumped at the opportunity to see more of Malaysia and get a look at where he lived and worked.

After touring the National Museum the following morning, we joined Jack for a bus ride through lush country, rubber tree plantations, and villages of wooden thatched-roof houses built on stilts. Such construction helped cool the interior of those houses in the warmest parts of the year. In Jack's village, we visited one of his Malaysian friends, who gave us a tour of his sandalwood home, visually beautiful and filled with the scent of the aromatic wood. Jack's home was much smaller, but wood-framed and perched on stilts. He loved his work, and found his local colleagues to be generous, friendly, and outgoing.

Though we had only a day and a half in KL, that short visit combined with our experience on Penang Island left us with a very positive impression of Malaysia. The tropical environment, multi-cultural makeup of the population, and delicious fusion of local foods were an attractive mix. Malaysia, we sensed, might be a great place to volunteer for a second hitch in the Peace Corps.

CAMBODIA

Next on our itinerary was a three-day visit to Siem Reap and Angkor, the old capital of the Khmer Empire. For 500 years, from roughly the ninth to the fourteenth century, the Khmer civilization flourished in what is now the northwest portion of Cambodia. Angkor Wat and numerous other Khmer temples in the area were so majestic they had been described, in the literature we read before the trip, as the "Eighth Wonder of the World." The fact that Cambodia bordered on Laos and Vietnam had been the source of some concern as we planned our trip months before. While Cambodia was officially neutral during the battle for supremacy in Vietnam, the Ho Chi Minh trail, used by North Vietnamese combatants, traversed portions of Cambodian territory near its eastern border. Since Angkor was in the country's northwest, far from the conflict, we assumed we would not be in harm's way. Our assumption proved correct, but we did find the presence of armed Cambodian military personnel at the airport intimidating.

Any fears we had faded as we made our way into town. Siem Reap was small, located within a dense tropical forest. Distinctively French, the little village provided the closest accommodations to the Angkor complex, just over three miles away. While Linda enjoyed negotiating in French for a room at the tiny Hotel de la Paix, I met an English couple familiar with the area. They graciously gave us a short walking tour of the city and pointed out a shop where we could rent bikes, an easy and affordable way to get back and forth to the historic sites.

Since the decline of the Khmer kings, Angkor had continued to be an important spiritual site for Cambodians. Despite significant jungle overgrowth by giant banyan and fig trees, the temple sites were accessible. For nearly a hundred years, the French, beginning in the 1860s, worked to reclaim some of the Khmer architectural treasures. The beauty and majesty of what we saw during our visit was primarily the result of work done by those French archeologists.

With only two full days to explore, we were up and out of the hotel by six o'clock the following morning. We planned to be gone most of the day and knowing there were no food vendors within the perimeter of the temple area, we purchased oranges and bananas at an outdoor stall on our way out of town. Armed with a good map and sturdy bicycles, we rode through the jungle on both paved and dirt roads, listening to the birdcalls and monkey shrieks.

Owing to the season, and perhaps because of the military conflict in Vietnam, we saw no other tourists. We did see local hunters with crossbows off in the distance and women collecting berries and greens on the forest floor. We had never seen betel nut chewers; they were distinctive, with blackened teeth and red juice coating their lips. All the locals seemed accustomed to seeing folks like us riding along the roads on our bikes. They never paid us any attention as they went about their business.

Children were a different story. They approached us with satchels of soft drinks and souvenirs, hoping to make a sale. Always polite, we enjoyed their enthusiasm and solicitations in French. As I noted, there were no shops, vendors, or commerce of any kind other than the ambitious kids. The whole area was regarded as sacred for its historic and religious significance.

Our map revealed many temples within biking distance of Siem Reap, far more than we could visit. Each built by a different Khmer king, the temples were created to represent the king's interpretation of the Hindu cosmos. They all, therefore, had the same central design, most having been constructed between 900 and 1200 AD. At the center of each complex was a stone representation of Mount Meru, the center of the world in Hindu and, subsequently, Buddhist cosmology. Lesser peaks often surrounded Meru. They looked like tall stone blossoms laid out in a square with Meru in the middle. Buildings housing the temple's sanctuary sat within the perimeter of the mountain peaks. Surrounding the stone mountains was typically a border wall or colonnade depicting the edge of the known world. Beyond was a moat representing the ocean. Finally, a bridge spanning the water, often reminiscent of a rainbow, served as an earthly connection to the temple complex.

Over the centuries, temple design evolved into larger and more complex depictions of Hindu cosmology and ultimately became the final resting place for the temple's designer king. The most dramatic temple was Angkor Wat, the last genuinely Hindu structure in the succession of Khmer kings. Later in the same century, Angkor Thom began to reflect the increasing influence of Buddhism within the Khmer Empire.

When we visited, the Angkor Thom complex had not been totally recaptured from the huge trees that had overgrown even the most significant structures within its outer wall. Tree roots looked as though they had been literally poured over the stonework, like how hot fudge flows and then solidifies over an ice cream sundae. The Bayon, the central temple within Angkor Thom, had forty-nine stone towers, with a giant smiling face on the four sides of each tower. Just who those faces represented and what their faces were meant to convey is a matter of speculation. But whatever their intent, the sight might well have intimidated worshippers during the king's reign.

We didn't want to feel rushed, so we saved our exploration of Angkor Wat for the afternoon. It was the most well-known, most photographed, and best preserved of all the temples, a stunning sight from a distance with its tall stone mountains surrounding the large temple at the center. A bridge stretching across a water-filled moat served as the entrance to the Angor Wat complex. As we walked the colonnade along the outer wall, we found every square inch filled with exquisite bas-relief depicting mythical Hindu stories as well as a history of the king's exploits and his contributions to the Khmer Empire. When the sun began to set, the sandstone towers and sculpture took on hues of orange and gold that reflected, together with massive thunderheads overhead, in the still water of the moat.

Next morning, a complex some twenty-five kilometers to the north known as Banteay Srei was on our "must-see" list. To get there, we hired a personable little man and his pedi-motorbike, really a rickshaw pulled by a motorcycle. Once at Banteay Srei, we were captivated. The contemporary name for the temple built in the tenth century was translated as "Citadel of Women" or "Castle of Beauty." The temple's title reflected its diminutive size, color, and beautifully sculpted walls and lentils. The entire complex, constructed of red sandstone, appeared to glow soft pink. The structures, all miniature, were less than half the size of those in other temples we had visited. The delicate architecture contained detailed carvings cut deeply into the sandstone. Despite over a thousand years of exposure to the moist climate and aggressive jungle growth, the bas-relief carvings were still stunningly beautiful. Their three-dimensionality had not been lost to the forces of erosion. The human figures, animals, and floral designs were all sensuously carved. We found the entirety of Banteay Srei just as memorable as Angkor Wat.

Our ride that morning took us through small villages. Children, chickens, pigs, dogs, cats, and even water buffalo were co-mingled into a memorable collage. The dirt roads and yards, though carefully tended, gave us an impression of poverty and economic distress. Despite that, the children we saw were friendly and full of curiosity. One small group of boys latched onto us during one of our rest stops and offered to guide us on a shortcut to the ruins of a nearby lesser temple. As we followed a narrow path through the brush, a wild pig started to charge us. One boy probably about ten years old challenged the pig with his machete and beat it back into the brush. We were impressed and appreciative. With the civil war that ravaged Cambodia in subsequent years, we have wondered what became of those cheerful boys.

RETURN TO HONG KONG

Before returning to Seoul, we had one more stop, a return trip to Hong Kong for three days. We planned to rendezvous with Barrie and Jerry, our friends stationed in Yechon, to hear about their own Asia experience. And we wanted to get together with Evey and Ira to pick up our goods and do some shopping for the Lee family.

While we shared stories about our travels with the Raiks, we found some great places to enjoy culinary treats. Our favorite was an all-you-can-eat buffet at the Hong Kong Hilton, where a wide variety of delicacies cost the equivalent of $1 US. We enjoyed it so much we went back each of the three days we were there!

When we called Evey and Ira, they invited us to join them for a tour of the territory beyond Kowloon. We visited resettlement houses built to relocate families from houseboats and squatter villages near Aberdeen on the backside of Hong Kong Island. Each tenement apartment was a single 12' x 14' room with an occupancy requirement of five adults. Often, an entire family lived and worked in their apartment making inexpensive goods to sell—things like plastic flowers or woolen mittens. Though the people reportedly felt privileged to live there, crowding in those buildings seemed an issue.

As was true throughout our trip, the hospitality shown by Evey and Ira seemed heartfelt. Everywhere we went new friends had shown us extraordinary kindness. They enriched our brief glimpses into each destination. Our takeaway impressions of each place, no doubt superficial, emphasized their differences. Hong Kong was bustling with commerce; Bangkok was noisy and seemed to be hanging on to the past; Malaysia was relaxed, tropical, and diverse; Cambodia's antiquities were magnificent while the population struggled for an economic foothold. We saw how people lived in drastically different environments and how our lives back home contrasted to their lifestyles and living conditions. We made strong memories, still vivid to this day.

Chapter 29

ACCOMMODATING CHANGE

Frigid temperatures and a blanket of snow greeted us as we returned to Taegu from Hong Kong in late January. We had just a few weeks of teaching before the term ended, then another four-week break before the new school year was to begin in March. After not thinking much about our teaching responsibilities during our trip, Linda and I suddenly had a lot of catching up to do.

A stack of mail awaited us at the post office. As I made my way through it, I opened a letter from home that contained tragic news. While crossing a street near her home in Southern California, my maternal grandmother had been struck by a hit-and-run driver. The incident happened mid-December but my parents, so as not to cast a dark cloud over our Asia trip, held back in notifying us. Mom was so busy caring for Granny that we didn't receive updates regularly. Two or three weeks went by with no news, and then when we did receive a note in the mail, it was invariably troubling. Granny had sustained significant brain damage and was in a coma. In subsequent weeks she was plagued by a series of infections and then pneumonia. Hospitalization was followed by admission to a rehabilitation facility and, ultimately, a nursing home. My grandmother clung to life for most of the following year, but never regained consciousness. She passed away in the fall, less than a year after the accident.

News of Granny's condition took the wind out of our sails. Busy February and March schedules provided some distraction, but we didn't have the same enthusiasm for our work. I felt shrouded in an emotional veil. It helped to connect with friends and share stories about our trip, to teach, and to work on completing my graduate school applications. It was a difficult time for both Linda and me.

Despite the cloud that seemed always to hover over us, Linda felt optimistic about her situation at Chae Il. Her students performed well in class; they followed her English instructions, initiated simple conversations, and demonstrated understanding. That was heady stuff for a novice teacher. The downside was her awareness that, as her students moved to eighth-grade, they would really have no further instruction in using the language. Their Korean English teachers relied on memorizing textbook material with no focus on building an ability to converse. It was discouraging to hear her fellow English teachers discount their students' abilities to think or be creative; they believed forced memorization was the key to learning.

Another disappointment surfaced when, despite her success, Linda learned that she would be teaching eight seventh-grade classes only once weekly in the new term — the same issue she had faced during her first month at Chae Il. A big difference was that she was to have no eighth-grade classes. Her teaching schedule was literally cut in half. She knew that such limited exposure to spoken English would be of little benefit to the new seventh-grade students. Whatever they learned wasn't likely to stick. To supplement her schedule in the new term, she arranged to teach six hours per week at the elementary school where the Lee children, Yooni and Wani, were students. She had requested that assignment before the holidays and expected it to be in addition to her regular Chae Il teaching schedule. The new schedule precipitated a change in her plans.

Linda was uncertain about the reasons behind the reduction of her classroom hours. Perhaps, she thought, it was because our Peace Corps assignments were scheduled to end in the middle of the school year. Her new students would have less disruption in their class schedule during the second half of the year with her teaching load halved. On a positive note, Linda thought the change might provide her sufficient time to initiate a community project during the spring term.

We knew the Ministry of Education planned to assign new PCVs to teacher education colleges. Because another PCV was not likely to be assigned to Chae Il, Linda decided not to contest her new schedule. Instead, she accepted the reduced teaching load and chose to think of it as an opportunity. She imagined putting together a community project that would allow her to continue working with some of her first-year students who would be moving up to eighth-grade.

Upon my return to Kei Sung, a radically different assignment surprised me as well. Beginning with the new school year in March, instead of teaching eight classes twice each week, I was to teach just two seventh-grade classes six times per week. I was to be the only English teacher for those two classes, responsible for reading and grammar in addition to the aural-oral conversation approach I had been using. Our friend Kathi, before she was medically evacuated, had a similar responsibility at her school. She was the only English teacher for her classes. Her students had performed as well on final exams as the students taught by her Korean colleagues, and their speaking abilities exceeded those of students taught only by Korean teachers. I thought it possible that Kei Sung had heard of Kathi's success and wanted to try it out.

Being the sole English teacher for a couple of first year classes challenged me. I was to have six different lessons to plan each week instead of just two. That would take a significant chunk of time. Theoretically, the new schedule provided additional time for me to prepare materials and recordings for the language lab. However, I doubted the new schedule considered the additional planning involved. Fortunately, two other Peace Corps couples with flexible teaching schedules took an interest in my language lab project and volunteered to help.

As Linda and I settled in again at our schools, in the Lee household it was time for the Lunar New Year celebration. During a three-day weekend in early February, extended families often gathered for a reunion. Dressed in traditional clothes, they ate rice-cake soup, paid respects to ancestors with prayers and offerings, and caught up on each other's news. Even in Christian homes, the Confucian philosophy of paying respect to one's ancestors remained a significant value. For the Lees, the celebration included visits with extended family members,

Yute games, and gifting the children with new clothes, colorful items for elementary students Yooni and Wani, and a new black school tunic for Googi. Still reeling from our sad news from home, our inclusion in the family's holiday celebration was comforting.

With the new school year just around the corner and the fact we would be leaving sometime in July, the Lee kids asked for additional help in learning English. Linda had shared with the younger ones that she would be teaching at their school a few hours each week in the new term. As Googi prepared to begin his second year of middle school, he also let us know he wanted more English practice. We decided to challenge all three kids to work together, with Googi as coach for his sister and brother. Informal lessons became a regular part of our playtime as the weeks passed.

An opportunity to participate in a "hundred-day" celebration for a newborn child provided another welcome distraction for Linda and me. Historically in Korea, surviving one hundred days of life was celebrated as a positive predictor of a baby's healthy future. With a reduction in infant mortality, the tradition had become less a celebration of life and more an opportunity to party with friends. One afternoon, in true Korean fashion, we received an invitation to one such celebration that very night.

Four couples, the husbands all teachers at Kei Sung, gathered at another teacher's home — the same teacher whose marriage ceremony we attended not long after arriving in Taegu. That couple was celebrating their first child's hundredth day. The party that evening departed from tradition in several ways. First, inviting couples was unusual. More often, the sexes would engage in gender-specific events. Second, all the husbands worked at the same Christian school, meaning there would be no drinking or smoking. Among non-Christians, social celebrations were often occasions for drinking. Third, the men and women were all seated together, the women in elegant traditional dress and the men in Western suits. More typically, men and women would congregate and eat in separate rooms. Fourth, all the couples were young, married for only a few years at most.

Hundred days celebration

As we all got seated on the floor around a low table, it was clear the women were more comfortable than the men as the conversation began to flow. Since the group expressed curiosity about our January trip and our American way of life, it wasn't long before everyone was engaged. Our primitive Korean and everyone else's limited English presented only minor barriers. I enjoyed the opportunity to be with some of the younger teachers at my school, and Linda always hit it off with the women, who were more open and curious.

The entire evening was a delight. The meal was a typical Korean feast. The dishes were tasty and the presentation beautiful. As always, our hostess welcomed us by saying in Korean, "Despite the fact we have almost nothing, please eat a lot!" Of course, there was enough to feed a much larger group. By then we understood that the rest of the family would be waiting to eat until we finished. The new mother, who prepared and served our meal, joined us as we ate, talked, and laughed. One custom that did not change was the way our hostess dressed for the evening. In contrast to the elegant traditional dress of the other women, she wore her everyday housedress. As a sign of humility, Korean hostesses typically dressed plainly, symbolizing their respect and deference to the guests.

Before February ended, we had more troubling news from home. Mom had been tending to my critically ill grandmother around the clock, sharing responsibilities with her sister, my aunt. Amid all their emotional pain, Mom had to undergo an emergency appendectomy. She spent time in the hospital, distressed at not being available to help care for her mother. We were so far away. Our anguish was a constant ache.

Amid that distress, Linda began to suspect she might be pregnant. She did not share her suspicion with me until she had symptoms of a miscarriage one evening. Luckily, we were both at home, but we were shaken. Linda figured she might have been six weeks along at the time. The next day, we hustled the small, wrapped package of discharged tissue over to Dr. Scholten, who confirmed what we thought and helped us understand what had happened. He reassured us that miscarriages were common in first-time pregnancies and told us not to be concerned; one miscarriage did not predict difficulties going forward. Relieved, we made a commitment to double our efforts at preventing another pregnancy. We weren't yet ready to complicate our post-Peace Corps lives with the birth of a child.

Still more distressing news arrived later in the mail. At the suggestion of my UCSB adviser, I had hastily applied for admission to a graduate counseling psychology program at an eastern university before we left on our Asia trip. I had requested permission to take the required Graduate Record Exam later in the spring when it was to be offered in Seoul. The letter I received from the university notified me that one of my required letters of recommendation had not arrived. At that point, I had missed the application deadline and was back to square one. We decided to hold off on further graduate school inquiries until we returned stateside in the fall. Instead, we turned our full attention to making the best of our last few months in Taegu.

Chapter 30

OF YIN AND YANG

The circular symbol of yin-yang, with its swirling half-circles of dark and light, has its roots in Chinese philosophy. Yin, the dark swirl, is associated with shadows, cold, and hostile energy. Yang, the light swirl, symbolizes brightness, heat, and positive energy. The yin-yang circle represents a balance between opposites, complementary forces that form a whole greater than their parts. For us, March and April contained elements of both yin and yang.

THE YANG

The weekend before beginning the new school year in March, the Raiks invited Linda, me, and five other PCVs to visit them in Yechon. We would all be staying in one room at the Raik's host family's home. Linda and I had stayed in the same room with Barrie and Jerry previously and thought it full. With the head count now numbering nine, sleeping was wall-to-wall.

The weekend's major event was a fried chicken dinner party for all of us at Sang Hae Won orphanage in honor of our contributions to the day-camp we had all helped lead the previous summer. After dinner, the Raiks narrated a slide show of their Asia trip. For most of the orphanage children, that show was their first exposure to places outside of Korea. It was great fun hearing their comments and questions; they literally overflowed with curiosity.

On Saturday I had my spirits lifted again when, in a 2:2 basketball game, I was finally on the winning side against Jerry. While it wasn't a 1:1 victory, I do admit to gloating a bit. To my chagrin, despite several more opportunities, it was my only win on the basketball court during our remaining months in Korea.

Back at our schools in Taegu Monday morning, Linda began investigating a potential community project. A missionary friend had shared with her that the young children in an understaffed Taegu orphanage struggled to develop intelligible speech. The children, all of whom were under seven years of age, had little interaction with Korean speakers and, as a result, they were creating their own ways of communicating with one another.

Linda imagined a project in which some of her middle school students would lead language development activities with the orphanage kids. The students could use visual aids, songs, games, and stories, like those Linda used to teach English. She wondered how her vice-principal, never one to embrace innovative ideas, would respond to her vision. Before presenting her idea to him, she shared it with Helen, our missionary friend who had alerted Linda to the problem. Helen loved the idea and offered to introduce Linda to the orphanage director. Over tea at the orphanage, the three of them talked about how such a project might unfold.

The orphanage housed children from infancy to age seven. The highest priority children, the five- and six-year-olds, would be starting school soon; they needed a basic understanding of the Korean language. In all, 178 children resided at the facility. The fact that only thirty-six were boys confirmed Linda's understanding of Korean gender preferences. With about sixty children in the five- to six-year-old age range, the director thought it best to divide those kids into smaller groups, each led by several middle school girls.

With those parameters in mind, Linda prepared to talk with her vice-principal. Her new teaching schedule left her Fridays open. She decided to seek permission to recruit students from the new eighth-grade class, all of whom she had taught for an entire year. Of those 480 students, she thought she could recruit a couple dozen to participate in a new English club. She would then pitch the idea to those students to gauge their enthusiasm for an orphanage project. Finally, she planned to propose that the school permit the students to visit the orphanage on Friday afternoons beginning in April.

On the day Linda decided to present her proposal, she arrived to find the vice-principal had been promoted and transferred to a different school. The head teacher, historically very supportive of Linda's presence in the school, was the interim administrator. As they talked, he expressed support for the concept and encouraged Linda to pursue it.

Before long, thirty of Linda's former students had volunteered to join an English club that would have a community-focused project. From that group, Linda selected four girls who might be good leaders for what she imagined would be four teams. Prior to the first club meeting, Linda arranged for those four potential team leaders to join her for tea with the orphanage director. The director described the problem to the girls and shared her vision of what would most help the children. She suggested dividing the five- and six-year-olds into four different groups that could meet weekly with the Chae Il students. Each group of children would have three or four students who could guide them in language building activities.

Back at Chae Il, the girls began meeting on Mondays and Wednesdays after school to plan activities focused on helping the orphanage kids develop their understanding and ability to speak Korean. At the club's first gathering, Linda asked the prospective leaders to describe their meeting with the orphanage director. There was a buzz as the members asked questions of their peer leaders. Linda listed the activities she used in teaching English and asked the girls if they thought the orphanage kids would respond well to games, songs, and stories. The students were unanimous in their support, especially for telling stories with puppets.

The club members were all enthusiastic about helping younger children, and the fact they would be able to leave school on Fridays for what sounded like an adventure was added incentive. They planned a field trip to the orphanage each Friday. Half the club members would go one week, and the other half the next, on a rotating basis. During their meetings Linda worked with the whole group to plan the activities for that week's visit. They used English as much as possible as they planned. Then, at the orphanage, the students would lead the activities in Korean.

Within two weeks, the students were ready. On March 28, they made their first trip to the orphanage. Since there were to be four groups of five- and six-year-olds, fifteen students made the trip. Each group of orphans had either three or four middle school students to lead the activities. Linda looked on, pleased with the spirit and imagination shown by her students as they interacted with the kids and acted out stories.

At the club meeting the following Monday, the first group shared their experience with the other club members, who listened with rapt attention. From Linda's vantage point, the second group seemed shyer and more tentative than the first, but they did fine when their turn came at the orphanage. By the end of April, the club had led four language-learning experiences for the orphans. As the girls taught popular children's songs, introduced vocabulary for food items, acted out stories, and played physically active games, they learned each child's name. Linda even included herself as they played the Korean version of London Bridge.

The project was not without some frustration. Linda found her limited Korean prevented her from collaborating as effectively as she would have liked with both the students and the orphanage director. She saw ways to improve the experience for both her students and the orphanage kids but had difficulty getting those ideas across. She could have used a translator.

Chae Il students teaching at orphanage

Back at Kei Sung, I was teaching two seventh-grade classes daily for an hour each, Monday through Saturday. I liked the challenge of teaching, but found the time passed very quickly during the instructional hour. At Blue Knob we learned the use of oral-aural methods, but I had to experiment with teaching reading and grammar. Because my students would face the same end-of-term written exams used throughout the school, I needed to keep pace with the other teachers. I tried to use English exclusively, relying heavily on visual aids. To keep the students engaged, I personally acted out the meanings of words and phrases. I tried to make each lesson as entertaining as possible.

One of my challenges was the limited space we had in the classroom. I had sixty students sitting at small desks in six rows. Narrow aisles between rows left little space to move about. Students didn't have much room to get out of their seats and practice with one another. Except for some role-play practice with pairs of students at the front of the room, students had to stay in place. I hoped the quick pace of each lesson, my animated teaching style, and the practice they did in their seats, held their attention.

When I wasn't teaching and doing lesson plans, I prepared programs for the language lab. For each hour-long lesson I chose the content, created an illustrated workbook, and developed a script for a master recording. Lessons were derived from the textbook used in all the classes. I assumed each English class would have one hour per week in the lab. That meant my co-teacher and I had to map out lessons that would keep pace with what the other teachers did each week in their classes; the fact that I was teaching those same lessons helped. The school asked me to create self-contained lessons for the lab that kept pace with the weekly instructional objectives for first-year students. That amounted to about forty lessons — a tall order.

I had a mixed reaction to that assignment. I liked the creative aspect of the design work and Linda and the two Peace Corps couples who had volunteered, helped me with recordings. One couple had secondary school assignments like ours, and the other taught at the university. One or two of them came over to Kei Sung about once a week when we typically reviewed one or two lessons, made revisions, and did a recording. I thought that variety of recorded voices would enhance the listening experience for the students. The encouragement I received from my fellow teachers, as they saw the number of completed lessons slowly increase, motivated me to keep working. Still, I didn't see how I could accomplish what the school wanted in my remaining time there. From start to finish, I could only complete about one hour-long lab lesson each week. At that pace I was going to fall short.

Unconvinced about whether the teachers would use the lab as my co-teacher and I envisioned, I had reservations about how useful the lessons would be after I left. The Korean English teachers had limited ability to speak the language. I knew they would be hesitant to reveal their limitations. Loss of face, especially with students, was something most traditional teachers tried to avoid.

As the new school year began, my fellow teacher, friend, and hiker, Gi Suh, knew it would be my last term at Kei Sung. In a casual discussion he mentioned a wish to improve his English, and I told him I wanted to keep learning Korean. We committed to squeezing some time into our daily schedules to coach each other. While priorities sometimes interfered, we managed to get together semi-regularly. Those moments were a bright spot in my day. I think both of us wished we could have taken our friendship to a deeper level, but our mutual language limitations posed a barrier.

THE YIN

While fully engaged at our schools during the day, troubling events began to occur at the Lee home. One March night, a burglar entered the house, not an uncommon event in Taegu. The slender stealthy man squeezed through a small, unlocked window. Samonim awoke when he opened the door to their room in the middle of the night. Mr. Lee stirred, and the burglar beat a hasty retreat without taking anything. Later, Mr. Lee cautioned all of us in the home to be vigilant about locking windows and doors. At night, before sleeping, he wanted us to close all interior doors in the house to make any intrusions more audible. Moreover, since Linda and I were the only occupants upstairs, he wanted us to lock our room door at night, something we had never done.

Curious to us, there was no thought of reporting the attempted burglary to the police. Koreans thought of burglars as desperate people; they believed burglars should be expected to do what burglars do. Responsibility for securing the home rested with the residents. If robbed, it was a family security issue, not a matter for law enforcement. The crime was not the burglary, but the failure to secure one's property.

The security breach wasn't the only shadow cast on the household that spring. Sometime during the week following our night visitor incident, Linda and I discovered some cash missing from its usual storage place in our armoire. Thinking the bank might have shorted me when I withdrew our monthly allowance, we chalked the loss up to a learning experience. Still, the missing cash puzzled me; I was always careful about such things. That said, Linda and I didn't think to change the location of where we kept our cash. We continued to stash it in the back of one of our armoire drawers.

A couple weeks later, Linda discovered more cash missing from the same place. Altogether, 6500 won had disappeared (the equivalent of $25), about a quarter of our monthly living allowance. We couldn't imagine anyone in the family violating our trust. Security within the family had never been a concern and we were hesitant to bring it up with Mr. Lee. After the second incident, however, we decided we had to say something.

With just the three of us in the room at breakfast, we raised the issue. Mr. Lee said he wished we had mentioned it earlier. He disclosed that he, too, had recently been missing some cash. He suspected Kihyun, the young live-in household assistant who had been with the family since our arrival. Samonim had confided to him earlier that she found Kihyun in our room a couple times with no adequate explanation for why she was there. Added to that, a neighbor shared with Samonim a rumor that Kihyun was planning to run away. Mr. Lee suspected she might have given stolen cash to a neighbor kitchen girl for safekeeping. Fearing the rumored escape might occur, the Lees decided they could never leave Kihyun alone in the house, a decision that upset daily routines for everyone and made all of us uncomfortable.

In Korea, a face-to-face confrontation was the absolute last resort in resolving a conflict. Any accusation made directly to Kihyun would result in a loss of face so severe that she would not be able to stay. Contrary to all cultural norms, Mr. Lee considered talking with her and threatening to take her to the police if she didn't return the money. He suspected, however, that if he discharged her and forced her to return to her rural village, she would probably face rejection by her family. The family's loss of face and disgrace would be intolerable. He decided against that strategy. Instead, he planned to have a padlock installed on our upstairs door to prevent Kihyun from entering our room. That act would also alert Kihyun to the fact that we all knew the room's security had been breached.

Gradually things got back to normal, and tensions eased. Mr. Lee and Samonim offered to repay the lost cash, but we had no desire to accept their offer. Given the additional security precautions, we assumed Kihyun would consider herself warned to transgress no further. We felt terrible for everyone. In our hearts, we feared our presence in their home had become a burden to Mr. Lee and Samonim.

Then, near the end of April, the unspeakable happened again. One morning, after we made an early visit to the public bath, Linda discovered some cash was missing from her purse. We had left our room before six o'clock and been gone less than an hour. In the Korean sense, we were at fault. It simply had not occurred to us to lock up at that time of day. We apologetically raised the issue at breakfast and asked Mr. Lee what he thought we should do. Immediately, he bolted out of the room, and lit into Kihyun. His fierce shouts echoed throughout the house. His reaction, so contrary to how Koreans typically deal with conflict, shocked us. We didn't know what to do. Amid his shouts, we retreated to our room. Before long, Samonim came upstairs to check on us and apologize. The situation was awful for everyone.

Linda returned home from school early that day and visited with Samonim alone. Despite feeling terrible about what had happened, Samonim's suggestion was to "just forget about it." We assumed she wanted to reassure us, but we knew a dark cloud had descended upon the family. Our presence in the household was a temptation for Kihyun. She was unhappy in her role, and although the Lees knew they should do something, they felt trapped. They couldn't manage without a household helper. We wondered if it would be better for us to move; we loved the family but did not want to be the source of escapable problems.

Within two weeks the mood lightened within the house. To our relief, the kids seemed their usual selves, and Mr. Lee and Samonim appeared less stressed. Kihyun avoided us for several days, but our relationship with her gradually thawed. Still, we sensed cordial politeness had replaced the relaxed congeniality and light-heartedness we had enjoyed since our arrival. We settled into what felt like a tentative peace, perhaps an unspoken acknowledgment that our time with the family would soon be coming to an end. Nevertheless, the yin of that situation precipitated a sad discomfort from which we never fully recovered.

Chapter 31

A SECOND SPRING

Bright spots appeared in our April calendar as tension within the Lee home gradually eased and we accepted the critical nature of my grandmother's injury. First, the Raiks and their Korean family planned to host a ceremonial Seder commemorating Jewish Passover. Jerry and Barrie wanted to introduce their tradition to friends in Yechon and invited us and some other PCVs to join them. So, on the first Friday of the month, six of us boarded an evening train bound for Yechon.

Rolling through a late winter blizzard in a chilly rail car, we arrived in Yechon shortly after ten o'clock that night. Jerry met us at the station and, after dropping our things off at their house and picking up Barrie, we struck out for the local Chinese restaurant. Over a late dinner, we learned about plans for the following day. Free in the morning to explore, it was to be all hands on deck Saturday afternoon to prepare for the Seder. Eighteen people had been invited. The evening was going to be a true cross-cultural celebration, and we expected to learn a lot about Jewish history and tradition.

Midnight curfew was fast approaching when we departed the restaurant. We all slept that night in the Raiks' host family's home, filling two of the three rooms in the house with wall-to-wall bodies. As morning broke, we all became aware of our differing wake-up habits. Some of us got up and out early to exercise; others chose to sleep in as the sun rose. The hand pump in the tiny courtyard got a workout as we all washed up and made ourselves presentable. While Linda and I explored the town's streets and paths along the river, Barrie and her Korean mother made plans for the cooking to begin mid-day.

Mrs. Lee, the family kitchen girl, and three PCV women spent the entire afternoon preparing the Seder meal. Almost everything was kosher, even the fat used for frying chicken and potato pancakes. Kitchen space was tight, with just two coal yonton cylinders on which to cook. The Raiks' family back home had mailed much of the food, although the Army rabbi in Seoul had sent some as well. Fresh ingredients came from Yechon's open-air market.

A lot of thought went into planning the evening and the elaborate menu. In addition to the pancakes, we had matzo, chicken and matzo ball soup, fried chicken, gefilte fish, cabbage rolls, and applesauce. Charoises, made of crushed walnuts, apples, and a touch of wine, was available to spread on the matzo. Each dish had its place in the Passover celebration.

To accommodate all the guests, we slid back the partitions between the rooms where we had slept and put out four floor tables borrowed from the Chinese restaurant. We placed the tables end-to-end in the expanded room. Symbolic ceremonial cloths were laid out to recall the events of the Passover. As the sun set guests began to arrive. Everyone wore their best: Korean women in traditional hanbok, Korean men in Western-style suits, and Americans in dresses or coats and ties.

Jerry began the evening by inviting us to hear the Passover story of how the Egyptians enslaved the Jews, and how Moses saved the Jews from God's wrath by marking their homes with lamb's blood, to be passed over and left unharmed by God's plague on the Egyptians. Speaking in Korean, Hebrew, and English, he reminded us to appreciate human resilience in overcoming adversity. The Korean adults related to that message, given that all of them had experienced foreign occupation, post-world war strife, and the internal war between North and South. As the story unfolded in segments, Jerry and Barrie shared the symbolic meaning of the foods traditionally prepared for the Seder meal. Everyone left late that evening, full of good food and a greater understanding for the meaning of Jewish Passover.

Linda Cooking for the Seder

Jerry (second from left) presiding at the Seder

Given the train and bus schedules on Sunday, the late morning bus proved our best option for returning to Taegu. The weather had warmed and the snow from Friday's freak storm had melted. The bus-ride, a typically slow, uncomfortable, bouncy four-hour endurance test, left us exhausted but still spiritually full from our previous night's experience.

The following week, while we dove back into our teaching roles, we attended a birthday party one evening at a downtown tabang for Howie, another PCV. The tabang was ubiquitous in 1960s Korea, found easily in all cities and towns. Typically located on the second floor of a retail building, dimly lit, and crowded with patrons, the tabang provided a gathering place for social encounters. A variety of tea and coffee drinks was available. Décor was typically tasteful, with artwork adorning the walls. Set apart from city noise, the tabang was a pleasant place. Tables were usually situated close together, arranged for groups of two or four. Aside from restaurants, the tabang provided the only place people could meet to have business discussions, socialize with friends, or study. We often arranged to meet Korean and American friends at a tabang to visit or rendezvous on our way to an evening event. The atmosphere, although not as subdued as a library, was not as noisy as a café. Patrons tended to be male, but as months went by, we noticed an increase in the number of women who chose to socialize in those establishments.

Howie's birthday celebration took place in a tabang new to us. When we walked in, we immediately sensed it differed from other tearooms. Booths lined the edges of the room, not just tables and chairs. The artsy atmosphere included musical instruments and colorful abstract paintings on the walls. The owner, a retired musician, had lived several years in Japan. An innovator and an eccentric, he cultivated his tabang as a hangout where college students could study, and professors could gather to discuss issues of the day. He encouraged patrons to bring musical instruments in the evening for jam sessions.

Howie and some of our other PCV friends, musicians in their own rights, had begun in recent months to frequent that tabang, becoming well known to the owner. They impressed us when they broke out guitars, a banjo, an Autoharp, and harmonicas. The crowd, Koreans and Americans alike, listened to the music with rapt attention and appreciation.

By mid-April, we began to feel like short timers. Mel, our regional rep, suggested we think about mailing things like winter clothes back to the States, especially if we thought we could not fit everything we wanted to ship in our two Peace Corps trunks. That prompted us to think about our departure's potential impact on our schools, our friends, and ourselves. We wondered if some of the more recently arrived PCVs might be interested in teaching at the elementary school, or for those teaching in middle schools, using our lesson plans and visual aids.

At about that time Mel passed along a request from the Ministry of Education. Linda and I were asked to lead a ten-week workshop to a small number of Taegu English teachers as a parting professional development event. Given our remaining responsibilities we had some hesitation but agreed to put a plan together.

On the recreation front, our friends Gi Suh and Duk Hee encouraged us not to miss a quintessentially Korean spring event. Every April, huge crowds descended on Chinhae, a small town on the south coast, to enjoy the thousands of cherry trees that grew throughout the city. Our friends insisted we could not leave Korea without taking in that festival, so we proceeded to plan a Sunday excursion for later in the month. Together with Gi Suh and Duk Hee, we invited Gary and Sharon, our Mennonite friends, to join us.

The night before our trip to Chinhae, we all gathered at the Mennonite farm to map out the following day and put together a picnic lunch. When Duk Hee expressed curiosity about how Korean and American lunches differed, we decided to make it a Western-style picnic. We filled a basket with three different kinds of sandwiches – tuna, ham, peanut butter and jelly – carrot sticks, fruit, and a chocolate cake. While some of us prepared the food, the rest taught Gi Suh how to make hand-cranked chocolate chip ice cream for a treat to top off the evening. As we enjoyed the ice cream, the topic of first names came up. Since we were going on an American-style picnic, someone proposed giving Gi Suh and Duk Hee American names. They liked the idea, and after some possibilities were tossed about, we settled on names that sounded like their Korean names, "Chris" for Gi Suh, and "Debbie" for Duk Hee. The names stuck! After more than fifty years, the Kwons are known in Chicago, where they now reside, as Chris and Debbie.

Next morning, we caught a jam-packed train at half-past seven for the three-hour ride to Chinhae. A beautiful morning in Taegu turned gray and cloudy by the time we arrived on the south coast. The cherry trees, however, were in full bloom. Despite the overcast sky, the little town was stunning, all decked out in pinkish-white blossoms. So many people had flocked to Chinhae that it looked as if the entire country had turned out. As we had seen elsewhere at public celebrations, groups often assembled in circles later in the afternoon and danced to the beat of a traditional drum, sang, and drank wine.

As we strolled after lunch, I was grabbed by one of the *halmoni* (grandmothers) and pulled into her dance circle. Red-faced and obviously intoxicated, she had a twinkle of mischief in her eyes. When she grasped my arm in a vice-like grip, I really had no choice; she was not about to take "No" for an answer. As we danced, the wine jug being passed around the circle eventually made its way to me. I chose not to partake. Perhaps sensing my readiness to move on, my dance partner gestured toward my friends. However, she still had firm hold of my arm. My release was out of the question until we had our picture taken together. Linda did the honors.

The train ride home got even wilder. Some in our car were continuing to drink. People danced in the aisle and sang at the top of their lungs. Our little group remained seated, taking it all in and feeling some anxiety about what might happen as the merriment continued. We had seen how such celebrations sometimes ended. Sure enough, as the train approached Taegu, a fight broke out among some men. Fists flew as we hastily migrated to the back of the car. When the train pulled to a stop, the fighting continued. We hustled off and waited on the platform to see what would happen next. Two policemen approached, yelled through the window at the combatants to knock it off, and then turned and walked away as the fight raged on. It was a typical law enforcement response to domestic conflict. The fight lent a sour ending to what had been an otherwise sweet day.

The spectacular cherry blossoms in Chinhae prompted Sharon and Gary to suggest we take another day trip to Pulgooksa, the historic

Chinhae Cherry Blossom Festival

temple on the outskirts of Kyungju, hoping for better weather than we had on our previous visit. We went the following weekend, and the weather was glorious, with multitudes of cherry trees in full bloom. The most interesting part of the day, however, was a chance encounter we had with a rural funeral procession.

Traveling in Sharon and Gary's car as we neared a parade of mourners, we stopped as the procession passed nearby. The deceased, a village elder, had a coffin adorned with colorful fabric and ribbons, over which flew a shading canopy. A group of thirty men

Rural funeral procession

carried the coffin on their shoulders, balanced atop a large, webbed rope. The bearers had wrapped towels around their heads to absorb sweat. They slowly made their way along a narrow dike between rice paddies, singing a beautiful and respectfully slow dirge. Dressed in traditional sackcloth robes and conical mourning hats, the silent mourners followed behind.

The funeral procession stopped a short distance beyond the place where we had pulled off the road. We approached and had a chance to ask some questions. If we understood correctly, the paid coffin bearers took periodic rest breaks. Before resuming, the mourning family was expected to give them a little more money to continue their journey to the family burial mound where the deceased would be interred. What we witnessed that day was a classic example of traditional rural Korean culture.

At the beginning of May, I took the Graduate Record Exam in Seoul. Linda stayed behind to attend the wedding of Shinja's sister. Shinja, the former household assistant with whom we felt a special bond, had remained close to the Lee family since her marriage in January. Linda had been drafted earlier to take a few photos of the younger sister's wedding. After she agreed to do so, the family decided she should serve as the official wedding photographer. Why, the family reasoned, should they hire a professional photographer when Linda possessed a perfectly good camera?

As the wedding date approached, Linda's anxiety escalated. Because the responsibility rested so heavy on her shoulders, she invited Sharon to assist and provide moral support. By the morning of the wedding, Linda was scared to death. But when the pictures came back from the developer a week later, she was relieved; the results pleased her.

The wedding itself had been a departure from what Linda and Sharon expected. As had become popular, the ceremony was more Western than traditional, not a positive trend from Linda's perspective. The bride's day was anything but relaxed and joyful. Two hours before the ceremony she was due at the beauty shop next to the commercial wedding hall. While there, she had cosmetics applied, had her hair coiffed, and borrowed a dress and jewelry. Immediately following the brief ceremony, she was rushed back to the beauty shop to return all the rented items, change into her own clothes, and have her hair quickly redone.

The whole event lacked a sense of excitement and was, as tradition dictated, absent of smiles. The fact that the marriage had been arranged probably contributed to a sense of apprehension, at least on the part of the bride. That night, as the celebrations concluded, the

Lee home overflowed with out-of-town guests. The house was so crowded downstairs that Googi, Yooni, and Wani slept upstairs with Linda. They had fun while I coped with the GRE in Seoul.

One more fete of spring remained on our calendar. The second "Stepping on the Coat" ceremony in Yechon was scheduled to take place the second weekend in May. The first event, held the prior year, had been a small affair. The Raiks and Gallons had been the only participants, accompanied by a handful of curious Yechon residents and the Raiks' host family. During the intervening year, word and photos had spread among the Peace Corps community. So interested were our friends that Yechon became flooded with young Americans anxious to participate in the event.

Twenty of us filled an entire yogwan. There for the whole weekend, our merrymaking proved to be an economic windfall for local merchants. Sunday was warm as we all donned our winter garb. Jerry led a long solemn procession on the route through town and up Namsan Hill, culminating in the hilltop ceremony. Perhaps because our numbers had swelled, a huge turnout of town folk gathered and watched in wonder. Their facial expressions radiated concern as we trudged up the hill, followed by visible relief as our spirits lifted on the walk back into town. We were all curious to know what the villagers were thinking.

Due to the large crowd of followers, Linda and I, with our tongues planted firmly in our cheeks, speculated about the possibility of "Stepping on the Coat" becoming an annual "right of spring" celebration. At the very least, it seemed the procession might live on in the memory of those in attendance. We mused that it might become the stuff of legend, a tribute to the young American couple that introduced such a puzzling custom to the community. In all probability, however, the ceremony in Yechon likely died that day. For us, it was great fun while it lasted.

Chapter 32

CHANGES ON THE HORIZON

In mid-May, just over two months remained until our departure from Korea. We had a week-long, end-of-service Peace Corps conference scheduled in June, last-minute work requests were coming in from our schools, and friends began making dates to get on our social calendar for farewell meals. In addition to all that, we were presented with a major surprise.

Early in the month, we learned our friend Sharon was pregnant. Upon hearing her morning sickness symptoms, Linda began to suspect the discomfort she was personally experiencing might not be the flu, but something else. When her nausea continued, she scheduled an exam at Dong San Hospital to check out her suspicion. Sure enough, a new Gallon family member was on the way. The doctor predicted a December 27 arrival.

In response to the news we were surprised, thrilled and uncertain about how best to handle the news. Given the miscarriage Linda had experienced earlier, we decided to keep it to ourselves until mid-June, the estimated end of her first trimester. In the meantime, Dr. Scholten provided powdered milk, vitamin supplements, and regular check-ups to make sure everything progressed normally. Korean food, for Linda, quickly became totally unappealing. She was so grateful for the freshly baked bread she received each week from our Mennonite friends. That bread proved to be the only food she could tolerate during her period of morning sickness.

The news prompted us to reconsider our post-Peace Corps options, which seemed few at the time. I don't recall feeling anxious about it, but I probably should have. We immediately crossed off several possibilities. Additional Peace Corps service in another country was out since in-country childbirth for PCVs was not allowed at that time. Budget cuts had eliminated Peace Corps recruiting on college campuses. Beyond my singular failed attempt to secure fall admission, I had not submitted any additional graduate school applications. The only other opportunity we considered was a position in a Peace Corps training program where we would help prepare future PCVs for overseas service. The status of that option was still unknown. The idea of trying to nail down what to do when we returned home seemed impossible with everything else that was happening. Ultimately, we again decided to put further planning aside for the time being, other issues needed our immediate attention.

Near the end of May, we received formal notice that our tour of service in Korea would officially end during the third week of July — the beginning of the summer break for our schools. We knew leaving Korea would not be easy. Our lives would change radically as we untethered ourselves from everything that had become familiar in the two years since our wedding: the Lee family, our Korean friends, our teaching responsibilities, and our Peace Corps chums. We had no idea what was next, with the exception that we were to become a family of three in about six months. Still, we felt confident.

As Linda and I considered our trip home, we decided to give ourselves a bit of time between leaving Taegu and reuniting with our families in California. We suspected the transition might not be easy. The itinerary we settled on began with a flight from Pusan to Fukuoka, a seaport on Japan's southern island of Kyushu, a little over a hundred miles off the coast of Korea. We then planned to spend three weeks traveling by train and bus to Tokyo. Friends had told us about Japan's impressive gardens and antiquities; we didn't want to miss the opportunity to visit some of them while we had the chance. From Japan, we wanted to spend ten days in Hawai'i before returning to California in late August. With our plans set, we tackled our "to do" list.

The staff at Peace Corps headquarters in Seoul reminded us that our two government-issue trunks, the ones we had first packed at Blue Knob, would be shipped home at government expense. With a weight limit of one hundred pounds each, anything in addition was our responsibility. We quickly filled a couple of boxes with winter clothes and shipped them off. A half dozen more would ultimately be packed and mailed before we were ready to go. While packing, we found our summer clothes to be in marginal shape, having endured rough hand washing over the previous two years. Without question, Linda's wardrobe needed a makeover since she would be nearly five months pregnant when we arrived home in August. We added commissioning a tailor to our list.

Toward the end of May, Barrie and Suki, the youngest child of the Raiks' host family surprised us with a visit. They were on a trial day trip away from home to see how eight-year-old Suki traveled without her parents. She had been diagnosed with a potentially fatal heart defect that needed surgical intervention. The Raiks were hoping to take her with them back to New York where she could get the operation and follow-up care she needed.

When the Raiks became aware of Suki's health problem, Jerry began researching the treatment options with physicians known to the Peace Corps. His investigation led him to a well-known missionary physician and surgeon in Kwangju, Dr. Paul Crane. Dr. Crane took an interest in Suki's condition. He was able to diagnose her problem and, after considerable effort, connect with a pediatric heart surgeon in New York City who offered to do the needed operation without charge. Coincidentally, it was Dr. Crane who wrote *Korean Patterns,* one of the few published works about Korea to which we had access during our training program at Blue Knob.

Since the Raiks were from Manhattan, they planned to serve as Suki's guardians during the trip and provide her care for several months during her post-surgical recovery. It was likely to be a challenging experience for all concerned. Suki's family would remain in Korea, ten thousand miles away. She would endure the trauma of both the separation and the surgery. Adding to all that, the Raiks would be providing care and comfort for a distressed girl who spoke no English and who would likely not be fully aware of what was happening to her. That commitment was a great illustration of the close relationships some PCVs developed with their Korean host families.

As our tenure in the Lee home was drawing short, Samonim disclosed she would like us to prepare some American meals for the family. With the addition of a wooden floor in her kitchen and warmer springtime weather, she had lost some of her hesitancy to invite Linda into her domain. On Korean Mother's Day, we served the family spaghetti and meatballs. Except for two cans of tomato sauce, all the ingredients were fresh from the local market, including the noodles. The meal was a big hit and, as had become our tradition, it was followed by a game that included the whole family. That evening the women's team won a spirited game of Monopoly.

A couple of weeks after Linda's successful debut as guest chef, Samonim requested a steak dinner. That request gave us pause; local beef seemed a bit of a gamble. The open-air market lacked refrigeration, the meat quality was questionable, and we weren't confident about cooking steak over the coal cylinder. We decided to ask the local butcher to grind some meat into hamburger, which we could cook thoroughly. We supplemented the "hamburger steak" with baked potatoes and green vegetables. After negotiating the entire meal with chopsticks, everyone gave it a thumbs-up.

Another unique dining opportunity presented itself unexpectedly on a sunny May afternoon. That day I decided to forego the crowded bus in order to visit one of my favorite Korean bakeries for a snack as I walked home from Kei Sung. Upon exiting the bakery, I noticed a sign across the street announcing the grand opening of a new eating establishment. The sign spelled out in phonetic Korean, "Kentucky Fried Chicken." That was the very first time I had seen anything that indicated Korea might be opening up to American fast-food businesses. For me, the restaurant would be a "must try" experience as soon as it opened.

Several weeks later, Linda and I invited another couple to join us for the "KFC" premier. We were very curious to learn if Koreans could improve on their previous attempts to replicate American cuisine. When we arrived on opening day, I wasn't surprised to find an empty restaurant. I suspected few Koreans had any knowledge of Kentucky Fried Chicken. While it didn't have the distinctive KFC logo, the bright yellow, red, and white décor was clean and attractive. We sensed some authenticity might be in the offing. As we awaited our order, our expectations rose.

When our chicken arrived, an entire bird — looking like a deep-fried rubber replica of the real thing — lay across a ceramic platter. Long and slender, it was golden brown from its beak and comb down to its feet. On close inspection, there were a fair number of quills protruding from its crispy skin. None of us found the presentation appetizing, but we wanted to give it a try. We prodded the bird, trying to free up some meat with our chopsticks but the poor creature was skin and bone. We concluded it had probably succumbed to starvation. We didn't regret our optimistic anticipation of a delicious fried chicken dinner, but again the delivery fell well below expectations. We thanked the proprietor but departed the establishment disappointed; our entrée was left largely untouched.

In early June, we spent a week in Seoul. Our schedule included an end-of-service conference, medical exams, FSI language tests, financial reconciliation, the purchase of airline tickets for our trip home, and goodbyes to lots of friends. During that week, the Peace Corps staff arranged a day trip to the Demilitarized Zone (DMZ), a potentially hostile place not normally open to visitors. The DMZ, a 155-mile-long strip of land, stretched from coast to coast at roughly the 38th Parallel, just thirty miles north of Seoul. Heavily guarded, the area had been the site of multiple military skirmishes during our nearly two years in Korea. Incursions from the north had resulted in the deaths of dozens of American and Korean military personnel, and scores of South Korean citizens and North Korean soldiers.

I wasn't sure why Peace Corps thought it important for us to visit the DMZ. Perhaps they sought to reinforce our understanding of the contrast between the communist North and the budding democracy in the South. Or maybe they wanted to give us a more accurate sense of the threat posed by the aggressive Democratic People's Republic of Korea (DPRK). More likely, it was an opportunity for us to witness the propaganda battle that waged daily along the DMZ.

All seemed peaceful that day, but we were not allowed to leave the bus. On the southern side of the DMZ, we saw lookout towers guarded by both Korean and American soldiers and the underground bunkers where the soldiers stationed along the border lived and slept. We could not see across the zone's two-and-a-half-mile width, but we heard messages blasted from loudspeakers on the North's side, praising "The Great Leader," Kim Il Sung. The South's side also had powerful speakers that broadcast positive messages about daily life in South Korea and traditional Korean folk music, perhaps intended to promote nostalgia among North Koreans who had long been separated from South Korean family members.

Our two-day "End-of-Service" conference took place at Academy House, made memorable during our meeting there in January 1968, when North Korean commandos attempted to assassinate South Korean President Park Chung Hee. The conference's formal agenda included executive briefings and candid discussions of our Korean experience, facilitated by Peace Corps officials from DC and elsewhere.

Just as important to us were the emotional farewells with fellow volunteers, friends with whom we had first bonded at Blue Knob two years earlier. No longer a naïve group of young idealists, we had all faced challenges while living in Korea and had internalized multiple lessons. We had witnessed political turmoil and aggression, been the targets of discrimination, felt the frustration of trying to be agents of change, managed a language barrier with varying degrees of success, and lived in sometimes harsh and risky environments.

As we gathered for a final assessment of our experience, we recounted our successes, failures, and frustrations with a collective sense of accomplishment. Most of us weren't sure how much our efforts would benefit those with whom we had worked. We had no idea whether our contributions would have lasting impact. We knew only that we were taking valuable lessons with us. Our experiences in Korea would stay with us for the rest of our lives. They were anything but forgettable.

Members of our group were bound for diverse futures in law, medicine, government service, academia, and various business pursuits. No matter what our futures held, our Korean experiences united us all. Introduced to Korea's history, culture, and economy firsthand, we had made valued friendships, lived through unexpected challenges, endured physical hardships, and come to see our own country from a different perspective. Feelings about the experience varied from person to person. Consistent among us was the knowledge that we had grappled with uncertainty and were the better for it.

Following the conference at Academy House, we all headed back to Seoul for medical exams, a language test, and to wrap up final financial arrangements. Those interested had a chance to interview for positions in an upcoming Peace Corps training program to prepare a new group of TESL educators for assignments in Korea. The training was to be staged at the Hawai'i Center for Cross-Cultural Training and Research in Hilo. I interviewed and was encouraged by the feedback I received. Linda and I thought it might be a good idea to include a visit to the center while in Hawai'i on our way home.

When we returned to Taegu, we still had five weeks before we had to say our final goodbyes. With the school term nearing an end, Linda wrapped up her orphanage project — one of the highlights of her Chae Il experience. Her students bonded with the kids at the orphanage, and while the project was just over two months old, the director seemed happy with the progress the five and six-year-olds had made in building a minimal set of language skills. Throughout the project, the Chae Il students never lost their enthusiasm. Linda loved coaching them and seeing their self-confidence blossom. She became so attached to one of the little five-year-old boys at the orphanage that I jokingly reminded her that we could not take him home with us.

Back at school, the head English teacher asked Linda to make an audio recording of the entire first-year textbook. She only had about a month before we would be leaving but the recording turned out to take less time than she first imagined. While she was uncertain how the school might use the recording, Chae Il's English teaching team had a more understandable request. They wanted Linda to recommend potential contestants for the provincial English-speaking contest in November — the same contest that Pong Sook had won the previous year. Chae Il would be the defending champion; the teachers wanted to identify students with the best chance of performing well in the contest.

At Kei-Sung, I finally began to accept that I would not accomplish everything the school had in mind for the language lab. I would finish only about half the seventh-grade lessons. I hoped they would serve as a model for whomever might tackle those I could not complete. Linda and I had given some thought to extending our tour for another year to continue working on the lab and teaching in either secondary schools or the teachers' college. Kevin O'Donnell, however, reaffirmed that PC/Korea policy did not allow in-country childbirth for PCVs. That policy eventually changed, but not before we were scheduled to leave.

The most wrenching aspect of leaving my school was that the academic year was just half over. I was invested in the two classes of seventh-graders I taught daily. Probably because I wasn't a stern authoritarian presence in the classroom, I had begun to experience some disciplinary issues with one of the classes. The issues were minor, though, and I wanted to stay with those students for the entire year. They were improving in their ability to use elementary English during class. Instead, I was going to leave just as my students were beginning to sense themselves making progress.

By mid-June, we calculated Linda had successfully emerged from the first trimester of her pregnancy. The morning sickness had subsided, and she felt more comfortable. She didn't yet show any physical signs of the pregnancy, but we thought it safe to share our status with family and friends. In an aerogram home, I drew a picture of a large green dill pickle with a caption that read, "Send Pickles!" That was all we said about the pregnancy. We knew our mothers would understand the message. Sure enough, within the month we received a small package from my mom with a foil-wrapped pickle and a suggestion that Linda pair it with the Korean equivalent of ice cream, referring to the odd cravings women sometimes experience during pregnancy.

Our doctor's wife, whose first baby had arrived earlier in the year, loaned Linda some patterns for attractive, practical maternity clothes. The tailor she commissioned did a terrific job. By the end of June, she had several beautiful summer-weight maternity outfits.

With less than a month remaining, our calendar began to fill with invitations for goodbye dinners. Missionary friends and faculty members at our schools made us feel both appreciated and sad. We found it especially difficult to say goodbye to close friends like Gi Suh and Duk Hee, Sharon and Gary, Barrie and Jerry, our Korean co-teachers, and most of all, the Lee family. We struggled that entire last month with the knowledge that we would really be leaving soon.

Samonim once again demonstrated her thoughtfulness as June turned to July. She knew which of the Korean dishes she had prepared for us since our arrival were our favorites, and for one of our last dinners she did something unexpected. As a total surprise, the menu one night consisted of all our favorite dishes. We feasted on special rice, savory noodles, side plates of lotus root, potatoes, fried sesame leaves, and to cap it off, our favorite duk, the soft slightly chewy rice pastry. We have never forgotten that meal or Samonim's satisfied expression when she saw our delight.

On one of our last weekends in Korea, we headed out of town to picnic with another volunteer couple and to get some final photos of the picturesque countryside. We loved the contrast between Korea's agricultural villages and the grit of its cities. Spectacular colors were the epitome of rural Korea in spring, summer and fall.

Barley harvest was ending, fields were plowed with oxen, and rice seedlings were planted by hand in flooded paddies. In the courtyards of village homes, older women tossed barley high in the air to allow the chaff to separate from the grain. Peaceful quiet was all around; there were no sounds of engines, traffic, or factories. As we walked earthen pathways several friendly country children approached to chat. Those sights and sounds were the yang of everyday life in rural Korea, balanced by the yin of backbreaking work, a lack of electricity, and outhouses perched atop pigsties. PCVs who lived in the cities had a very different experience from Volunteers who lived in smaller towns and villages.

Barley harvest, rice planting, and typical scenes of a rural village in summer.

Chapter 33

HOMEWARD BOUND

Travel preparations, formal goodbyes, and farewell gatherings filled our last days in Taegu. We packed trunks, lunched with fellow teachers and principals, had dinners with friends, and joined other volunteers at a party hosted by Mel and his family. Sandwiched in between, we tried to spend as much time as possible hanging out with the Lee family.

Mr. Lee shared his plans to continue his religious studies at a seminary in Japan. He hated to leave the family in Taegu but believed it essential to complete a divinity degree. Samonim, who still had not learned a word of English, sweetly shared how much she was going to miss us and how much she wished she could see and hold our baby. Two years had passed quickly. They said we arrived as guests and were leaving as members of their family.

We shared a special bond with Googi, then fourteen years old. He was a great kid – enthusiastic, playful, and intelligent. His grasp of English continued to grow; we could now communicate on a whole range of practical topics. When we played a card game with him, we used English most of the time.

Yooni's and Wani's language skills had also improved but being younger and not as familiar with the basics, they hung back, deferring to their older brother. Our hearts ached when we imagined them growing up without us. We hoped we would be able to keep in touch through the years.

Linda and I needed to wrap up one last work project – leading the ten-week teacher in-service workshop with a half dozen English teachers from the Taegu area. All men, the group worked to improve both their ability to speak and to teach. For the last class session, we went out for a celebratory dinner. We knew well by then that Koreans never failed to show appreciation for any effort taken on their behalf.

Linda bids farewell to students and faculty at Chae Il Girls Middle School.

During those final weeks, we felt genuinely appreciated, not only for the work we had done but also for having been willing to spend time in Korea and learn about the country. We felt humbled by the outpouring of gratitude and thoughtfulness from those with whom we had lived, worked, and shared adventures.

As we engaged in final goodbyes, the mood in the greater Taegu community shifted dramatically. We were caught unaware as demonstrations against the government erupted on an almost daily basis. President Park Chung Hee, a former military general, was a controversial authoritarian leader. He made it known that he intended to continue as president beyond the limit authorized by the country's fledgling constitution. As a result, protests were mounted in cities throughout the country. The Kei Sung principal, concerned about maintaining control at the high school, requested assistance from the police and the army to help keep student demonstrations from getting out of hand. During my last week of work, newspapers covered the loud student protests; the entire city seemed on edge.

During our time in Korea, we knew the government to be strong armed. Censorship was a reality. American magazines like *Time* and *Newsweek* that we purchased from street vendors often had words, paragraphs, and sometimes, whole pages and covers blacked out. Fear of communist incursions was real. A midnight curfew had been in effect since our arrival. Military service, mandatory for all young men, exemplified the intensifying struggle between the heavy hand of government and democracy.

With turmoil as a backdrop, Linda and I departed the Lee home for the last time on July 21, 1969 and made our way to Taegu Station to board a train to Pusan. A whole host of friends and school officials came to the station to see us off. Flooded with a mix of sadness and excitement, we shared hugs, handshakes, and well wishes all around until it was time to board.

When Mr. Lee and Samonim came aboard the train to say a final goodbye, our tears flowed unrestrained. Linda and I were both puddles. It was wrenching to think they and their children would not be part of our everyday lives in the future. They had welcomed us into their family for nearly two years, acting as our mentors, parental figures, supporters, and friends. Their home had been our refuge, a place where the roots of our own relationship deepened and grew. The experience of leaving seemed surreal; through our tears we couldn't adequately express our gratitude and appreciation to them. We hoped they sensed how we felt.

As the train pulled away, we felt the familiar fabric of our lives being torn apart. We knew the separation had to happen, that our life in Korea was a temporary commitment, but leaving was terribly difficult. It took a while for us to catch our breath and focus on what lay ahead.

Sharon and Gary had volunteered to accompany us as far as Pusan. They knew how difficult it was for us to leave. By the time the train pulled into Pusan mid-afternoon, we had gathered ourselves emotionally. Our flight to Fukuoka was scheduled for early evening. With time to kill, the four of us taxied out to the airport on a typically hot, humid afternoon. We found a small bar outside the terminal and went in to get a cold drink.

The old, gray building had faint primitive signage. As we entered, our eyes took a few seconds to adjust to the dim lighting. People crowded around the bar and peered up at a small black and white television tucked high on a shelf in a far corner. We looked up at it as well, and at that moment, we saw Neil Armstrong exit the Apollo 11 lunar lander and take his first "small step for man and one giant step for mankind" on the surface of the moon. The fuzzy screen made it difficult to make out the images, but the moon landing seemed a fitting event for our last day in Korea, another in a long string of historical events that took place while we were there from 1967 to 1969.

Later at the airport, Linda and Sharon, both in their fourth month of pregnancy, shared a tearful goodbye as Gary and I lent moral support. The flight to Fukuoka still lives vividly in our memory. We left the small Pusan airport, located on a dirt road some distance from town, and flew barely a hundred miles across the Sea of Japan. As

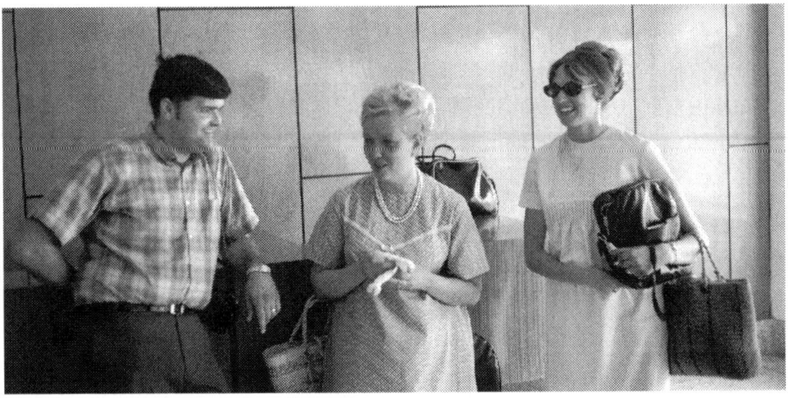

Gary, Sharon and Linda at Pusan Airport

we descended, bright lights below illuminated a baseball stadium on the city's outskirts. Upon landing, we exited the plane, entered the airport, and instantly felt overwhelmed by the clean building, colorful neon lights, tasteful décor, and carpeting. We were experiencing environmental shock! The modernity of it was such a surprise, so different from what we had just left behind in Korea.

That first impression carried over to our check-in experience at the downtown inn where we had reserved a room. The nicely furnished, bright lobby had attractive plants and a big color television tuned to a professional baseball game. Our room, replete with tatami mats on the floor, starched linen sheets, colorful comforter, and beautiful artwork, was far nicer than anything we had expected. It even had air-conditioning! We had entered a very different world.

During our three weeks in Japan, Linda relished the easy availability of milk in vending machines located just off the sidewalks in every city and town we visited. The only milk available in Taegu came in powdered form and was typically mixed with room temperature water. In Japan, whole milk was inexpensive and sold cold in single-serving bottles. We rarely passed a milk vending machine without buying a bottle. Linda's new diet seemed to affect the growing baby in her womb; we referred to our unborn as "HP," short for Half-Pint. By the time we arrived in Tokyo, Linda felt HP moving; I heard an "Ugh!" now and then when the baby got restless.

As we traveled, we noticed how well the Japanese maintained their cities and preserved their antiquities. The architecture, structural craftsmanship, and landscape designs were works of art. The city of Kyoto had once been the nation's capital, and we especially loved the temples, gardens, and palaces there. We thought Korea's remarkable temples and other historic sites could be similarly attractive if the country chose to develop and preserve them.

We found traveling by bus and train through Japan to be a great way to transition to life outside Korea. The gardens and other antiquities captivated us and eased the painful loss of our Korean family and friends. Gradually, we became accustomed to refined transportation, shopping, dining, and lodging. We loved Japanese food and were grateful for the helpful plastic models of menu items displayed in restaurant windows.

Most of the Japanese people we met could not speak or understand English. At a bookstore, we found "instant Japanese" resources – little books that came in handy to help us meet our daily needs. Structurally, the Japanese language had much in common with Korean, and if we kept our inquiries simple, we were able to understand most directions, purchase whatever we needed, and secure answers to questions. Like Koreans, the Japanese appreciated our attempts to use their language.

One exception to our success in communicating occurred with an innkeeper in Kyoto. We found a delightful *ryokan*, an inn not unlike a Korean yogwan, in a central part of the city. The single-story, traditionally designed building had a small number of rooms that formed the perimeter of an attractively landscaped courtyard. Pleased with our find, we registered for a weeklong stay and moved into a bright tatami room with minimalist, tasteful furnishings.

All went well until we attempted to use the bathing facility across the courtyard. The bath, like an upscale, mini version of the public bath we used in Taegu, was in a room just big enough for one family. It consisted of a tiled floor around the perimeter of a deep tub filled with clear hot water. Shortly after we entered the bath, we heard a knock on the door. The innkeeper shouted an exhortation that we not use soap in the tub. In our admittedly limited Japanese, we acknowledged that we understood. Again and again, she shouted the same instruction, and we tried to reassure her that we understood. However, nothing we said seemed to diminish her anxiety.

We finally exited the bath and, after repacking, checked out of the inn. We assumed that the innkeeper had experienced some unfortunate incidents with foreign guests. While we understood her anxiety, we suspected that, had we stayed, we would likely have been the subject of more suspicion and harassment. We quickly found a more accommodating hotel, and our stay in Kyoto was so enchanting that we quickly set the bathing incident aside.

After our week in Kyoto, we had three days in Tokyo where we discovered we much preferred smaller towns and country villages to the big city atmosphere. The crowds, the distances from one venue to the next, and the higher prices overwhelmed us. After two days, we were ready for the next leg of our journey home.

The next day, August 13, we boarded a plane for a red-eye flight to Honolulu. After flying all night, our friend Lindsey greeted us at the airport. Lindsey, the K-I PCV with whom we had been so close in Taegu, gave each of us a lei and his trademark warm smile. We were glad to see him and had many questions about his life since his departure from Korea a year earlier. He had just as many questions about our year and our plans.

Lindsey dropped us off at the Friends Meeting House, where we had secured a room. After settling in, he picked us up again mid-afternoon and took us to the Chart House Restaurant, adjacent to Honolulu's small-boat marina. Lindsey insisted on treating us to our first dinner back on American soil. We had a wonderful reunion, gabbed for hours, and made plans to get together again later in the week.

Of Hawaiian heritage, Lindsey had grown up on Oahu. His family owned picturesque property on the island's windward side. We spent hours at his family cabin that week, swam in their tropical freshwater lagoon, and made Hawaiian poke while we caught up with one another. We mentioned that we had no definite plans for the future but had interviewed for a Peace Corps training program scheduled to begin later in the year. Lindsey told us the training center, operated by the University of Hawai'i, was on a different island, the Big Island of Hawai'i, but Oahu had a Peace Corps office located not far from the Friends Meeting House. I made a mental note to drop by the office sometime during the week.

Ann and John, the managers at the FMH, were the kindest folks. Knowing this was our very first time in Hawai'i, they invited us to spend a day with them at Hanauma Bay, the famous ocean wildlife preserve located a short distance from downtown Honolulu. Our Hanauma Bay visit introduced us to snorkeling, tropical fish, and coral. Floating above the shallow coral landscape felt like glimpsing another world.

Later that day, on our way back from the beach, I asked Ann and John to drop me at the Peace Corps office, conveniently located on our route back to the Meeting House. Wearing beach jams, a tank top, and flip-flops, I went in to inquire about serving on the staff of an upcoming Peace Corps training program.

After introducing myself, I asked the receptionist's forgiveness for my casual appearance. She mentioned that the director of the Center for Cross-Cultural Training and Research, located in Hilo, happened to be on Oahu that day and was in the office. She asked if I would like to speak with him. I had surmised that, at best, I might be able to have a telephone conversation with someone from the center. Happy for my good fortune, I said, "Sure!"

Over an hour later I offered my thanks to Mel Beetle, the center director from Hilo, for the impromptu interview. He explained that staffing for an October program had not yet been set. I jotted down my contact information and gave it to him as I left. I felt good about the interview but had no idea of my potential for being offered a position.

Our plan for transitioning back home to California had worked well. Traveling in Japan had eased the pain of leaving friends and family in Taegu, and we became accustomed again to more modern amenities. Reconnecting with Lindsey, someone who knew well the life of a Peace Corps Volunteer, had given us insight into some of the adjustments we might have to make upon returning home. He helped us recognize that our friends and family in California would have no concept of what our lives in Korea had been like, despite all the letters we had written.

On August 22, mainland re-entry day, we touched down at Los Angeles International Airport, where we shared hugs and kisses with members of both of our families. At five months pregnant, Linda was definitely "showing" signs of her condition as we walked off the plane. She immediately became the star of the show as our families reacted to seeing us for the first time in nearly two years. Because we had so much to talk about, we felt a bit awkward. We didn't know where to start – with our lives in Korea, their lives while we were gone, the immediate present, the future? Again, we felt overwhelmed.

About ten days later, on a sunlit afternoon, Linda and I we were chatting with her parents in their Santa Paula living room. I will never forget hearing the loud ring of the black rotary phone. Sitting closest, I answered. On the other end of the line was the training center director calling from Hilo. After exchanging pleasantries, Mr. Beetle said he had a question for me: "How would you like to have your baby in Hawai'i?"

I instantly experienced a rush — disbelief, elation, relief — as I put my hand over the receiver and asked Linda, who sat across the room, "How'd you like to have the baby in Hawai'i?"

Her face burst into a big smile…"Yes!!"

EPILOGUE

Moving to Hawai'i was another adventure. We loved the tropical warmth, the cultural diversity, and the island environment. Everything about our life there was different: our lodging, the food, the work, and the people we worked with. To us, our new home was a blend of Pacific Island, Asian, and Western cultures — a complex mix. Adding to all of that, we were soon to become parents. We had a lot to learn.

The Center for Cross-Cultural Training and Research (CCTR) at the University of Hawai'i in Hilo, located on the campus of a former hospital, contracted with the Peace Corps to train volunteer recruits to work in countries throughout Asia and the Pacific Islands, not just Korea. Having an opportunity to do that kind of work weaned us from our lives as Peace Corps Volunteers, not abruptly but gradually. We were provided an opportunity to integrate our Korean experience as we moved forward with our lives in America.

Linda and I were both hired to work on a three-month program preparing recruits to do the work we had done — teach English in Korean secondary schools. Linda was assigned to the cultural awareness track, while I was part of the TESL team. Because our baby was due in late December, Linda planned to work just the first half of the program. Then, when the training transitioned to Honolulu in mid-December for practice teaching, she would accompany me and, most likely, have the baby there.

My contract went through January, with no promise of future

employment. Continued work at CCTR was possible but depended on my performance and the availability of an upcoming training program. We decided to cross that bridge when we came to it down the road. In the meantime, we had interesting work to do and the birth of our baby to look forward to.

I thrived in my role as a trainer, especially when coaching practice teaching sessions. During off-hours, Linda and I often found ourselves responding to trainees' questions about life in Korea, the things we enjoyed, the challenges we faced, the relationships we built, and the successes we experienced. Those discussions were exactly what we needed to help us bridge our experience in Korea with life in mainstream America.

When the training program shifted to Honolulu in mid-December, our baby's birth was close at hand. Linda's first tasks were to contact the physician her doctor in Hilo had recommended and make arrangements for her future admission to a maternity hospital. As she did that, we settled into an apartment at the Kuhio Palms in the heart of Waikiki.

The week before Christmas, we had surprise reunions with old friends from our hometown in Southern California. Dean was in Honolulu with his wife on R&R leave from his military posting in Vietnam. Allen, best man at our wedding, and his wife were in town for his college roommate's wedding. Despite Linda's apparent readiness to give birth, the six of us planned to meet for dinner on December 26. As we prepared to leave our apartment that evening, Linda's water broke. Instead of meeting at the restaurant, we all converged on Queen Kapiolani Maternity Hospital.

During Linda's admission, I requested permission to stay with her during the entire birthing process. I really had no clear picture of what to expect, but we wanted to be together for the birth. Soon, I understood why they had me sign a waiver swearing I would stay seated when we got to the delivery room. I was not expecting the amount of blood that soaked the sheets as the doctor worked to help extricate our baby from the warmth of Linda's womb. Finally, after eight hours of labor, our healthy baby daughter, Kristen, announced her arrival by letting us know she did not appreciate the cool temperature of the delivery room. It was the morning of December 27, the exact date predicted by the very first Korean obstetrician Linda had seen back in Taegu. Our family had become three.

As the three of us began adjusting to life together, we received news from our friends the Raiks. The corrective heart operation they helped arrange for Suki, the child of their Korean host family, had been successful. The three of them had traveled from Yechon in July, and Suki's surgery was scheduled soon after. During her recovery, Suki's homesickness had been difficult for all of them, but after three months, she was well enough to return to Yechon, in the company of a nun from the Catholic mission. Theirs was a heartwarming and miraculous story, a testimony to the power of the Peace Corps experience.

In late January, when our baby was just a month old, we returned from Honolulu to Hilo. Our wish to continue living in Hawai'i was granted when I was offered a contract extension to work on another program to prepare more English teachers for Korea. Instead of being a TESL instructor, however, I was asked to co-direct the first half of the program and then lead it during the latter half, scheduled for the first time to take place in Korea.

That news thrilled us. Kristen would be nearly four months old by then, and we would be able to introduce her to our friends there, especially the Lee family. We couldn't believe our good fortune. While the leadership role I was asked to shoulder was intimidating, I received assurances that I would have ample support. It was time for me to stretch myself again.

Never having been in a management role, I was to oversee a program for dozens of new volunteers as they traveled halfway around the world to enter a totally new culture, while continuing their high intensity language and technical training. The goal was for those recruits to get a more accurate picture of their assignment and the conditions under which they would be living for two years.

In late March, our family of three arrived in Seoul, after an eleven-hour flight, during which three-month-old Kristen slept no more than thirty minutes. We were all exhausted! Fortunately, I didn't have to hit the ground running; we had time to settle in. I had a chance to get a handle on the training calendar and better understand what my responsibilities would entail once the trainees arrived two weeks later. My team included a very capable group of managers for the language, cultural, and technical tracks of the program. My job was to coordinate, troubleshoot, evaluate, and make recommendations for the improvement of future training projects. I relished that role.

One of the initial challenges I faced involved how I was to get around to the various places I needed to be. As a volunteer, I had not been allowed to operate a vehicle, nor did I ever want to. Korean traffic and roads were downright scary. To do my job, however, I had to overcome that anxiety. I needed to navigate both the traffic crush in Seoul in a tiny Jeep, and the narrow, rough, unpaved roads out in the country in a larger four-wheel drive Land Rover. It was sink or swim. After the first few days, I navigated the crowded chaotic multi-lane traffic circles at major intersections. I never really got comfortable in city traffic, but I managed to avoid trouble.

Our plans were to be in Korea from March through May. After about a month, on a free weekend, we decided to take the train to Taegu to introduce Kristen to the Lee family. Mel, our Peace Corps regional rep who was still in Taegu, informed us the Lees had moved. With the help of a taxi driver, we found their new home, much smaller and more traditional than the two-story house in which we all had lived together. Since the family had no telephone, we surprised them on a Saturday afternoon.

Samonim and the three children were at home, but Mr. Lee was not. As he had hoped, he was studying for his advanced theological degree in Tokyo. We were disappointed, but we knew attending seminary was his dream. We were glad for him and thought we might have a chance to meet him on our return trip to Hawai'i.

We spent the afternoon introducing Samonim, Googi, Yooni, and Wani to Kristen, and catching up on their family news. Our limited

Korean and Samonim's total lack of English made it difficult to share in much depth about what had transpired for both of our families during the eight months that had passed since our emotional good-bye. Googi contributed but his English was limited. We wished Mr. Lee had been there to facilitate our exchange of information. As the afternoon turned to dusk, we bid the Lees another sad farewell. We didn't know if or when we might see them again.

While in Taegu, we also had reunions with Gi Suh and Duk Hee, and Gary and Sharon. Both couples had new babies, born since we had last seen them. We relished the introductions and catching up on each other's news. We all made commitments to stay in touch.

After two months, the in-country portion of the training program on which I worked was deemed a success. The trainees had a taste of Korea before making a commitment to serve, and Peace Corps decision-makers were able to assess how the trainees responded to their new environment before making final selections. A decision was made to host at least a portion of all future training programs in Korea. Peace Corps eventually adopted that policy for almost all countries they served worldwide.

My experience of coordinating and troubleshooting the program's various activities was a positive one. I learned that trainees found my observations helpful, as did Peace Corps/Korea staff, and my colleagues at CCTR. Problems predictably arose as the program unfolded, but solutions were found. The touchiest involved trainee insensitivity to the impact of their behavior on others. Coaching and the establishment of clear limits resolved most of those issues. As my confidence grew, I began to think my interest in counseling might be a good fit.

Back in Hawai'i, Linda and I faced a dilemma. While in Korea, I received an invitation to begin graduate studies in counseling psychology at the University of Oregon. Then, upon our return to Hawai'i, CCTR offered me a one-year contract to continue leading future Peace Corps training programs. We found ourselves in a dilemma. It was the beginning of July and we had to quickly make a decision. Our first inclination was to stay in Hawai'i. We loved everything

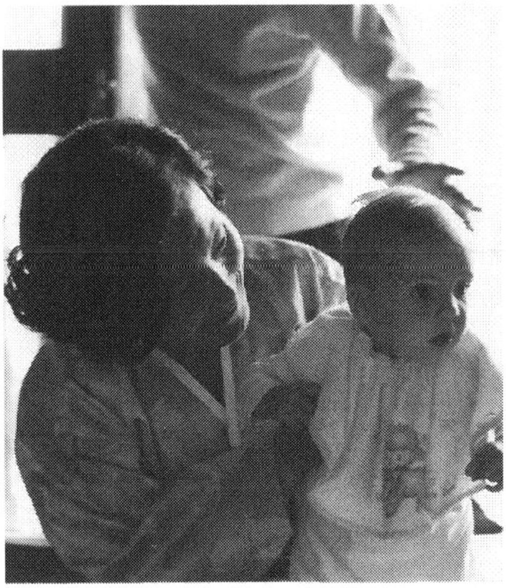

Samonim and Kristen

Kwon Gi Suh Family

Mr. Lee and Kristen in Tokyo

Yooni, Googi, Kristen and Wani

about being there. It seemed a great fit for the three of us.

I contacted the University and asked if my admission could be deferred for a year. The answer I received was a firm "No, but you could reapply for admission next year." Discouraged, I failed to appreciate that I would likely be an even more desirable degree candidate with another year of experience under my belt. Instead, the value of earning further academic credentials won the day. I knew I needed the sheepskin to pursue my interests and provide for our growing family. We decided to head for Oregon.

While leaving Hawai'i was tainted with sadness, it helped provide closure to our Peace Corps experience. We had shared what we learned with trainees preparing for their own adventure in the "land of the morning calm." The lessons we took with us from living and working with Koreans never dimmed. We learned to trust and have confidence in ourselves, and each other. Our life in Hawai'i had helped us integrate those lessons. We prepared to move on.

We did get to have our reunion with Mr. Lee in Tokyo on our return from Seoul, but we gradually lost touch with the Lees. None of the letters we wrote to them over the years were returned. We didn't know what happened to any of them until, one day in 2006, our telephone rang. It was Googi, then fifty years old. He had found our phone number on the web.

Googi shared that the entire family had migrated to the United States in the 1970s, after Mr. Lee completed his graduate studies. All three children had married, and each had two children of their own. Mr. Lee and Samonim lived with Googi's family in Nashua, New Hampshire. Yooni's family lived in Pennsylvania and Wani's in New Jersey. Without hesitation we quickly began to plot a visit.

The whole family planned to be together in Nashua that Fall to celebrate Chuseok and Mr. Lee's eightieth birthday. As fate would have it, we had planned a trip for that same month to Montreal to visit relatives. Nashua was only a five-hour drive from Montreal. A much longed-for reunion was going to happen.

That reunion, in the fall of 2006, was special beyond measure.

Everyone was there, including all six Lee grandchildren. Our hearts were warmed as we hugged grown-up Googi, Yooni, and Wani. Mr. Lee and Samonim had aged but were otherwise the same. Mr. Lee's wisdom and patience as the respected patriarch were evident. Samonim, ever the shy but skillful behind the scenes matriarch, still had not learned a bit of English, despite having spent more than thirty years in the States. Despite the barriers, our curiosity about one another made for non-stop storytelling. The teen-aged grandchildren, all of whom spoke perfect English, devoured our Korea scrapbook. They couldn't get enough of the pictures of their parents as children and our stories about living with the family in the late 1960s.

We celebrated Chuseok and Mr. Lee's birthday the weekend of our visit. Favorite traditional foods and shared stories culminated with a declaration from Mr. Lee that Linda and I were, indeed, members of their family and that we were all finally having a proper family reunion.

In the years since that wonderful weekend, we made other discoveries. Gi Suh and Duk Hee, our close friends in Taegu, migrated to Chicago sometime in the early 1980s. For many years, Gi Suh operated an Asian cafe in the shadow of the Sears Tower while Duk Hee was a department assistant at Northwestern University. Linda

Lee Family Reunitied in 2006

and I have since visited them in Chicago and stay in regular contact.

Nak Kyung, our young friend who introduced us to his family in the Korean countryside, remained in Korea to successfully manage a high-tech sub-division of a company headquartered in California. We found him before making a return trip in 2009 when the Korean government invited all former Peace Corps Volunteers for a visit. By the time we arrived, Nak Kyung had retired from his corporate leadership position. He met us at the airport and spent the best part of a week unselfishly driving us to visit friends in distant parts of the country. Before departing, we visited his home, met his wife and shared a traditional home-cooked Korean meal. We stay in regular contact with him via Facebook and e-mail.

The Korean government has remained steadfast in its support of all former Peace Corps Korea Volunteers since the last group served there in 1981. During our 2009 visit, the government provided us with lodging, meals, educational programs, interpreters, and trips back to our work sites. In Taegu, each of our schools welcomed us with banners and gifts. At Kei-Sung we were greeted by several retired faculty with whom I had taught. The principal greeted me with a question: "Do you remember me?" He introduced himself as a seventh-grade student of mine, 40 years earlier! We had a wonderful visit and tour of the school, which had been totally modernized since I taught there.

At Chae-Il, we were surprised to find a whole new school had been built on the site of the old one. Several of Linda's former students surprised her with a big bouquet of flowers. Those girls, now women, insisted on treating us to dinner, where they regaled us with stories of learning English from Linda. They spoke, too, of how women's roles in Korean society had changed and how they loved being businesswomen.

Korea in 2009 had indeed transformed itself into "The Miracle on the Han River." Modern, clean, and prosperous were adjectives we could scarcely have imagined using to describe the country fifty years earlier. Today, they seem like understatements. Conversely, it would be hard to overstate the positive impact of starting our marriage and our family while serving as Peace Corps volunteers in Korea. The experience profoundly shaped the course of our lives. Our fellow volunteers and Korean friends have remained part of our world ever since.

Korea's generosity and our gratitude continue to the present. During the worldwide pandemic, the government sent each former Peace Corps/Korea Volunteer a COVID-19 Survival Box, filled with useful gifts as an expression of their appreciation for our service. We were overwhelmed when we opened a large package containing, among other things, high quality masks, antimicrobial gloves, backpack, silk fan, ginseng candy and a pair of silver-plated chopsticks and spoon. Prior to the pandemic, our Korean consulate in the Pacific Northwest hosted an annual dinner program to acknowledge all who have formerly worked and remain friends with Korea, including but not limited to Peace Corps Volunteers. Those thoughtful gestures remain an expression of the culture we first encountered 55 years ago.

As we look back on all that was memorable during our time in Korea, we recall the 33 great granite steps that transported us up to the grandeur of Pulgooksa in the summer of 1968, and how those steps were symbolic of the 33 steps to Buddhist enlightenment. The 33 chapters recounted here chronicle the steps we took as we sought to find our way in a historic land, home to a culture so different from our own, and the warm, generous, passionate people who became our lifelong friends. We took from Korea far more than we gave. We are, and will forever be, grateful.

ACKNOWLEDGEMENTS

Writing this memoir was something new for me. Telling a story, I quickly learned, was quite different from the grant applications and professional journal articles I had produced during my working years. Linda and I had long wanted to recount and reflect on our Korean adventure, to turn it into a readable narrative for family and friends curious about our Peace Corps experience. Thanks to our parents who had saved almost all our correspondence, we had over a hundred letters and countless photos to jog our memories. When the COVID pandemic arrived, I had an opportunity to get started.

As I began, Bruce and Katy Peet, long-time friends and writers, provided insightful editorial suggestions as they reviewed early drafts. Friends who served with us in Korea also stepped forward to help. Kathianne Crane, a fellow K-III, offered steadfast encouragement as she provided timely feedback on each chapter. Another K-III alum, Richard Wiley, himself an accomplished author, steered me to Peace Corps Worldwide for assistance with publishing. Other K-III PCVs, including John Cushing, Neil Waters, Jerry Raik and Tim O'Brien, all lent suggestions as they read over drafts of the manuscript. Without the help of all those friends, this book would not exist.

While the COVID pandemic was a trial for many, the fact that I had to sequester myself for months at a time was a blessing in disguise. It afforded me time to focus on synthesizing our letters and recollections. If I had not been forced to remain indoors for extended periods, I would no doubt still be writing. Then, after multiple drafts had been refined, came the copy editing and book design. Major thanks to Dania Zafar who created the look and feel of the attractive final product.

Finally, while we collaborated on every page of what you hold in your hands, I cannot thank Linda enough for her undying support, commitment, and tolerance as I sat hunched over my laptop for hours a day. As this project draws to a close I envision getting to those tasks on her "honey, do..." list that I have long neglected. Hugs to you, Linda, for being my loving and gracious partner in this enterprise!

PHOTO CREDITS

To Mark Brown:

- p. 45: Kei Sung Middle School Teachers Room
- p. 62: Using visual aids, Lunch with colleagues, Linda at work in classroom
- p. 63: Class begins with a bow, Warming in teachers room, Steve in the classroom

To Caroline Schlattmann:

- Author cover photo